# Words of Torah

RABBI JOSEPH MESZLER

Copyright © 2015 Joseph Meszler

All rights reserved.

ISBN:1515269744

ISBN-13:9781515269748

# DEDICATION

To Rabbi Julie Zupan for making all things possible. I love you.

CONTENTS

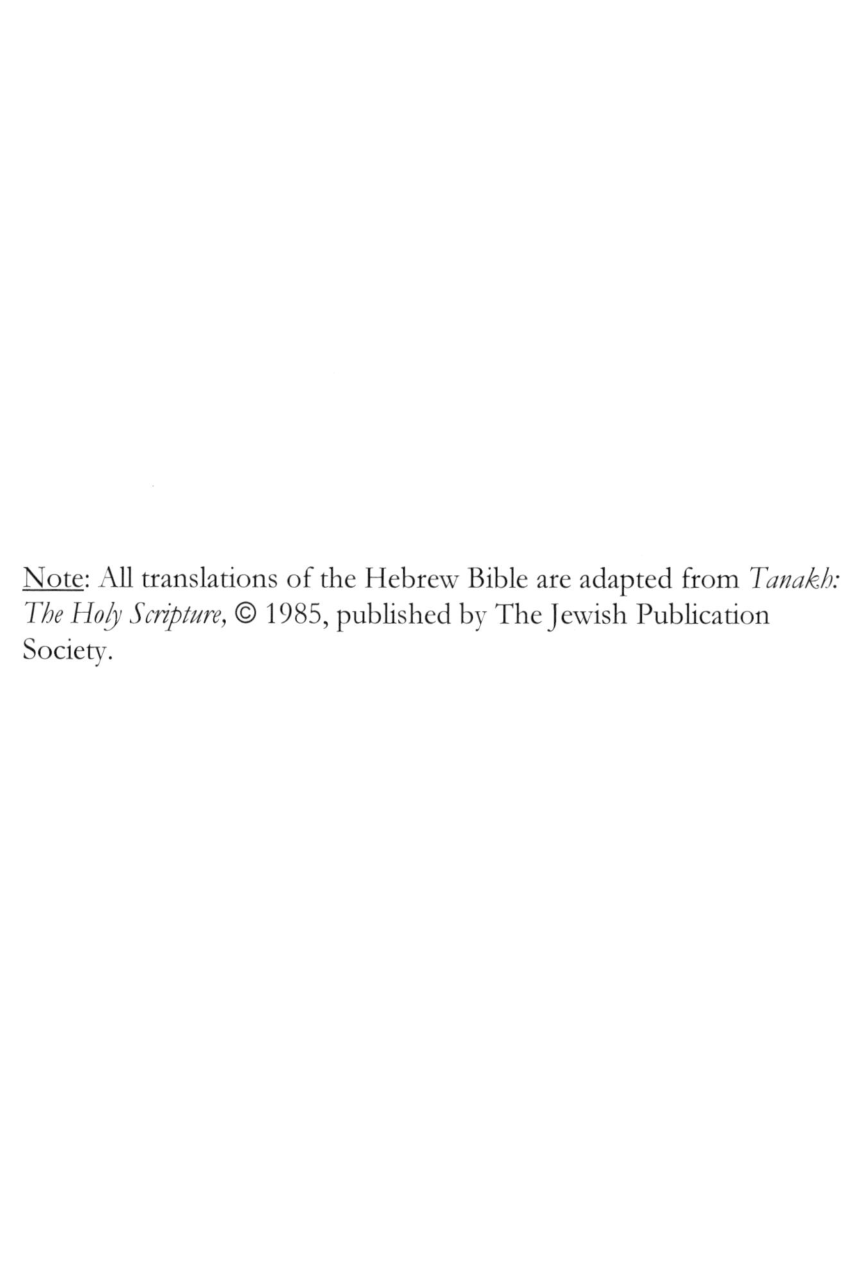

Note: All translations of the Hebrew Bible are adapted from *Tanakh: The Holy Scripture*, © 1985, published by The Jewish Publication Society.

# AN OPENING WORD

One of the centerpieces of the Jewish Shabbat service is to hear a *d'var torah* or a "word of Torah," from the Five Books of Moses. As a congregational rabbi, I have been giving sermons, or *divrei torah*, every week. This volume is meant to help you in your own personal study of the Hebrew Bible. Torah study is a sacred act.

The words of Torah in this volume are a selection based upon the traditional weekly Torah portion, arranged by their Hebrew names in the traditional order of the year. I have given many more sermons than these. Many times I have spoken about issues of social justice or the political events of the day, but these sermons are not included here. The purpose of this volume is a journey through the text of the Torah itself, so excluded from this volume are topical sermons or addresses centered on holidays.

The best way to read this book is to imagine that you are sitting in a seat in a synagogue sanctuary, listening to the sermon. Allow yourself to be transported there on a Shabbat evening or morning. Connect yourself to a larger community through time and space. If you feel you have learned anything, even one letter, I will feel gratified.

I want to thank the members of Temple Sinai of Sharon, Massachusetts for listening to these "words of Torah" week after week, whether at Friday night or Saturday morning Shabbat services or other occasions. I also want to thank our Shabbat morning Torah study group who have joined me for weekly Torah study as we have learned together, line by line. The deeper purpose of this volume is to preserve a conversation that we have been having together for many years in hope that the memory will make you smile.

## *Bereishit* (Genesis 1:1-6:8)

### The Jewish Story of the Creation of the World

In the beginning, way back when, in olden days, once upon a time, over the hills and far away, a long time ago, you know how it begins, the world was born.[1]

And if you lived in Greece in ancient times, you knew that the world was born when the gods went to war. Gaia, the Earth, gave birth Uranus, Hades, Eros, and the Titans, who were horrid hundred-armed monsters. Chief among these was the terrible Kronos, who killed his father Uranus and spilled his blood everywhere, creating the other gods and goddesses and the rest of the universe.

But if you were to journey north to Scandinavia, the Vikings would tell you that they knew how the world really began. There were once two places, the place of fire and light in the south and the place of ice and dark in the north. When these two places met, the moisture formed the evil frost giant Ymir. From his body melted ogres, and from the ice melted a large cow that fed all of them. The grandchildren of these creatures were Odin and other gods, and they rose up and killed Ymir and the other creatures. They turned Ymir's body into the earth and his blood into the seas. His bones became the mountains and his teeth and jaws the rocks and stones. And his skull became the sky, with each of its four corners held up by a dwarf, and his brains became the clouds.

But if you were to travel across the seas to the Navajo in the Americas and to attend a nine-day ceremony called the Blessing Way, they would enact a ritual for you to tell you how the world really began. Out of the dark emerged one world, and then another, and then another, and then another, until a fifth world formed which was inhabited by people. The first world was inhabited by insects, and the second world was inhabited by swallows. The third world was run by grasshoppers, and the fourth world was a world of black and white in

---

[1] The following sketches of world myths are taken from David Leeming and Margaret Leeming, *A Dictionary of Creation Myths* (Oxford: Oxford University Press), 1994.

which Coyote and Badger appeared. The First Man appeared in the fifth world, but there is still another world, a sixth world in heaven above, that is a place of perfect harmony.

In Japan, however, the world began when the female Izanami and the male Izanagi took a bath in the primeval sea. When Izanai washed his eyes, the sun and the moon were released. As they scrubbed their bodies, heaven and earth sprang into being. And when the spear of Heaven was thrust into the watery Sea, the tip raised the first islands of the earth.

And yet, if we were to go to a modern bookstore today anywhere in the world, we might read about how the world was created in a great explosion that happened in only a few minutes. Even now, we can see that moment of creation because the light from that big bang is still on its 20 billion year journey, expanding into solar systems, of which we are an infinitely small part. Stephen Hawking, when he was once trying to explain the Big Bang theory to an audience of non-scientific people, was interrupted by an older woman who told him that he was dead wrong, that the world was made of turtles, one on top of the other. When he asked how far this stack of turtles goes, she replied, "It's turtles all the way."[2]

And so, on Rosh Hashanah, we unroll the scroll of the Torah, and we tell the Jewish version of the story of creation. We do not tell it because we believe that this is literally how it happened and that every word is fact. We tell it because, just as the ice of the north shapes Norse mythology and the islands of the Japan appear in Japanese storytelling, our story tells something about what we believe is the basis of the world. We are not unique because we might believe in creation; many peoples believe that. Jewish civilization is unique because of what we believe about creation and the kind of world we live in.

*Bereishit*, in the beginning, there was one God, and the One God created the world out of nothing. The One God differentiated creation in a series of six days, beginning with separating light from darkness. After this first separation, God continued to separate and differentiate. On the second day, God separated the waters to form sea and sky. On the third day, God separated the dry land from the oceans and caused plants to grow. And then God went back and

---

[2] Stephen Hawking, *A Brief History of Time* (New York: Bantam Books, 1988), 1.

made manifest physical beings and life onto these settings. On the fourth day, God made the light into the sun, moon, and stars. On the fifth day, God caused the sea and sky to be inhabited with fish and birds. After each day, God says that the work was good. And on the sixth day, God caused animals to appear on the dry land to eat the vegetation, and the rulers of all were human beings.

"God said, Let us make a being in our image, after our likeness" (Genesis 1:26). Who is the "us" that the One God is referring to? While later rabbinic legend suggests angels and offers other explanations, from the story itself it seems that God is addressing the animals that God has just created. God is saying to them, "Let us make a being in our image," that is, in the image of an animal and in the image of God. This being would be part spirit and part physical being, an animal and yet with a divine aspect. And God announced that this was very good. In this way, people came to rule the earth, and the story of Adam and Eve is told in the next chapter.

But before that story is told, it says that God rested on the seventh day. On the seventh day, God created rest by ceasing to create. God created a moment of holy reflection.

What differentiates the Hebrew story of creation from the others? First of all, and most importantly, there is no war or bloodshed. There are no giants or ogres that are killed. There are no spears that are thrust forward, and there are no explosions or big bangs. No corpses are made into mountains, and no blood is made into seas. There are no Titans or hundred-armed monsters. There is no violence at all. Instead, one God creates everything out of nothing, and after each day, God calls the creation "good." To affirm the Jewish story of creation is to affirm that we live in a good world, a world that was not meant for bloodshed, a world that has people, who are a mixture of animal and spirit, to preside over everything in goodness. The Hebrew story of creation is an affirmation of the way the world was meant to be.

Secondly, the world is ordered and harmonious, with each thing in its place. God creates by dividing, with everything following after its kind. God sorts and calibrates. The world, so chaotic to us, actually has laws of nature and a rhythm to its seasons. It is up to us to try to live in harmony with it, not to destroy it, waste it, pollute it, or heat it up with carbon gasses. It is our job to find our place in the balance of nature, and if we don't, the world will undoubtedly balance us out of the equation.

A rabbinic parable tells us this moral: We were created last in the order of creation to teach us humility, that even insects were created before us. It says in Genesis that God gave the world to Adam and Eve so that they might "till and tend to it." "Till it" means that we are supposed to use the world to our benefit. "Tend it," however, means that we should also humbly protect it. We can use but not abuse. We are thus supposed to be stewards of God's world, for it is as if God said, "This world pleases Me; take care and protect it, for after this, there will be no other" (Ecclesiastes Rabbah 7:20).

Finally, the Hebrew creation story ends with peace. The mythologies of the world lack the seventh day, the day of Shabbat. Rabbi Abraham Joshua Heschel expounds:

"The meaning of Shabbat is to celebrate time rather than space. Six days a week we live under the tyranny of things in space; on Shabbat we try to become attuned to holiness in time. It is a day on which we are called upon to share in what is eternal in time, to turn from the results of Creation to the mystery of Creation, from the world of Creation to the creation of the world."[3]

Shabbat, in other words, adds a dimension of being conscious of the passing of time to the story of the world. We remember that ultimately, life, the universe, and the story of creation, *ma'aseh Bereishit*, are all ultimately a mystery that we have the privilege to protect and explore. This is the Jewish version of the story.

What differentiates Judaism from other religions and peoples is not that we believe in creation or tell flood stories or other such things, for many other peoples do that, and some many years before we did. What differentiates Jews is how we tell our stories and how we look at the world and at life. We can either accept the world as a place that, from conception, is about conflict and chaos, or we can aspire to a vision of the world that is about balance, goodness, and *shalom*.

Let us continue to be partners with God in the work of creation. Let us, we who are both animal and divine, retell our vision of a world that is good, that is harmonious, and that is peaceful.

---

[3] Abraham Joshua Heschel, *The Sabbath* (New York: Farrar, Straus, and Giroux) 10.

## The First Family

There they were, two naked people in the midst of a garden, a paradise of fruits, vegetables, and animals. Then along comes a snake and asks Eve to break the one commandment God gave them, not to eat of the fruit of the Tree of Knowledge. She eats, then he eats, and then this perfect picture all falls apart. God shows up, asking, "Where are you?" (Genesis 3:9) Confronted with their rebellion, these children of God do the natural thing. He blames her, she blames their pet, and everyone gets kicked out. But now they put on some clothes.

A great deal of our understanding of the story of Adam and Eve, a story that we feel we all know reasonably well, actually comes to us from Christian art. When we think of the First Family, of the first man and woman and their famous encounter with a piece of fruit and a walking snake, the images that inevitably come to mind have been provided for us by the likes of Michelangelo on the Sistine Chapel. Naked bodies with appropriately placed fig leaves holding an apple, while a snake with a human face winds around a tree spring up from our collective unconscious.

And as much as we cannot help but respect this visual cultural inheritance, a return to the Hebrew text will give us a more Jewish perspective on this sacred story. The fact that the fruit that Adam and Eve ate is never once referred to as an apple in Hebrew, or that two trees are described, the Tree of Life in the middle of the Garden of Eden and the Tree of Knowledge of Good and Bad, are things that we might never discover unless we go back and read the text. The story of Adam and Eve's expulsion begins with the words: "The two of them were naked." The Hebrew word for naked is "*arum*," which also means "shrewd," and it is used again in the very next sentence to describe the serpent, "the shrewdest of all wild beasts" (Genesis 3:1). This pun with the word "*arum*" is lost in translation, and without it, we would lose the play on words that Adam and Eve were seduced equally by their own nakedness as well as by the snake. Also lost in translation is when Eve says that the snake deceived her. The Hebrew is alliterative; it might best be translated as, "The ssssnake sssseducccced me" (Genesis 3:13).

Adding to our difficulties are the theological beliefs that are predominant in our society. All of us have absorbed through osmosis an understanding of Original Sin and the Fall of Man, things that are not at all a part of Judaism. It was Rashi, the 11$^{th}$ century commentator from France, who made sure to write that, according to a Jewish reading of the story, Adam and Eve conceived Cain while still in the Garden of Eden, placing the sexual act in paradise, and not afterwards as a result of some kind of fall. The values of chastity and celibacy have a much greater weight in other religions than Judaism for this reason. For some, sexuality is a result of sin, whereas in Judaism, it is a part of the natural course of the garden God planted. Whereas rabbis are encouraged to marry and have families, priests, monks, and nuns are not.

In this spirit, let me add some Jewish legends that have been spun from a Hebrew reading of the story of Adam and Eve. It is helpful to balance out our cultural inheritance by religious education. Perhaps we might think of our own origins differently as well as want to seek out greater Jewish knowledge.

According to Jewish legend, called *midrash*, when Adam was created out of the dust of the earth, Adam was both male and female. God created Adam, male and female, in the divine image, and then divided them. The Hebrew word that is later called "rib" is also the word for "side," so that God does not create Eve from Adam's rib but rather splits Adam in two, down the middle, separating female from male. And it is because they were originally one human being that each wedding couple under the *chuppah* is likened to Adam and Eve in the *sheva Berachot*, the seven wedding blessings. Each couple seeks out the original wholeness that Adam and Eve once enjoyed. It says in the Torah that God brought Eve to Adam. In the Jewish imagination, God also personally designed a chuppah for them and adorned Eve in a wedding dress. And Eve is referred to as an *ezer knegdo*, a helper across from him. If male and female seek that unity, one sage explained, then they will be a help to each other. If not, then they will be across from each other, ready to confront each other. The Jewish take on this story tries to be realistic.

According to legend, the fruit that Adam and Eve ate might have been a fig, for they were found hiding under a fig tree and sewed fig leaves together. Others felt it was a bunch of grapes, which can sometimes be bitter, for this act brought them some bitterness. Rabbi Abba of Acco felt that the fruit was none other than the etrog. But Joshua ben Levi taught: We should not try to guess the identity of the tree. If God did not reveal it, it was because God wanted to spare the tree's honor. We should spare another person's honor whenever we can and leave out names (Genesis Rabbah 15:7).

A number of things happened after the eating of the fruit. God told them that when they ate of it, they would die. But they ate the fruit, and did not immediately die. What God meant was that they would become mortal, not living forever. Instead, they would have to reproduce and work to sustain a family. They would become like gods, with the power of creation.

And still another legend has it that originally Adam was a giant, and light from his body radiated from one end of the earth to the other. After his rebellion, God diminished him and put out his light, and Adam needed light from other sources. It was then that Adam and Eve experienced their first nighttime. The sun went down, and they became very afraid. They thought the darkness was an additional punishment to toil and childbirth. When God saw their fear, God taught them to strike two flints together. From these came fire, and Adam uttered a blessing, "Praised are You, who creates the lights of fire." It is this blessing that we say at Havdalah, at the conclusion of Shabbat, when the Sabbath has ended and darkness comes. When they saw the dawn, Adam and Eve said, "Such is the way of the world, and we, we did not know it" (Genesis Rabbah 11:2, 19:9).

The Jewish version of the story is a story not about sin and punishment, but more about growth and painful discovery. The Jewish legends inspired by Adam and Eve teach us of a dawning of manhood and womanhood, of a crisis of coming of age, of a learning to take responsibility. The awakening of Adam and Eve's sexual maturity inevitably expels them from a garden of childhood to the risky land of working for a living and raising children. It is about seduction as well as beauty, about individuality but also wholeness, about creation but also mortality, about darkness but also light. It is a story we all go through, again and again, and it is true not because that is how it literally happened but because we all relive it.

May we embrace these beautiful parables, so that, like Adam and Eve, we can go through the process of self-discovery and work for a world upon which our future may be well founded, a well-watered garden giving life and knowledge.

### Cain and Abel

Imagine a family with two boys. The brothers have different talents, especially academically. The older one is very good at math. The younger one really struggles with math. They come home from school. It is report card day.

Mom is waiting in the kitchen. The older one hands over his report card. Under math it says, B+. "Thank you," she says to her older son. The younger one comes into the kitchen and hands over his report card. Under math it says, B+. "I am so very, very proud of you," says the mother. She gives him a big hug.

Later that day, the older son "accidentally" shoves the younger son down the stairs.

This is the story of Cain and Abel. It is the story of the offering of two brothers, apparently the same, but underneath, very different. It is the story of parental blessing that is uneven but consistent. It is the story of anger, jealousy, and revenge. It is the desire to strike back at God but settling for the more convenient target. It is the story of how violence comes into the world.

Why is there violence? Why do people kill other people? Strangely, the Torah only alludes to the reason and has a literal gap in the text.

> Cain said to his brother Abel… and when they were in the field, Cain set upon his brother Abel and killed him. (Genesis 4:8)

What did Cain say to Abel? Did an ancient person invent whiteout? A line is missing…

Some might take this as an ancient scribal error. The rabbis, however, felt that the omission was deliberate. For hundreds of years they wondered what the conversation was before the world's first murder (Genesis Rabbah 22:16).

One interpretation has it they argued about possessions. Cain was said to own the fields, and Abel was said to possess flocks of sheep. Abel's sheep still needed to graze on Cain's fields, and Cain became furious. Cain said, "Get your sheep off of my property," and then he killed him. The point of this interpretation is that violence comes into the world because of strife over material possessions.

Another interpretation has it that they were arguing over a woman. Cain and Abel desired the same woman, and Cain was willing to fight for her. "You care to take this outside," Cain must have said. Never mind the fact that this woman has made a magical appearance out of nowhere. The rabbis' point here is that violence is a product of passion. Cain slays Abel out of lust.

Still another rabbinic interpretation is that Cain was jealous of Abel's relationship with God. Cain had offered a sacrifice to God, and so did Abel. Abel's was found more worthy. In a religious rage, Cain lashed out. "Death to the infidel!" Cain must have cried. The rabbis of old were willing to admit that religion could be a source of bloodshed.

If we turn to our modern parable of the two brothers and the report cards, we could say that the source of violence is anger at God or the unfairness of life. Cain cannot shove God down the stairs, however, so he has to settle for his brother.

But there is a deeper lesson to be learned from the Torah's silence. Ultimately, after Abel was dead, Cain's motivation is irrelevant. Violence, no matter what the cause, is ultimately wrong. By not giving us a reason, the Torah is teaching that what Cain said is no longer matters. Of course there are deep psychological and societal reasons why people commit violence, but at the end of the day, you are responsible for what you do. *Adam mu'ad l'olam* – a person is always responsible (*Bava Kamma* 26b). The first murder is still murder. It is one of the few things a Jew is commanded to martyr him or her rather than do.

Today, I think that we often rationalize violence. Somehow, if we can explain why someone commits a crime, we can excuse it. Or we compartmentalize it into a different, safer part of our minds. But understanding why someone acts out and holding someone accountable are two separate issues. It is our duty to find our social responsibility in how our community contributes to violence through a lack of family care, the media, and failing to provide resources for those who are suffering. But it is also our duty to indict those who have acted immorally, no matter what the rationale.

Shabbat, the seventh day on which God rested, is supposed to be a day of peace. But there is no peace without justice. Let us be mindful of what it takes to bring peace to the world. Let us face our responsibilities, especially the difficult ones. Then we will have a time when the words that are shared between siblings are ones of love and support, and then it will be a Sabbath of the wholeness and harmony that we call, "*shalom*."

## *Noach* (Genesis 6:9-11:32)

### Noah's Word

We all think we know the story of Noah. God sees that the world is full of corruption and violence, and the Torah says God's heart was grieved. God decides to start over by flooding the world, so God picks Noah and his family to be the sole survivors.

At God's command, Noah builds what we read in Hebrew is a *teivah* or a boat that we commonly call in English an ark. (By the way, the ark that we put our Torah scrolls in is actually a different, unrelated Hebrew term.) The story continues that Noah brings two of every animal onto the boat, and they sail away when the rains come. After the flood, Noah finally finds dry land.

Words are important in the Torah. They have symbolic meaning. Noah's name in Hebrew means, "rest," and his quest is to find a place for the ark to rest on dry land. And interestingly, the Hebrew word for Noah's ark - the *teivah* - is used in only one other place in the Torah. When Moses' mother puts him into a basket and floats him down the Nile River to the Egyptian princess, the basket is called a *teivah*. In a miniature version, Moses' life is saved in a *teivah* from the waters of chaos and death.

Whether it was the big ark or the little ark, the Hebrew word *teivah* seems to mean a vessel that floats and saves. It is a sanctuary that keeps death at bay.

But what native Hebrew speakers will tell you are that the Hebrew word *teivah* also has a completely different second definition. Sometimes words can mean two different things, as different as the word "sack" can mean either a bag or what you try to do to a quarterback.

The second meaning of *teivah*, apparently unrelated to the first, is that *teivah* means "word." A common rabbinic phrase refers to the *teivot* of Torah, the words of Torah.

So a *teivah* either means a kind of lifeboat, as in the cases of Noah and baby Moses, or it means a word.

These seem to be apparently two completely different definitions, but to Rabbi Nachman of Breslov, the two had to be connected. Rabbi Nachman taught: "Noah was righteous person who was able to draw words of Torah to himself. This *teivah* became his protection against the floodwaters that engulfed the rest of humanity and rejected God. Yet Noah's *teivah* was not capable of saving others. In contrast, Moses also entered an 'ark' when his mother placed him in the river as a baby. Since Moses was destined to receive the Torah and bring it to all humankind, his *teivah*, his word of Torah, was great enough to save everyone."

It completely changes the story if we switch the definitions around and understand Noah's *teivah* to be a word and not a boat, reading the tale metaphorically instead of literally. Instead of physical water, we can understand the flood to be surrounding corruption, violence, and rejection of God. And instead of a boat, we can understand the *teivah* to be life-saving words that one person offers another.

This interpretation of Noah reminds me of the story of Rabbi Leo Baeck during the Holocaust. Leo Baeck, even though he had numerous chances to leave Germany, stayed with his people and went with them to Terezin. This labor camp was not as horrible as a death camp but was still hell on earth. And yet, on Wednesday nights, Leo Baeck would gather people together and give a lecture from his memory on history, philosophy, or Jewish ethics. The Nazi guards allowed him to do this because they found it amusing. But survivors testified that for that moment in time, those who listened to Rabbi Baeck's words were transported out of the camp and into a kind of imaginary university lecture hall. They engaged in a kind of defiance, spiritual resistance, and transcendence. His words gave them - at least temporarily - new life. His words were an ark against the flood.[4]

But let's understand Noah's *teivah* on a more everyday level. Has there ever been a time when someone else's words have been a life raft for you? Have you ever felt lost or depressed, but someone else's unexpected, kind words suddenly turned things around? Have you ever clung to what someone else once said to give you hope or help you get through?

Or maybe, you are the one who has been privileged enough to have given someone else a *teivah*. Maybe you are even now responsible for showing compassion to another by being sensitive with what you say and reaching out.

God, help us remember that words are powerful. Words matter.

---

[4] Leonard Baker, *Days of Sorrow and Pain: Leo Baeck and the Berlin Jews* (New York: Macmillan Publishing Co., 1978), 287.

They can teach Torah. They can give hope. They can save life. They can even give a moment of Noach, of rest, when we are lost at sea. Let us not take the kindness of others for granted, and let us offer the compassionate word whenever we can. And while we may not be worthy of giving words as powerful as Moses who was able to bring them to all humankind, maybe we can be like Noah, helping our circle of loved ones and creating our own sanctuary of life.

**The Window in the Ark**

It is fitting that we have had a week of rain for the week when we read the story of Noah. It is supposed to start precipitating now, for Sukkot initiates the rainy season in the land of Israel, and our Shemini Atzeret service contained our prayer for rain. Still, we cannot help but notice it has not only gotten wetter but also darker. The sun does not come up until later in the morning, and it goes down earlier and earlier.

Before we risk feeling a little gloomy, we should take comfort in the fact that for Noah and his family, it must have been much worse. Nothing like a little glee at another person's misery.

The Torah tells us that it rained for forty days and nights, flooding the earth and wiping out all life. Noah and his family were trapped inside the ark, which God had commanded him to build. The instructions for building the ark were very clear:

> Make yourself an ark of gopher wood; make it an ark with compartments, and cover it inside and out with pitch. This is how you shall make it: the length of the ark shall be three hundred cubits, its width fifty cubits, and its height thirty cubits. Make an opening for daylight in the ark, and terminate it within a cubit of the top. Put the entrance to the ark in its side; make it with bottom, second, and third decks. (Genesis 6:14-16)

This was to be Noah and his family's home for the entire time of their ordeal, holed up also with all the animals of the earth. Such a time must have particularly unpleasant, and yet we cannot help but think that they probably did not complain. After all, they were inside the ark. Death and destruction reigned supreme outside. Noah and his family were safe.

One of the most interesting features about these building instructions that God gives to Noah is that he is to make "an opening for daylight." In Hebrew, the opening is referred to as a *tzohar*, an obscure word. Some translate it simply as a "skylight." Later in the story, however, we find that Noah sends out a raven and then a dove to see if there is dry land. The Torah tells us: Forty days later, Noah opened the ark's window that he had made (Genesis 8:6). A different Hebrew word, *chalon*, is used, and here we can see that it can open and shut to keep the water out.

The question is if these two things, the *tzohar*, the "skylight," and the *chalon*, the "window" were the same thing or two different openings. Almost all commentaries say that they are the same thing, such as Kimchi when he says that the two openings are "identical." But if that is the case, then why use two different terms? In reference to the *tzohar*, Ibn Ezra tells us that there must have been numerous skylights in order to give sufficient light to the ark, not just one. Another explanation found in a *midrash* is that the *tzohar* wasn't really an opening at all but rather a magical gem that shone with daylight for the day and dimmed during the night. But this would mean that Noah, of his own accord, made the additional *chalon*, the window (Genesis Rabbah 31:11, 33:5). This is what the Torah explicitly tells us, "Noah opened the ark's window that he had made."

If this is the case, that Noah had plenty of sources of light, magical or otherwise, why would he make another window, adding to the instructions that God had given him? Why would he add a shuttered door, perhaps in the side near the roof?

While all of this is speculation, perhaps it is because while Noah and his family were safe inside the ark, it would have been impossible to ignore the suffering that was happening outside. Lights in the ceiling would not have allowed Noah to bear witness to the destruction, but a *chalon*, a window in the side, would have enabled him to look out and see. Noah, of his own accord, felt compelled to witness the scene around him.

In Judaism, we have a strong tradition that tells us not to look away and ignore the pain of the world. Maimonides teaches us "anyone who sees a poor person begging, averts their eyes, and does not give *tzedakah* commits a transgression" (*Mishnah Torah Hilchot Matnot Aniyim* 10:3). The Torah commands that in biblical times, when a neighbor lost an animal, such as an ox or a horse, and then we see the animal wandering, we may not hide ourselves but rather should stop what we are doing and help chase the animal down. In addition, when someone's burden falls and needs help lifting it on the road, we may not conceal our presence in the hope of dodging the responsibility of getting involved. We cannot simply drive by, pretending not to see but must stop and help.

Noah looked out the window out of empathy. And we who live in our insulated homes, protected by green lawns, and fenced by trees, ought to remember Noah's window. We are obligated to look out from our comfort and security, to be sensitive to the suffering of others, and to get involved when we can.

It might have been easier for Noah to shut the window and not look, to turn up the radio and keep our eyes focused on only what is in front of us, but inside we would know that we were choosing not to see. We can try to inoculate ourselves with endless entertainment and headphones in our ears, but these tools of self-deception have their limits. Denial and self-afflicted blindness are contrary to the Jewish values of compassion and truth telling. But these must begin with "truth-seeing," to bear witness to the truth.

We live in a world where we can be easily overwhelmed. We can be overwhelmed by information, by chatter, but the incredible size of the events our day. In a time of globalization, it is very tempting to tune out. We must protect ourselves.

But let us, even as we each build our respective arks in order to make it through this day and age, also remember to build a window, a window to look out and see the world around us. Let us pray to have the courage and sensitivity to look out that window. And even more so, let us endeavor to reach out and help whenever we are able.

**"Going Where No One Has Gone Before"**

Like many of us, I grew up watching "Star Trek" on TV, and it was great entertainment. When the opening credits would role and the theme music would play, it was very exciting. The star ship "Enterprise" would zip around, and it didn't matter how fake or ridiculous everything looked. And the narrator would always say, with great drama in his voice, that the voyage of the starship, "Enterprise," was to "boldly go where no man has gone before."

We human beings have great pride in our desire for exploration and conquering. We consider Columbus, Magellan, and others to be great figures that illustrate the power of the human will. But as far back as the Bible we find that the will to go where no one has gone before often comes with a price, and we are cautioned in this tale from Scripture to carefully examine our motivations before we go out and conquer. The story of which I speak is only nine verses long, and it has come to be known as the story of the Tower of Babel. Interestingly enough, whereas the stories of creation and of the flood can be found in different versions in other ancient cultures, the story of the Tower of Babel only appears in the Hebrew Bible. It is unique to Judaism. It reads, in its entirety, as follows:

> Once, the whole earth was of one language, and of one speech. It came to pass, as people journeyed from the East, which they found a plain in the land of Shinar, and they settled there. They said one to another, "Come, let us make bricks, and burn them thoroughly." Thus they had brick for stone, and they had slime for mortar. Then they said, "Come, let us build a city and a tower for ourselves, whose top may reach to heaven; and let us make a name for ourselves lest we be scattered abroad upon the face of the whole earth."
>
> The Eternal came down to see the city and the tower, which the mortals had built. God said, "Behold, the people are one, and they have all one language; and this is what they begin to do?!? Now they will restrain themselves from nothing that they scheme to do. Come, let us go down, and there confuse their language that they may not understand

> one another's speech."
> So the Eternal scattered them abroad from there upon the face of all the earth, and they left off the building of the city. Therefore the name of it is called Babel (meaning, "confusion") because the Eternal confused the language of all the earth there and from there God scattered them abroad upon the face of all the earth. (Genesis 11:1-9)

This ancient story raises more questions than answers. On the surface, it appears to be a story that explains how different languages came to be on the earth and why it is that people live in so many different places. We can imagine a little girl asking her mother why is it that some people speak French and other people speak Spanish and how did they get to live so far away, and the parent quickly cooks up a tall tale to explain how things came to be.

But our sages of old and modern day teachers see something more serious in the story of the Tower of Babel. They see lessons that apply to our lives today, for just as we fantasize about going where no one has gone before, so did the citizens of the land of Shinar. They built a tower into outer space, and it cost them dearly. Are we to understand that God does not want us to cooperate with one another? What was so wrong about having one language for all humanity? What sin did the people of Shinar commit that caused God to directly intervene into their lives to disrupt their so-called "scheme"?

One rabbinic teaching was God approved of human cooperation, but God did not approve the project itself. The project of building a tower, they claim, came out of the arrogance of the people. The story says that they wanted to "make a name for themselves," and therefore their motivation was all wrong. Building a tower into heaven was seen as a direct affront to God. The people didn't know where their strength ended and where the heavenly powers began. Their project was an arrogant invasion into heaven that called for a response (*Pirkei D'Rabi Eliezer* 24).

Not only that, the rabbis continue, but also the project must have been more important than the people themselves. If we think back to the ancient world, the amount of labor and danger that is involved in building such a monument must have meant a huge loss of human life. Think of the pyramids or the ziggurats of the Middle East, or even the stone carvings of Petra. We might ask ourselves, How many human beings must have died in the construction of these grand plans? One rabbinic legend has it that when the Babylonians lost control and dropped a brick from the structure of the tower, they would wail and bemoan the loss. But when a human being fell during this risky escapade, they would shrug and simply say that it was a necessary sacrifice. In the eyes of these rabbis, then, the problem with the Tower of Babel was that it was a project of arrogance and a waste of life.

We must always be sure that our motivation is correct. Our endeavors should not be to make a name for ourselves, for personal pride or domination. Rather, our projects should reflect the sanctity of our lives and the gifts that God has given us.

If we move ahead to the middle ages, however, we find another explanation for the Tower of Babel offered by our tradition. A rabbi named Obadiah Sforno who lived during the Italian Renaissance. He claimed that the sin of the Tower of Babel was that it was conceived by a few but imposed upon all of the people. The one language of humanity was used to impose one ruler, one religion, and one point of view onto the mass of humanity. The tower, claimed Sforno, was built through slavery of mind, body, and spirit. This was not an act of cooperation at all, he claims, but an act of oppression. When God caused everyone to speak different languages, therefore, God was not breaking up the camaraderie of the people. God was, in a sense, revealing the differences that were already there. God was trying to foster diversity in the face of tyranny. And perhaps it was only Rabbi Sforno, who came from a time of great openness to the universality of humanity, who could reveal this meaning hidden in the text. (See Sforno on Genesis 11:6.)

Rabbi Sforno thus has another lesson that is immediately relevant to us. Never should our efforts treat casually the freedoms that we hold dear. Never should a compelling vision turn into coercion or our devotion to a cause become another's slavery. True cooperation is the celebration of our diversity, recognizing our genuine differences while learning to work together.

But there is one more explanation that I would like to offer to you tonight, one that comes from the modern era. Rabbi Benno Jacob looks at the story of the Tower of Babel and sees a completely different problem. He simply sees this story as an explanation of misplaced priorities.[5] What use, asked Rabbi Jacob, is such a tower? The sin of the Tower of Babel is that they built a tower rather than build housing for the poor, that they raised these bricks rather than make sure there were enough hospitals with decent equipment, which they tried to make a name for themselves rather than supply enough accommodations for the aged or for schools. While the people of Shinar were boldly going where no one had gone before, they left the people who were in need of society's help behind.

Perhaps the most important lesson of the story of the Tower is Babel is that the expenditure of our resources should match our values. Our resources should surely be dedicated to the new frontiers of our existence, but we must first be sure to take care of our people, our schools and our hospitals, the dignity of our elders and the growth of our children. Without compassion for our neighbors laid down as a foundation for our society, no tower has any chance of succeeding.

If we look at all of these explanations of the sins of the people of Shinar together, it is hard not to find one of which we as a nation are not still guilty. We are a society whose technology and energy is unprecedented. We can build far more than towers that reach heaven; we can plunge into the human genome and we can take photographs of the furthermost stars. Our power over life and death has never before reached such potential, and it is only going to increase. The question we used to face is: Can we do this? We now know that the answer is yes. We can do just about anything we set our minds to. The question we should ask ourselves instead is: Should we do this? Is this a moral thing to do, and what are the potentials for abuse?

This reminds me of an incident that occurred with our high school students when they were studying American History. They started talking about the arrival of Columbus to America and how they were taught to memorize the names of the Nina, the Pinta, and the Santa Maria. They were also taught that, whereas the white men from Europe had these majestic boats with sails, nets, and hulls, the Native Americans only had canoes. Clearly, the European explorers were far more technologically advanced. They used these boats not

---

[5] Harvey Fields, *A Torah Commentary for Our Times: Genesis* (New York: UAHC Press, 1990), 33-34.

only to explore the world but often to make war and even engage in the slave industry. And so we asked ourselves: which kind of boat do you think was more beautiful? Which people used their boats in a more ethical fashion? Just because we have more knowledge, does that automatically mean that we are wiser?

Let us remember the lessons of our sages. All tools can be used for blessing or for curse. As our rabbis taught, let us hold every human life as holy and approach all of our endeavors with humility. As Rabbi Sforno preached, let us remember to celebrate the diversity that each country, language, and human face contributes to our humanity. And as Rabbi Jacob wrote, let us remember that our morality must be the foundation upon which all else is built.

In short, the Tower of Babel story does ask us to go where no one has gone before, but not in the use of our power. Rather, we pray to expand our hearts into new frontiers. We pray to bring our minds into compassionate understanding of one another. And we pray for unprecedented strength to build an ethical foundation and a life according to God's will.

## *Lech Lecha* (Genesis 12:1-17:27)

### A Revolution Begins with Two Words

When God called Abraham, two Hebrew words inaugurate the journey. *Lech lecha* – commonly translated as "go forth" – start Abraham on his way, and these words have echoed through history: "Go forth from your land, from your birthplace, from your father's house to the land that I will show you" (Genesis 12:1).

In Hebrew, these words are written in an emphatic form. The word *lech*, "go," would have sufficed, but by adding the second construction, *lecha*, a sense of urgency was added. When God called Abraham, God wasn't just saying, "Go when you have a chance," or "Go when you are ready," but rather, "Get going!"

Jewish commentators throughout the ages have pondered the depth of these two words and what it really means to "get going." Rashi says that the second word, lecha, should also be understood hyper-literally, "for you." In other words, "Go forth for your own sake, for you, for your own benefit and good." According to Rashi, Abraham needed to leave the toxic environment in which he found himself and find a new home where he could live the life he was meant to. Leaving was to his own benefit (Rashi on Genesis 12:1).

Centuries later, Hasidic commentators would take Rashi's understanding to a new level. They understood "*lecha*" to mean not just to go "for yourself" but also go "to yourself." This was not just a leave-taking of a place but a journey inward, to himself, to go to his roots, to live an authentic life. In other words, *lech lecha* can also mean "be true to yourself."[6]

This understanding is complemented by what it means to leave one's birthplace and home. Hasidic teaching continues that more than a change of place, *lech lecha* means to get out of one's way of thinking, to leave an old view of the world behind. It is a command to be open-minded and to try to transcend one's limits. It can be understood as being willing to find one's potential. Go deep into yourself. One *midrash* states that at home Abraham was like a bottle of perfume that was shut up tight. It was time to uncork the bottle and to go spread his fragrance throughout the world (Genesis Rabbah 39:2).

---

[6] For example, *Kedushat Levi* on Genesis 12:1.

Aviva Zornberg points out that this journey is the first journey that is not a matter of dismissal but one that is made willingly in a positive direction. Previously, Adam and Eve were kicked out of the Garden of Eden. Cain was exiled to wander the earth. Noach needed to escape a flood. The makers of the Tower of Babel were scattered. But Abraham sets out willingly because there is a divine imperative.[7]

Some interpreters have pointed out the strange order of the biblical verse. Physically, whenever we leave somewhere, we first leave the house, then our home town, and then our land, but the Torah lists it in reverse order. "Go forth from your land, from your birthplace, from your father's house…" Perhaps it does so because God is breaking Abraham in slowly to the emotional difficulty of the task: you are going to leave the country, which means you need to leave the place you were born, which means that, as hard as it might be, you need to leave the home that you grew up in.

Another commentator looks at the numerical value of the Hebrew words "*lech lecha*." In Hebrew, there is not separate set of symbols for letters and numbers. Letters and numbers are the same. So *lech lecha*, which adds to exactly 100, also indicates the age at which Isaac will be born to Abraham. Abraham left in order to have a child and a new future, and the age at which his dream would come true was embedded in the command. (*Baal HaTurim* on Genesis 12:1).

Still another commentator, Rabbi Zalman Sorotzkin, points out another facet of the words *lech lecha*. He points out that these two words are used by God twice, once at the beginning of Abraham's journey, and once at the end. Abraham is told to go forth into the world, and then, finally, when he is with his son Isaac, he is told to "go forth" – *lech lecha* – to a mountain to offer up his son to God. Sorotzkin states:

> We customarily say that our forefather Abraham began Jewish history with *lech lecha*. Now, the rabbis tell us that our forefather's lives presage our own. The Jewish people have spent little time "at home"; for most of their history they have undergone Abraham's first trial, wandering from nation to nation, from one

[7] Aviva Zornberg, *Genesis: the Beginning of Desire* (Philadelphia, Jewish Publication Society, 1995), 74.

> country to another. But frequently they have also faced Abraham's last trial, too: the sacrifice of Isaac. This other *lech lecha*, "Get yourself to the land of Moriah" was more significant than the first because it was the more difficult of the two. How often the Jewish people have sacrificed themselves on Abraham's altar since they became a nation![8]

There are elements of truth to all of these interpretations. Spirituality often begins with a leave-taking, of leaving behind a stifling environment or an old way of thinking. It is often to our own benefit to go, as emotionally difficult as it may be, but it is ultimately for our own good. No one I know enjoys unwanted or sudden change. Nevertheless, we sometimes only reach our potential when facing some adversity, when forced into something new. Perhaps even in the beginning is a hint of where we will end up. And too often, going forward means tremendous sacrifice.

But I think today *lech lecha* also has an added meaning: stand up for yourself. The Jewish people have indeed heard the call to leave for a better situation, going from country to country, and too often been compelled to offer our sacrifice, and we have proven that we can reach tremendous heights and spread beautiful gifts throughout the world. But going forth for yourself can also mean not to be complacent, to go forth and demonstrate and protest and write and speak out. Abraham was told that he would go out and be a blessing, but sometimes we need to make our own blessings. Sometimes we need to act on our own behalf. God will bless us if we take the initiative, if we act first. Waiting around, standing still, hoping that someone else will stand up for the Jewish prophetic vision doesn't work.

If we have a view of how our country is supposed to be according to our Jewish values, then we need to get out and do something about it. If we think that something needs to be done for the Jewish people, for Israel, or for the world, then *lech lecha* means to get off of our butts and move. The world is crying out for help. Israel needs our vocal and unapologetic support. Schools need our

---

[8] Rabbi Zalman Sorotzkin, *Insights in the Torah: Bereishis* (Brooklyn: Mesorah Publications, Ltd., 1991), 92.

attention. Energy reform has all but been forgotten. Providing affordable housing has been all but left behind in the foreclosure crisis. Pick an area of the world that is hurting, and do something about it. Get involved. Pick something that you are passionate about, and act. Move! Go forth!

I recently had a conversation with an Israeli who is living in America. He said, "You know, you Americans like to sit on your couches and watch a lot of television. You don't like to go out and do things." That astute observation reveals a real pity, because there is so much to do. There are things to learn and experience. There are causes that need volunteers. There is so much that can be done.

If we can still hear the command of *lech lecha*, to go forth, then maybe we can also recognize that this is for our own good. Stand up for yourself and for others, and do God's work in the world, just the way Abraham once did. The command comes, and it is not casual. It is necessary, and it is urgent.

**Abrahamic Faiths**

On Wednesday morning I found myself sitting in front of about seventy 7th and 8th graders at the Blessed Sacrament school in Walpole. This private Catholic school had invited me to participate in an interfaith panel. My friend Father Scott Euvrard from Our Lady of Sorrows Church here in Sharon took the lead and invited me along with a wonderful Muslim woman, Karin Firoza. We were to share a little about our similarities and differences. The students were incredibly polite. Dressed in their smart uniforms, attentively sitting and listening, and happily bringing us water were just some ways they showed their hospitality. And they were genuinely interested in what we had to say. After all, interfaith discussion is important not only to learn about others but about ourselves. Sometimes you can only understand something after comparing it to something different.

We began by discussing similarities. We talked about monotheism – the belief in one God – and Father Scott admitted that in Catholicism it is complicated because while they believe in one God they also believe in the Trinity. We talked about shared ethics of respect, love, and charity. We talked about how each religion is based on a Scripture, taking the form of interpretation of a written word. And finally, we talked about how the three religions are often grouped together under the umbrella "The Abrahamic Faiths." We all look to Abraham as a common ancestor.

In this week's Torah portion, we find this idea of Abraham being a common ancestor to be part of the story. Abraham's original Hebrew name was *Avram*, which means *av* – father, to *ram* – many. Abraham is the father of many nations, including Jews, Christians, and Muslims.

But then we moved on to differences. One of the most deceiving parts of comparative religion is that we want to line up questions to answers. For instance, we might be tempted to ask, "What do Jews, Muslims, and Christians believe about the afterlife?" The problem with that kind of question is that it neglects the issue of emphasis. In Christianity, the afterlife is very important. Much has been written and painted on church ceilings about heaven and hell. But in Judaism, the afterlife is not emphasized. Many Jews have believed different things, and there is no defining doctrine. Jews have been much more concerned about the life we know rather than what happens afterwards. More ink has been spilled on how a Jew should conduct him or herself in the morning than what happens after we die.

Trying to fill in a chart of what Jews, Christians, and Muslims believe, therefore, can be deceiving. Instead, we should ask about what kinds of questions preoccupy different religions. Whereas a Christian question might be, "How can I achieve salvation through Jesus?" an essential Jewish question is, "How can I fulfill the *mitzvot* or commandments?" In other words, there may be traces of commonality between the religions, but what does each emphasize?

After we got through discussing differences, including that Judaism does not see Jesus as the Messiah or Mohammed as the final prophet but can regard each as important teachers, we got to the heart of the matter. Many questions were raised about Islam and terrorism, stereotypes, and hate speech. What I wanted the students to take away from this session was this:

To risk deliberately oversimplifying matters, I believe there are two kinds of religious people. On the one hand, there are people who look to their religion for absolute certainty. These folks seek to abandon doubt and focus only on what they believe. Religion for them is a matter of moral clarity and unambiguous action. They believe they are the sole possessors of the truth, and not only disagree with their neighbor but can be moved to violence to defend their worldview. This is what the word "zealous" means – to be jealous of the truth. They believe, "I have the truth and no one else can." I told the students that the technical term for these people is jerks. "What should you learn from this panel?" I asked the students. "Very simple: don't be a jerk."

The other group of people is made of religious seekers. I count myself among them. We see ourselves not as possessing all of the truth but as fellow travelers on the same road. I come from my religion and culture. I celebrate and go deeply into my spirituality. But I can learn from other people. Religion for me is not so much a matter of clarity and certainty as it is a way to cope with the mysteries of life and death. It is a source of learning for living wisely and an instrument to affect change for more compassion and justice. The first spiritual step is humility, which means admitting our smallness and how much we do not know. This is the kind of religion that does not promote vandalism or even war but instead starts soup kitchens and builds hospitals.

The world needs fewer zealots and more seekers. We should seek to learn from all people and also learn how to healthily live and let live. Our piety will ultimately not be proven by arguing doctrine or Scripture but by how we conduct ourselves. We should ask, "How can Judaism help us lead a more meaningful life and make the world a better place?" We are – after all – first human and then Jewish. We should resist the tribal instinct that makes us want to reverse that priority.

I would like to close with a story by Gotthold Ephraim Lessing from 1779 from a literary work entitled *Nathan the Wise*. The story is a parable I will retell (Act 3):[9]

There was a king who was blessed with many children. He ruled his kingdom wisely, and much of his wisdom was due to his magic ring. This magical ring made him love others freely and be loved.

Eventually, as he grew older, he did something foolish. In different moments of pious weakness, he managed to tell each one of his many children that, when he died, they would be the one to inherit the ring. And each one secretly felt enormously blessed and proud.

---

[9] sites.google.com/site/germanliterature/18th-century/lessing/nathan-der-weise-nathan-the-wise

Well, the king realized he had done something foolish, and so he took the ring to a master jeweler, and told the jeweler to make fakes, copies so precise that no one could tell them apart or from the real thing.

Eventually, the king died, and it was quite a funeral. As the casket was lowered, all the children noticed that they each wore a ring. And then the argument began. "I have the real ring!" "No, I do!" The children argued with each other.

Finally the palace judge broke in and scolded them, "At the moment, it doesn't look like any of you have the real ring. If the ring is supposed to make you love and be worthy of love, then only time can tell who has the real ring. You must live a life pleasing to the eyes of God and humankind rather than expect a ring to do it for you."

Our religion is our ring. We have many diverse brothers and sisters. It is only how we as seekers conduct ourselves that determines whether or not we have the real thing.

## *Vayera* (Genesis 18:1-22:24)

### Who is Honored?

A story from Eastern Europe, recorded in a commentary by Rabbi Harvey Fields,[10] tells us that there was once a young student who was privileged enough to visit the home of the famed teacher known as the Chafetz Chaim. The student arrived later than he thought and immediately joined the rabbi at the dinner table just before Friday night dinner. He had been on the road for many hours. He was hungry and weak from travel.

The rabbi was just about to sing Shalom Aleichem, which is customarily sung before lighting the Shabbat candles. *Shalom Aleichem malachei hashareit, malachei elyon.* Greetings and peace to you, angels, servants of the Most High. It is believed that at the beginning of Shabbat, angels come down and accompany us through the day. Instead of singing, however, the rabbi skipped the song and quickly went through the blessings, rushing to the meal.

"Why did you skip singing Shalom Aleichem?" the student asked.

The Chafetz Chaim answered, "You were hungry. A hungry person should be fed as soon as possible. Angels can wait!"

This week's Torah portion speaks of the *mitzvah* of hospitality, *hachanasat orchim.* It begins when three men approach Abraham and Sarah's tent. Abraham gets up, rushes to greet them, and brings them into his home. Sarah prepares a meal. The men, who turn out to be angels, then announce that Sarah will become pregnant in her old age. She laughs, not believing them, but their words come true. In a year's time, Isaac is born.

This display of hospitality and its reward is contrasted with a second story in the Torah portion, which takes place in the home of Abraham's nephew, Lot. One of the angels stays behind with Abraham and Sarah, while the other two continue on to the city of Sodom. There they are greeted by Lot and brought into the house. The people of Sodom find out about it and surround the house, demanding that the guests be turned over to the mob. Lot, in a strange act of defense, tells the crowd not to be so wicked, that they can have his two daughters instead of the guests. The mob charges

---

[10] Fields, 47.

the house, and the angels blind the crowd with light. Lot and his family make their escape, and the angels caution them to run and not look back. Fire and brimstone rain down on the city. Lot's wife gazes behind her, and she turns into a pillar of salt.

It is hard to compare the two displays of hospitality. Abraham behaves graciously, and he is rewarded. Lot, however, lives in a hostile place. While he tries to protect the strangers, sacrificing his daughters is incomprehensible to us. We also do not know exactly why Lot's wife turns around. The *Midrash* teaches that Lot's wife did not want to leave, that actually she was the one who sent word to the town that they were hosting strangers and to come and get them. In this instance, Lot's wife did her best to take advantage of the strangers, whereas Abraham and Sarah did their best to honor them (Genesis Rabbah 50, 8-9).

At the heart of the *mitzvah* of hospitality is an issue of power. The act of hospitality is the voluntary giving up of power, of welcoming a person into our domain and making someone who could be subject to our will into an honored guest. The heads of the house lower themselves to be servants; the poor traveler becomes a king to be waited on. Power is given away freely, and God smiles. Pirkei Avot teaches, "Who is honored? The one who honors others" (*Avot* 4:1).

How we behave towards people over whom we have power is a test of our character. It is one thing to act moral and righteous when we are powerless and our actions affect only ourselves. It was Nietzsche who wrote that morality was only a commodity of the weak. But Judaism teaches that there is such a thing as morality when we have power and influence over others. We hold ourselves responsible for the vulnerable in our society. We are supposed to bring in the hungry and weary from the outside. It is as the prophet Isaiah has taught us:

> To unlock fetters of wickedness,
> And untie the cords of the yoke
> To let the oppressed go free;
> To break off every yoke.
> It is to share your bread with the hungry,
> And to take the wretched poor into your home;
> When you see the naked, to clothe him,

And not to ignore your own kin.

Then shall your light burst through like the dawn
And your healing spring up quickly;
Your Vindicator shall march before you,
The Presence of the ETERNAL shall be your rear guard.
Then, when you call, the ETERNAL will answer;
When you cry, God will say: Here I am. (Isaiah 58:6-9)

Rather than the worship of power, we obey commandments that ask us to serve righteousness. When we shelter another, we use our power correctly.

Today, we do not live in a time when wanderers from off of the street come to our homes very often. If someone comes over, it is either because they are invited, because they are asking for money, or because it is Halloween and they want candy.

That does not mean, however, that we cannot practice the *mitzvah* of *hachnasat orchim*. We can still use our resources to empower others, to shelter them, and to raise them up. Rather than keep what we have for ourselves, we can give freely.

There are numerous opportunities. We can give to organizations like Habitat for Humanity that literally build homes for the homeless. We can participate in or support local programs like Children of Chernobyl or the Fresh Air Fund where we welcome children into our homes and our lives. We can support the State of Israel so it may serve as a refuge for many. In doing so, we can strive to fulfill God's command. And sometimes, simply welcoming another into our lives with a cheerful and positive expression on our face can have untold power. I can lift another's spirits and recognize our common humanity. In fact, people who are homeless remark that people walking by, ignoring them and avoiding looking them in the eye is one of the most difficult parts of their situation. To be looked at with kindness can be a tremendous lift.

Let us use our power for good, to think of Abraham and Sarah as role models who kept their tent and their lives open on all sides. Let us think of ways that we can be like Abraham run out and seize the chance to help another. Let us walk with faces of welcome, reflecting the verse from the Torah, "May God's face be lifted up to yours and give you peace" (Numbers 6:26). If we do so, we will bring blessing to others and to ourselves.

**Coming in During the Last Scene**

There has been a recent trend in movies for the last couple of years to show part of the end of the movie at the beginning. The movie starts with a particularly dramatic scene of some of the main characters in conflict, and the audience is left to wonder, "What's going on? How did all of this come to be?' The story then goes back in time and relates the events that led up to such a desperate situation. Such a movie is Stephen King's "Dolores Claiborne," where the film begins with a scene of the housemaid standing over a woman in a wheelchair with a rolling pin in her hands, ready to strike her down. It is at that moment that the postman comes in and sees her. The rest of the movie is a trip back in time to explain and resolve how this situation came to be. When we finally return to this penultimate scene, we find that the woman in the wheelchair is in horrible pain and has been begging to be put out of her misery, but the housemaid cannot bring herself to do it.

Much the same happens in our Jewish storytelling tradition. Every Rosh Hashanah, we read the last scene of the story of Abraham. He stands over his son, Isaac, with a knife, ready to sacrifice him to God. But we rarely go back in time to read the story that led up to this scene. As a result, the story of the near-sacrifice of Isaac, appearing in this week's Torah portion, is often misunderstood.

Abraham is a fascinating individual. He is a character who has left his homeland in search of the One God. He has negotiated and fought with kings, he has cultivated new lands, and he has committed himself to an everlasting covenant. But Abraham appears strange to us in this final scene, the story we call the "*Akeidah*," the binding of Isaac.

The scene is meant to disturb us. God says, "Take your one, your precious one, Isaac, whom you love and go offer him up on a mountain that I will show you" (Genesis 22:2). Your one, your precious one. What might we expect from Abraham? Protest! A cry of pain! A whimper of pleading! Something.

Instead we get... nothing. Abraham gets up early, splits the wood, saddles his donkey, and doesn't say a word. And the rest of the story is filled with silences and lack of detail. Where are they going? To the mountain I will show you. How long did they travel, and which direction? Three days... to somewhere. And what did they say on the way? We have no idea.

Is Abraham blindly obeying God's command? Is that what God wants? Well, that idea doesn't really make much sense either. The only time Abraham does open his mouth to say something, he says to Isaac, "God will see to the lamb my son." Does that mean that he believes God won't let him do it? Is it just a slippery way to dodge answering Isaac's question? Is he too much in shock to really give an intelligible response? The text is profoundly silent. And all the while, in this loud silence, we can feel the anguish and hurt of Isaac, the one, the precious one, the beloved.

So let us go back in time to earlier in Abraham's story, like they do in the movies, and let's see what led up to this event. Let's look at the figure of Abraham in the story of Sodom and Gomorrah, just a few chapters earlier. Here, we find an Abraham who appears to be the exact opposite of the Abraham of the *Akeidah*. We read about an Abraham that would stand up and challenge God with remarkable *chutzpah*. In that story, God tells Abraham that God is going to utterly destroy all of the inhabitants of the cities of Sodom and Gomorrah because they are so wicked. What does Abraham do? He protests.

"Would You, God, destroy the righteous with the wicked? If there are fifty righteous people in the cities, will you spare the cities for their sake?" (Genesis 18:26).

God agrees. Abraham then begins to bargain God down. "What about forty?' God agrees again. "Thirty? Twenty? What about ten?' God agrees, and Abraham stops there. Abraham backs off at ten.

Here, apparently, the test was to see if Abraham would speak out on behalf of others. God goads Abraham on, and Abraham argues with God in a passionate plea for the lives of human beings. We are left admiring Abraham's initiative and extolling his sense of righteousness.

At first, we might have only more questions: How can the Abraham who pled for Sodom and Gomorrah be so silent when it is his own child at stake? Is this the same Abraham? Where is his righteous protest at God's test when it is his one, his precious one, whom he loves? To answer these questions and to explain the final scene, we must look more closely for the connection between the stories.

The connection, as it was taught to me, is this. At Sodom and Gomorrah, Abraham bargains with God. He protests on behalf of anonymous others in numbers of fifty, forty, thirty, and twenty. He stops at ten. Why ten? Why did he stop there? Why not down to the last righteous person in those cities?

Indeed, God saves those few righteous people in Sodom and Gomorrah before the destruction starts. The narrative tells how Abraham's nephew, Lot, was rescued by God's angels from Sodom and Gomorrah shortly before the destruction. God does not destroy the righteous with the wicked.

So perhaps God was waiting for Abraham to keep going. Why stop at ten? Maybe Abraham was supposed to say, "What if there is one righteous person in the cities? How can you kill that innocent one, God?' But Abraham did not. He stopped at a nice round number.

And so God showed how important one life can be. Especially if it is your one, your precious one, whom you love. We may read the binding of Isaac as God's hard lesson to Abraham on the importance of the individual. You see, it is easy to speak in large numbers. Ten righteous people in Sodom and Gomorrah. Seven thousand missing people in Kosovo. Three hundred ten thousand people told to stay in their homes during the recent uranium accident in Japan. Six million Jews murdered in the Holocaust. In the words of the Hebrew poet Dan Pagis: "I won't mention names / out of consideration for the reader, / since at first the details horrify / though finally they're a bore."[11]

But if we remember the one, the precious one, the loved one, we get a different story. That is the path from the story of Sodom and Gomorrah to the *Akeidah*. The families of those who have been killed in Kosovo, the faces of the children walking to school in nuclear contamination clothing in Japan, and the Jews that fill this synagogue, the individual, the precious, the beloved, they mean something to us. They break the numbness of large figures and remind us that these are individuals, that these are lives that we cannot round off to the nearest set of ten. As the Talmud says, "If one saves one life, it is as if one has saved an entire world; and if one

---

[11] Dan Pagis, "Autobiography," *Points of Departure* (Philadelphia: Jewish Publication Society, 1981), 3.

destroys one life, it is as if one has destroyed an entire world." With Isaac this is literally true, for without Isaac, God's promised blessing of progeny and abundant descendants for all time means nothing. Isaac is one life, yet he is also the promise of an entire future world of Israel. And it is the same with any individual, no matter where they may live or what group they might belong to. We lose an entire world of feelings, of thoughts, of insights, of children.

Let me share one last story with you, told to me about the Jewish philosopher Abraham Joshua Heschel, although I have heard it in other forms as well. Heschel as a boy read the story of the binding of Isaac, and as he read, he became frightened. He could picture Isaac as an individual, a boy with a face like his own. He was scared on Isaac's behalf when Abraham laid the wood upon him. He trembled when Abraham put Isaac on the altar. He almost cried out when Abraham reached for the knife.

Heschel's father saw his son's fright and said, "What are you reading?"

Heschel answered, "The *Akeidah.*"

"And why are you so frightened?"

"I couldn't help but think of what would have happened if the angel had been too late."

"Abraham," Heschel's father answered, "angels are never too late."

"Yes," Heschel answered, "But people can be."[12]

Let us commit ourselves anew to seek out the face of others, not as anonymous groups or statistics, but as people who need us as we need them. Let the last scene be one where we remember the sacred value of each life, that each life is precious and beloved. And let us strive for the day where everyone has a place to be a recognized individual, honored in dignity and respect, in a time of peace.

---

12 Hillel E. Silverman, *High Holiday Highlights: Make Them Your Spiritual Adventure* (Jersey City: KTAV Publishing House, Inc., 2003), 51-52.

## *Chayei Sarah* (Genesis 23:1-25:18)

### Being Remembered

In the Torah, we read that Abraham's last gesture as he prepares to die is to make arrangements for a wife for his son, Isaac. After the death of Sarah, Isaac's mother, and with the approach of his own end, Abraham wants to make sure his son is not going to be alone in the world. Abraham's last words are that Isaac should start a family, and he should realize that life was meant to be lived in relationship with others. Abraham is a father looking out for his child, trying to ensure his future.

Similarly, in the Haftarah (I Kings 1:1-31), King David is very old, and he is worried about his child, Solomon. There is a dispute in the kingdom as to who will inherit the throne. David makes a pronouncement to his wife, Bat Sheva, and to Nathan the Prophet that Solomon shall be king, and it is this formal declaration that ensures Solomon's future. However, the passing of the throne is far from easy, and David tells Solomon that this will be so. David tells Solomon that only through great effort and hard work will Solomon become a great and wise king. And so it happens when Solomon reigns after his father.

Its seems that this week is a week of aging parents making sure that their children are safe and secure before they leave this world and giving last minute instructions. Of course, we do not need to be aging to worry about the future of our children.

There is another story that comes to us from the Chasidic masters of Eastern Europe, which tells us of a man who anticipated his death and wanted his son to feel secure. In the story, a certain rabbi had come to employ two orphans in his home, and these children lived with him and served him. The children came to depend on the rabbi, but as time went on he knew that these children must soon learn to become independent. So one night, the rabbi took a lantern from off of the wall, opened up its shutters, and lit it. He then told the children to come with him outside. The children did so, and soon they were walking out into a dark field, approaching the woods. The light of the lantern guarded their steps, and they followed the rabbi down the path and into the forest. When they entered the woods, tree branches and leaves surrounded them. It was very dark, except for the light of the lamp the rabbi held. Suddenly, the rabbi stopped. He turned to the children, and he snapped the shutters on the lantern closed. A huge darkness fell over them, and the children became very frightened. "Rabbi!" they cried. "Where are you?"

"I am right here," the rabbi answered. "You cannot see me, but I am right here. One day, you also will be on your own, and you will no longer be able to see me or touch me in a moment of need. You will have to find your own way. But that does not mean you are alone or need to be frightened. My voice can always come out to you from the darkness of your memory when you need guidance."[13]

In the fears that we have for our children, and also in the fears that children have in going off to be on their own, we might ask ourselves about what feels permanent, what is it that will ensure our future. The words of Abraham are words of instruction telling Isaac to make his own family. The words of David are professional advice, telling Solomon to solidify his career through effort and hard work. And the words of the Chasidic rabbi standing in the darkness are words of faith and memory, telling his children to always remember what he tried to teach them when they feel lost and to believe in themselves. These things, family, hard work, and faithful memory, are the foundation upon which we also rely to carry us into our future. We might add that another element, love, permeates all of these, for just as Abraham loved Isaac, David loved Solomon, and the rabbi loved the orphan children in his home, so are our words colored by emotion.

Many times parents work hard to make sure that we will have enough capital to sustain our children and give them all the opportunities they need. Abraham, David, and the rabbi offer us three models of what it means to pass on a secure future to our children. But what children want most of us is our time and our attention. They want our guidance and to know how to be. It may be obvious and simple but it is nonetheless true: the most important and lasting things in our lives that we have to give are things we can neither touch, define, or pin down and fit neatly into a box. Things like family, hard work, memory, faith, and love are the truest things in our lives even though they are intangible. If we bequeath these immaterial things to our children, then they will go forward into independent lives feeling secure.

---

[13] Roberta Louis, *Test of Faith* (Los Angeles: Torah Aura Productions, 2005), 7.

One last final story (Midrash Psalms 93:12): A story is told about a problem that the sages faced with a provision that a man left in his will. In the will it stated that "my son shall not inherit anything from me until he has learned to be a fool." A fool? The rabbis were mystified. They went to see Rabbi Joshua ben Korcha, and as they approached Rabbi Joshua's house they saw him through the window. He was on all fours, with a reed sticking out of his mouth, making donkey sounds, playing with his children. It was then that the sages understood. Just as Rabbi Joshua was acting like a fool, so too do we inherit the best things from those who came before us when we immerse ourselves in the love and values of family, leaving behind pride and pretense.

God, help us to make memories that will sustain the next generation, to instill them with a sense of faith, to teach them the value of hard work and initiative, and to permeate all of our words and attention with love. Then we will inherit the blessing of our ancestors.

### The Servant's Prayer and Isaac's Prayer

What is prayer? Why do we do it? More importantly, why does most everyone seem to do it? All over the world, people pray. Worship seems to be an integral part of every culture.

This week in the Torah we read the words of a man's prayer. The man is the servant of Abraham, and he is sent to find a wife for his master's son, Isaac. But the rabbis in their commentaries found the words of the servant's prayer very problematic. The servant is standing near a well where the women have come to draw water. He prays for a sign to help him choose the right girl for Isaac. Here are his words, and see if you can guess what problem the rabbis had with them:

> Eternal One, God of my master Abraham, grant me good fortune this day, and deal graciously with my master Abraham: Here I stand by the spring as the daughters of the townsmen come out to draw water; let the maiden to whom I say, 'Please, lower your jar that I may drink,' and who replies, 'Drink, and I will also water your camels'—let her be the one whom You have decreed for Your servant Isaac. Thereby

> shall I know that You have dealt graciously with my master." (Genesis 24:12-14)

The servant asks for a sign. Specifically, he designs a test. He can pick a beautiful young lady with his own eyes. But how can he find out about her character? Just to make sure she is also generous and kind, the woman who not only notices him and gives him water but also goes above and beyond and gives water to his camels as well will be the one he is looking for.

So what is the problem? Sages like Maimonides was concerned that the servant's prayer borders on sorcery (*Avodah Zarah* 11:14). He has created a test, and he is waiting for God to literally send him "good fortune" and make his words come true. He found it audacious that the servant should assume that the Creator of the universe would condescend to accommodate his particular words. Other sages disagree. They found the servant's prayer merely a description of a character test.[14]

Underneath there debate is a more basic question: what is prayer at its root? Is prayer simply wishing, or is it something else?

Occasionally, some people will try to answer this question by coopting science. There have been studies done of people who are having surgery, while unbeknownst to them people in another room or even another city are praying for them. Do they have a higher rate of recovery than people who don't have strangers – without their knowledge – praying for them? Many times the writers of these studies claim that there is a tremendous effect and this proves the power of prayer.

Any scientist, however, will tell you that this is nonsense. Science deals with empirical data. How are you supposed to measure prayer scientifically? Or a person's piety? Does their denomination count? Any review of these studies shows that remote, intercessory prayer cannot be measured scientifically. This also goes for sports teams and armies. As much as we may pray for a magical sign for victory or something else, there is no way to tell. How are we supposed to know, as the Bob Dylan song goes, that God is on our side?

Going back to our Torah story, like Maimonides, if we

---

[14] *Chullin* 95b, Nehama Leibowitz, *New Studies in Bereishit* (Jerusalem: Hemed Press, 1993), 225.

understand the servant's prayer at the well as sorcery, then, pardon the pun, it does not seem to hold much water.

Praying for signs usually is disappointing. So then why should we pray? We should pray because prayer is really about internal changes in ourselves in the emotional realm, not physical manipulations of our world. We can ask God to give us insight and see the world in a new way. We ask God for strength or courage to face something we need to face. We show thanks to God for the blessings in our lives, and this gives us a feeling of peace. Prayer helps the person who prays through inner transformation. The true sign of the efficacy of prayer is if it makes you a more humble person. It may also help another, but only if they know you are praying for them. It can help them feel less lonely. Prayer is not magic; it is meditation, perspective, and connection.

We have an example of this kind of prayer, prayer-as-self-reflection-and-meditation, also in our Torah portion this week. The Torah says when the servant brings Rebecca, the woman he has found to be the bride, home to Isaac, they find Isaac out meditating in a field. Isaac was literally just talking things over with God, alone outside. This kind of prayer makes more sense to me than the servant's prayer who asked for good luck and a sign. Traditionally, the rabbis understood Isaac to be establishing the *mincha* or afternoon prayer.

Rabbi Nachman of Breslov encouraged people to make prayer a daily part of their lives. He wasn't talking about knowing the Hebrew prayers, although of course he did want people to know them. The Hebrew prayers connect Jews to each other and speak of the Jewish people's values. But he was just as concerned that people take time each day to simply talk to God in your own language about anything you want. He also was ahead of his time because he insisted that – if you really wanted to see personal transformation – you couldn't just think your prayer. You had to go somewhere you were completely alone and talk out loud to God. Today we might call this a version of talk therapy, but Rabbi Nachman called it *hitbodedut*, which literally means "alone time." It was time to be alone and talk aloud to God. Rabbi Nachman taught that if you did this every day, you would live a less stressed and more balanced life. It would allow you to have more time with a *yishuv hada'at*, a settled mind (*Likkutei Moharan* II:122).

I would like to issue everyone the Rabbi Nachman challenge. I have spoken of this at Religious School, and I give the challenge to you as well. It is simply this: Talk to God by yourself out loud for one minute every day this upcoming week. See what happens to you. Don't pray for magic signs or for the Patriots' defense to move out of last place. Prayer can't help them. Instead, see if can just simply talk about how you are feeling. If you get stuck, just keep talking, even if it seems mundane. What do you need help with to be a better person? What would you like to thank God for in your life? What is confronting you this day that you need help facing? See if you come out after your conversation feeling lighter, more humble, or even grateful.

God, teach us to connect to You and to each other. "Eternal God, open my lips that my mouth may declare Your glory" (Psalm 51:15).

## *Toledot* (Genesis 25:19-28:9)

### Isaac: Between a Rock and a Hard Place

You have to feel sorry for Isaac. His father, Abraham, is the central character in twelve whole chapters in the Torah. His grandson, Jacob, gets ten. Isaac, the man in the middle, gets only one. One chapter in which he is the main character. In all the other places in which he appears, and even those are few, he is relegated to the background. Whoever was his publicity agent should have been fired.

As a result, we do not know much about the second of our three patriarchs. We know that as a child, he was traumatized by being dragged up a hill by his father to be offered as a sacrifice. We know that as an old man, he went blind and was tricked by Jacob into bestowing his innermost blessing onto the wrong son. And in between, what did he do with his life?

Our one chapter (Genesis 26) tells us that Isaac did three things. God appears to Isaac and renews the covenant with him. It says that God told him, "Reside in this land, and I will be with you and bless you; I will assign all these lands to you and to your heirs, fulfilling the oath that I swore to your father Abraham. I will make your heirs as numerous as the stars of heaven" (Genesis 26:3-4). From this we learn that Isaac maintained a relationship with God and renewed the covenant of his father. Just as his father was promised abundant descendants, residence in the land, and that God would be with him, so will Isaac enjoy those blessings. Isaac maintains the traditions of his father.

The second thing we learn about Isaac from this chapter about his life is that he was able to make peace with his neighbors. It tells us how Isaac made a pact with the local king, Abimelech, and how he avoided open war with the Philistines. Through painful sacrifice of resources and direct negotiation, Isaac and Abimelech exchange oaths, and this pact lasts throughout his lifetime.

The third, final, and perhaps most important thing we find related to us about the life of Isaac is that he dug wells. Isaac must have been very talented about finding water in the desert, at digging wells and thereby bringing prosperity to his family and to all of his household. His ability to find water in the desert became the envy of all of his neighbors, but when they would claim the wells for themselves, rather than fight them, he would simply dig new ones. In an expanding economy, all things are possible. And the Torah claims that the water in the wells were called, "living waters," (Genesis 26:19) a very unusual phrase.

It is because of this unusual phraseology, that the water in Isaac's wells are called, "living waters," that the rabbis of old brought an esoteric interpretation to what Isaac was doing. The sages of antiquity interpret the act of digging a well as a spiritual exercise. They read into Isaac's well-digging as a symbol that Isaac didn't just bring water to the people but also wisdom. In the *Midrash*, which is rabbinic legends and lore, the rabbis claim that Isaac dug five wells, corresponding to the Five Books of Moses (Genesis Rabbah 64:8). Even before Moses lived, Isaac was spiritually bringing living waters, meaning wisdom, to the people. Water, a sign of nourishment, was equated with nourishing words that sustain people.

So even though Isaac only gets one chapter in the Torah, he manages to do some important things: he maintained the covenant, made a peace treaty, and found vital resources so that he as well as those around him could live. The vitality of these resources were "living waters," either in a literal sense or in the sense of the rabbis, meaning the dispensation of wisdom.

Still, one wonders whether or not Isaac would have been satisfied with his accomplishments. He is literally stuck between a rock and a hard place, between an extremely famous father and a just as famous son. He does not nearly get the credit that he deserves.

It is for this reason that a Chasidic rabbi of 19$^{th}$ century Poland makes this sensitive insight: Rabbi Yechiel of Aleksandrow, Poland, claims that Isaac never felt he accomplished much in his whole life. All of his life he thought he thought of himself only as "the son of Abraham."[15] He never felt he did much in all of his days. And whoever edited the Torah must have felt so, too, for only giving him one chapter.

However, Rabbi Yechiel goes on to point out something even more sensitive and insightful. He also claims that Abraham never felt that he did anything particularly special, that he lived all of his days not knowing if his work for God was going to last or if anything he attempted was ultimately worthwhile. One thing he was certain of,

---

15 Lawrence S. Kushner and Kerry M. Olitzky, *Sparks Beneath the Surface: A Spiritual Commentary on the Torah* (Northvale: Jason Aronson Inc., 1995), 29.

however, that he felt was his one good accomplishment: he had raised a righteous son, Isaac.

Yechiel concludes that this is the way it is with all righteous people. The parents give all the credit to their children and the children give all the credit to their parents. In a sense of meekness and humility, their own accomplishments seem small, but their faith in others is large.

Perhaps we can identify with how the patriarchs felt. At the end of the day, none of us will be able to know if our accomplishments will be great or small, enduring or fleeting. We will never know if our labors will really last. But we can have faith in generations past and those yet to be and our connection to them. Our personal Torahs may be long or short, well-known or obliterated by time. But hopefully we can say, "I was part of a righteous family, I helped teach others wisdom, I was part of the chain of tradition and was therefore connected to something larger and more important than myself."

We grow in stature the more humble we are, and the more we see ourselves as part of a tradition and part of a larger whole. It does not necessarily matter if our contribution is famous or not, but it does matter to see ourselves as part of a chain going back and forward in time.

Isaac, it seems, was content to say that, and perhaps so can we.

## *Vayeitzei* (Genesis 28:10-32:3)

### *Rachel Imeinu*

Toward the end of Herman Melville's *Moby Dick*, Captain Ahab, while searching for the white whale, encounters another ship. The ship is called the Rachel, and the captain of the ship is desperate. The captain of the Rachel bumped into the famous white whale, and they put down boats to pursue it. The venture did not go well, however, and the captain's son (as well as other sailors) was lost at sea. Ahab parts company with the Rachel and her captain, and Melville states that Rachel continued to look for her lost children. At the end of the novel, when only the narrator survives, it is the Rachel that comes to the rescue.

One of the things that makes *Moby Dick* such a great novel is that Melville knew his Bible. Specifically, he was familiar with this week's Torah portion, *Vayetzei*, and one of its central characters, Rachel.

In this week's selection, a young man named Jacob leaves home, and on his way he dreams of a ladder connecting heaven and earth. In that dream, God, at the top of the ladder, tells him that God will take care of him. God will protect him and provide for him.

Jacob comes to a well, and he sees the people gathered there. There is a stone over the well's mouth, and the people are waiting for the shepherds to come and remove the stone. One of those people in the crowd is Rachel.

When Jacob sees Rachel, he is overcome with emotion. In the first act of macho prowess, he lifts the stone off of the well himself. He then comes over to Rachel, and wasting no time, kisses her. The Torah even says he bursts into tears.

But not all goes according to plan, as romantic love seldom does. Jacob agrees to work seven years in order to marry Rachel, but her father has other plans. After seven years, Jacob marries a veiled bride, only to discover that he has married her older sister, Leah. The father explains that it is there custom that the older is always married before the younger. Jacob then agrees to work another seven years in order to marry his beloved. In a sense, Rachel comes to represent love itself.

Still, the three of them make a strange family. The sisters, now wives to the same man, become competitors. Jacob fades into the background of the story, and Rachel especially comes to the foreground. Rachel competes with her sister, Leah, to have children. Leah produces child after child, and she praises God for each one. Rachel, however, has difficulty conceiving, and it is only after a great deal of time that she gives birth to Joseph, whose name, incidentally, means something to the effect of, "May I have another?' Rachel does give birth to another son, Benjamin, but she dies in childbirth.

This is not the end of the story. Even death does not end Rachel's struggle. In later Scripture, the prophet Jeremiah declares that, when the Jewish people went into exile, Rachel's spirit was present at the side of the road watching over her descendants leave the Land of Israel. In Jeremiah 31:14, we read that Rachel is weeping continually for her exiled children. It is this verse, incidentally, that Herman Melville referenced as the last line of his book when the narrator is rescued: "Rachel…in her retracing search after her missing children, only found another orphan." [16]

With all of this struggle and lamentation, we might think of Rachel as a tragic figure. I believe, however, that it would be a mistake to do so. Just as the Rachel is the ship that comes to the rescue at the end of *Moby Dick*, in Jewish legend Rachel is often depicted as the Jewish people's best representative before God. For instance, when God destroyed the Temple, we read in one rabbinic story that Rachel takes God to task for such an act, much in the same way that Abraham argued before God for the cities of Sodom and Gomorrah. "How could you have done such a thing?" Rachel asks, and the rabbis declare that God cried and wept in response to Rachel's accusatory finger pointing. It is perhaps for these reasons, for her compassion and her strength, that Rachel is called in the Talmud, *Rachel Immeinu*, "Rachel our mother."

A question that we may ask, as human beings as well as Jews, is what is it inside of each of us that has made Rachel into this kind of figure in our tradition? Why do we, in passing down our Torah from generation to generation, cling to the figure of a woman who is eternally present, waiting for us while we go into exile, weeping for us when we are in pain, and standing up for us when we feel that the world is too much for us to bear? What desire does *Rachel Immeinu*, Rachel our mother, satiate in our collective psyche?

---

[16] Herman Melville, *Moby Dick* (USA: Bantam Books, 1967), 521.

Perhaps it is that all people have a fundamental need. The need is for empathy. Rachel, as described in the Bible and rabbinic lore, is one of the most empathic figures of our tradition. She, to use an over-used phrase, "feels our pain." She is the comfort of Jacob who is on the run. She symbolizes the person in our lives who is worth waiting and laboring for. She represents the source of inspiration that gives us strength to move boulders and obstacles. She is the comforting voice in our conscience that makes us feel less lonely. While we might want to bottle up our emotions, Rachel teaches us that we all need to express ourselves and find fortitude turning outwards, in opening the well and letting the waters flow. Rachel represents our need to be heard and understood, our longing for connection.

This need for empathy presents itself especially during this time of year. Soon, when we approach our cars in the morning, the frost will have collected overnight on the hood. We will be able to see our breath when we exhale. The temperature has begun to drop, and it is only going to get colder. We have to remember to put on layers and to be sure to take our jackets when we leave our homes. Perhaps we can hear the voice of our mothers in our heads, reminding us to bundle up.

But there are those among us who might only feel the cold and might not hear Rachel's voice. Perhaps we need to be that voice for each other. Perhaps we might realize that we all have that need for connection and to think of those who are lonely and in need of a human touch.

And so, as the winter approaches, a little empathy, a little bit of the Rachel in all of us, should come into play. As we feel the cold, we should empathize with those who feel colder. And as we gather around the table to give thanks for our lives, our friends, and our families, we should also do something on behalf of others. Who knows? Perhaps we might be like the Rachel, the ship that comes to the rescue at long last.

Let us pray for the sensitivity to care for others and to be like *Rachel Imeinu* who lets us feel heard, understood, and connected. Let us dedicate ourselves to being aware of others' circumstances, and be moved to do something about it. Let it be our mission to nurture empathy within ourselves and our community, and, in so doing, perhaps we can help mend our too often broken world.

## *Vayishlach* (Genesis 32:4-36:43)

### Being Sent

I would like to invite you into a very special world, the world of Jacob, our father. The stories of Jacob are filled with a dream-like quality as Jacob travels on his journeys. His travels begin as he leaves the land of Canaan, fleeing his brother Esau, heading to a place called Haran. On the way, Jacob has a wonderful dream about a ladder connecting heaven and earth with angels going up and down. Actually, "angels" is a bad term for who these beings are. The Hebrew is *malachim*, or "messengers," obviously meaning messengers of God.

Jacob stays in Haran for twenty years, makes a family and gains wealth, and then returns to the land of Canaan, there to meet his brother Esau again. On the way back, Jacob has another dream-like encounter, this time with an angel who wrestles him to the ground by the banks of a river. Jacob overcomes the angel, and only after this battle, goes on to make peace with his brother who he hasn't seen in so long.

The Jacob stories are a kind of cycle, where Jacob travels from Canaan to Haran, has a divine encounter on the way, and travels from Haran back to Canaan, with another divine encounter on the way back. His life follows a kind of trajectory laden with dreams and divine messengers and passion. It seems like a magical world to us.

Jacob is a man with a mission, so to speak, and he encounters messengers from God. At the climax of the story, right before Jacob meets Esau again after so many years, the Torah tells us that Jacob sends some messengers of his own. He sends these messengers ahead to kind of "test the waters." They carry gifts with them to try to appease Esau just in case he was still bitter at Jacob after all that time. The unspoken reality is that these anonymous messengers will be the first casualties of Esau's wrath if he is still angry.

To prepare these messengers, Jacob tells them that Esau will ask them three questions, three questions that every servant should be able to answer. He says that Esau will ask them, "Who are you? Where are you going? And who are these others before you?" (Genesis 32:18)

If I were to pick out one thing that characterizes Jacob's travels, it is the sense of being a messenger, of being sent. Whether it is the divine messengers that go up and down Jacob's ladder, the angel that wrestles with Jacob in the dust, or the messengers that Jacob himself sends, Jacob's world is filled with a sense of mission, of being sent somewhere. Even Jacob's own life, from Canaan to Haran and back again, follows a path that gives his travels meaning, as if he was sent to be an example to future generations of what it means to be Yisrael, to struggle with God.

There is a Hebrew word for this sense of being sent somewhere. The word is *shlichut.* It means having a mission, of having a passion, which you would do anything to fulfill. Boldly stated, it means that down in your kishkas you feel that God demands something of you. The name of this portion shares the same root, *vayishlach.* It is a particularly Jewish notion, for Judaism is a religion of commandments, of serving a Supreme Authority that gives meaning and purpose to our lives.

The first question, "Who are you?" receives an ever-changing answer. Who we used to be is not who we are, and who we are going to be is yet to be discovered. Life itself is a journey, but nevertheless we seek to be grounded in our family, in our community, and to take a stand for the things we believe in.

"Where are you going?' Often we know that it is easy to simply react, to get by, to give up responsibility for ourselves. Do we live in a world where things solely happen to us, or do we also acknowledge that we are responsible for our choices, both good and bad? Someone once said to me that our lives are made up not just of unforeseen challenges but also our choices. We cannot control what happens to us in life, but we are culpable for our decisions, and they chart the course for where we are going.

"And who are these others before you?' To whom are we responsible? What will future generations have to say about us? Have we left the world a safer, better place, or is that a goal that is impossible to achieve? Before whom do we stand, and to whom must we be answerable?

It is far too easy to distract ourselves and not think about these questions. Often we used sanitized words rather than risk exposing how we really feel and what we really think. Fear may keep us from being honest about our sense of *shlichut*, our sense of mission, especially if we do not feel we have one. We should have faith, however that everyone is on a journey of some sort, even if we do not realize it.

We have the opportunity to compare Jacob's world, a world of dreams and ideals and conviction and *shlichut* to our lives. What are we passionate about? For what would we climb a ladder all the way to heaven or get down and wrestle in the dirt? On what path, to the best in our ability to ever know, do we believe that God is sending us?

Jacob's world makes demands on us. It asks us to be unafraid to be passionate about something. It demands that we dream of ideals and encounters with God. It asks for a Judaism of conviction and determination. And it reminds us that, in some way, we are all really messengers, charged to discover and fulfill our obligations, to live out our *shlichut.*

Who are you? Where are you going? Who is before you? Every messenger needs to be able to answer these questions, and there is so much good left undone.

**Jacob Was Left Alone**

*Vayivater Ya'akov levado.* Jacob was left alone (Genesis 32:25).

These words mark the beginning of Jacob's encounter with his long, lost brother, Esau. Years before, as an adolescent, he had left his brother Esau after a terrible fight. They have not spoken since that moment that Jacob cheated his brother and left him in a murderous rage.

The Torah now brings us, many years later, to the point when Jacob and Esau are grown men. They are about to be reunited. Jacob gets word that Esau is coming towards him with an army of 400 men. Jacob, meanwhile, only has his family, most notably his thirteen children. The Torah says that at this moment Jacob was "terrified and afraid" (Genesis 32:8). It is a strange phrase, "terrified and afraid." It is obviously redundant. The rabbis, however, jump on this strange wording and claim that Jacob had two basic fears: he was terrified that Esau would hurt him or his family, and he was also afraid that he would have to hurt Esau to defend himself.

And so Jacob does three things: He first sends gifts ahead to his brother. He then divides his camp into two. Finally he prays.

Jacob sends gifts because he hopes that there is a chance for peace. He hopes to win this brother's good favor and avoid bloodshed. But the second thing he does, dividing his camp, is an act of military defense. He divides his camp into two so that if Esau attacks one group, the other can flee.

Finally, he prays. He appeals to the One for strength to face this, his greatest trial.

The rabbis say so should all of us face challenges: with efforts for peace, with smart protection of ourselves and our lives, and with prayer and spirituality. These are the efforts that Jacob models for all of us for times of adversity.

In the end, however, after he has done all he can, Jacob is left alone. It is nighttime, and he is alone in the dark. Sometimes, we do everything in our power, but then we can only sit and wait.

There is a difference between being alone and being lonely. One can be alone and be very happy. Sometimes, it is nice to be left alone. But to be lonely is another matter. One can be lonely, even in the midst of people. One gets the feeling that Jacob is both alone and lonely in his anxiety. In his fear, he is left in the dark, isolated from the rest of the world.

It is in this state that Jacob famously wrestles with an angel of God. He struggles with himself and with the coming encounter. And it is only with the break of day that the wrestling match ceases. It is only with the light that the angel says, "Release me!" (Genesis 32:7)

Some of us have known how Jacob must have felt during that long night. Some of us know what it is to be alone, to be isolated, to be lonely and we are not sure when the light is coming. Some of us have our own wrestling matches that we go through each and every day.

This is the time of the year when the nights are at their longest and coldest. It is a time when day is short and the dark night comes quickly. It is instructive, therefore, that precisely during this time we light the lights of Hanukkah as a symbol of light and warmth. It is at this time that God commands us to kindle light, not just for ourselves but for the whole world. We traditionally put the menorah in the window to display the light and share it with others.

And all year long, on Friday night, we light two candles. We light them as day begins to disappear and night draws near because we human beings need light when it gets dark. It is hard to say prayers in the dark. It is hard to be left alone. And so part of our Shabbat worship consists of lighting the candles and simply being together. The gift of another's presence might be enough to get us through our own personal darkness.

Depression is a disease that hits many people this time of year. It feeds on isolation and darkness, but it is also, doctors say, often very treatable. Judaism asks that we do not leave another person alone, that we reach out to others, that we remember how Jacob struggled and seek to make each other's lives easier. Perhaps Jacob did not need to be so alone during his moment of trial.

A Hasidic parable teaches as follows:[17] the Rebbe was sitting among his disciples, and he noticed that Moshe Ya'akov was not there. Now that he thought about it, the Rebbe realized had missed the past few gatherings. "How is Moshe Ya'akov doing?" the Rebbe asked.

No one knew. No one had inquired after him, even though he had been absent. "What?" exclaimed the Rebbe. "You mean to tell me that you go to the same market, you study in the same room, and you share the same Sabbath, and you do not know how Moshe Ya'akov is doing? Whether he needs help or comfort? Whether he needs someone simply to listen? Or maybe something exciting has happened to him, but he has no one with which to share it! This is what it means to be a congregation, so that no one is left alone, either in their sorrow or their joy."

Let us remember the struggles of our patriarch Jacob, and also remember our duty to each other at this time of year. Let us reach out and remember what it means to be a congregation and to be a community, to remember the miracle of togetherness.

---

[17] Elie Wiesel, *One Generation After* (New York: Schocken Books, 2011), 206.

## *Vayeishev* (Genesis 32:4-36:43)

### The Long View

There are many expressions that we have all heard about time. "Time will tell" is one of them. One of my favorites that my grandfather used was, "This too shall pass." Another based on the biblical book of Ecclesiastes is "everything in its own time" (Ecclesiastes 3:1).

In many ways, this week's Torah portion is about being able to take the long view. The name of the portion is *Vayeishev*, which means, "and he settled." Jacob finally settles down with his twelve sons in the Land of Israel. The Talmud teaches us, however, that in the Torah when things begin to settle down, that's just when the trouble usually starts.

Of the twelve sons, the most famous is Joseph. Joseph boasts to all of his brothers that he will one day rule over them. Joseph is the smart one, a dreamer, and he taunts his stronger brothers with his visions. The Torah tells us that Joseph says:

> "Hear this dream which I have dreamed: There we were binding sheaves in the field, when suddenly my sheaf stood up and remained upright; then your sheaves gathered around and bowed low to my sheaf." His brothers answered, "Do you mean to reign over us? Do you mean to rule over us?" And they hated him even more for his talk about his dreams. (Genesis 37:6-8)

If I were to translate this biblical passage about Joseph's boast into modern-day speech, it would be something like a cheer I once heard at college. The geeks would get together and taunt the jocks: "That's all right. That's okay. You'll be working for us one day."

Understandably, Joseph's brothers did not like it. (Neither did the jocks.) Joseph's brothers hate him so much that they sell him to a caravan of Ishmaelites going to Egypt.

Of course, we know the story, and Joseph's dreams do in fact come true. However, as it often is with life, they do not come about as Joseph had planned. It took a long time for Joseph's prophecy to come to fulfillment: Joseph was seventeen years old at the time of this dreams. He was thirty years old when he stood before Pharaoh. There were then seven years of plenty followed by two years of famine before Joseph's brothers come begging to Pharaoh's court. At this point in time, Joseph had risen to be second only to Pharaoh. The Torah also tells us that Joseph described himself as being "like a father to Pharaoh," which means that the Pharaoh was probably a child. In effect, Joseph is the ruler of the whole country. And, twenty-two years after his first dreams, Joseph finds his brothers bowing down to him.

The price for the fulfillment of his dreams has been terrific. Joseph has been alienated from his family. He has been cut off from his father, served as a slave, and spent time in jail. When his brothers lay prostrate before him, there is no satisfaction in it. His last wish is that when he dies, his body is carried back to the Land of Israel, the land of his father, where he always wanted to be.

And yet, looking back over his life and being able to take the long view, Joseph senses a higher purpose in what has happened to him. When he reunites with his brothers, he gives one of the most famous speeches in the Bible:

> I am your brother Joseph, he whom you sold into Egypt. Now, do not be distressed or reproach yourselves because you sold me hither; it was to save life that God sent me ahead of you. It is now two years that there has been famine in the land, and there are still five years to come in which there shall be no yield from tilling. God has sent me ahead of you to ensure your survival on earth, and to save your lives in an extraordinary deliverance. So, it was not you who sent me here, but God. (Genesis 45:4-8)

Joseph does not take credit for his accomplishments. He explains that he was simply one part in a larger process. He sees God's hand working not only in his life but in the lives of others. And while this may mean that Joseph has not necessarily lost all of the arrogance of his childhood in that he still sees himself as God's chosen servant, there is something to be said for believing that one has a role to play in the mind of God, whatever that may be. Perhaps we all do have our own unique paths to fulfill.

Joseph is only able to come to this realization with the passing of time. He is able to make meaning out of his life, especially his life's tragedies and twenty-two years of experience, by seeing how they helped serve some kind of good. If he were able to go back in time and talk to that seventeen year old kid who was boasting towards his brothers, I have a feeling Joseph would have had some strong words about kindness and respect.

Perhaps for all of us today, we might be able to learn from the experience of those who have gone on before us. When things happen to us, when we face challenges, when we have to make a big decision, seeing that moment as part of a larger picture can be very helpful. We can sometimes be tempted to panic and react to an extreme situation in the moment, or perhaps we can take the longer view, realizing that we are part of a larger process in which we are only a small part.

The psychologist Viktor Frankl put it this way. In his ground-breaking work on logotherapy, detailed in his book *Man's Search for Meaning*, he asks us to occasionally perform a little thought-experiment.[18] When we are faced with a panicky moment or a big decision, he says, we might want to project ourselves into the future. If it were twenty years from now, and you were able to look back at the decision that you now face, what advice would you give yourself? If you are able to try to imagine the longer view, how would you judge your day-to-day actions? Are the things that we think of as terribly important really so significant in the larger scheme of things? What would an older you tell yourself?

One more expression about time is that "hindsight is twenty-twenty," but we are still responsible for our decisions and living with the consequences. Shabbat can be a time to stop, reflect, and try to have a larger perspective on our lives. It is a perspective that is terribly hard to reach, but nevertheless, its fruits can be a sense of calm and humility.

Let us pray to try to occasionally take the long view, even if it turns out to be imaginary. Let us live with the bigger picture of what is really important always in front of us. And let us never waste an opportunity to share our love and reassurance with one another, for being connected to each other is what it is really all about.

---

[18] Viktor E. Frankl, *Man's Search for Meaning* (New York: Simon & Schuster, Inc., 1984), 131-132.

## Joseph the *Tzaddik*

This week in the Torah we turn to the beginning of one of the most well-known Bible stories. This week we begin to read about Joseph and his brothers. The story begins with the famous coat of many colors that gets Joseph into so much trouble. Joseph's brothers are jealous of their father's favoritism of Joseph, and so they sell their brother into slavery in Egypt. From there, Joseph goes from rags to riches to become second only to Pharaoh and, through Joseph's intervention, winds up saving the world from famine, including his estranged family.

There is a little known episode within the story, however, that many movies and other retellings often skip over. After Joseph is sold into slavery in Egypt, Joseph becomes the property of a nobleman named Potiphar. Joseph helps manage Potiphar's affairs, and Potiphar becomes successful. Potiphar entrusts Joseph with his whole household.

However, the fly in the ointment is that Potiphar's wife takes a liking to Joseph. She approaches him day after day for an adulterous relationship, and day after day he refuses. Joseph says, "How can I do this great wickedness and sin against God?" (Genesis 39:9) One commentator, named Obadiah Sforno, understands this to mean that Joseph is saying, "How can I repay all of Potiphar's good to me with evil?" (Sforno on Genesis 39:9). At one point Potiphar's wife literally tears off his clothes and creates an embarrassing scene. In complete frustration, she then tells her husband that Joseph, the Hebrew slave, had raped her while he was away, and Joseph is thrown into prison.

This episode does not make the PG-13 version, but it is actually considered by many later Jewish authorities to be the most important part of the Joseph saga. Even though the Joseph story is long and exciting, it is different than the previous stories because God does not directly address Joseph in the same way that God spoke to Abraham, Isaac, and Jacob, and therefore he was not included in the list of patriarchs and not deemed to be as important. The incident between Joseph and Potiphar's wife, however, did catch the attention of later rabbinic authorities because of Joseph's display of virtue. Because Joseph resisted temptation and maintained his integrity, he is referred to in the Talmud as Joseph the *Tzaddik*, or Joseph the Righteous.

In the imagination of the rabbis of the Talmud (*Yoma* 35b), they retell this episode to make Joseph appear especially pious. When Potiphar's wife says, "Yield to me!" Joseph says, "No." She then threatens to have him thrown into prison. Joseph quotes from the Psalms and says, "God sets free the captive." When she tells him she will bend his back with labor, he replies, "God raises up those who are bowed down." And when she even threatens to have his eyes put out, Joseph finishes the Psalm by saying, "God opens the eyes of the blind."

Because of Joseph's integrity and piety, he became an archetype for the ideal righteous man who masters temptation and keeps himself pure. The character of Joseph became a symbol for righteousness.

Joseph the *Tzaddik* became a larger-than-life figure in the eyes of Jewish tradition, but if we think about it, he really didn't do anything that was larger than life. All he did was simply the right thing. The world is not black and white, but at the same time, sometimes we complicate things that are fairly simple. Sometimes in life, the difficult things in life are not very complicated at all. They are hard to do because they are emotionally hard or demand a real commitment from us, but they are not too difficult to figure out. All Joseph did was not sleep with another man's wife, and yet we know that we human beings fail in these simple commitments all the time. Perhaps Joseph was really righteous not because of his piety or devotion but simply because he was a *mensch* and insisted on doing the right thing by his friend.

In other traditions, we might hear of the idea that immoral acts or temptations come to us almost like an outside force beyond our control. Sin, for some, is understood to be a demonic force lurking and waiting to spring temptation upon unsuspecting good people. Judaism, however, feels that this explanation as why people fail each other is too easy. The responsibility for our choices, claim the sages, lies within each of us.

According to a rabbinic understanding, every human being has two impulses: an impulse for good and an impulse for bad. We can either choose to cultivate virtues in our life or vices through our free will. And yet, the more we do, the easier it becomes to follow the path we have beaten out for ourselves. As one proverb says, "One *mitzvah* leads to another, and one transgression leads to another." We are ultimately responsible for our own actions, not some outside force, and we can choose to be good people or bad. The power is entirely within us and the choices that we make.

This idea, interestingly enough, was illustrated by none other than Robert Louis Stevenson in his famous novel, *Dr. Jekyll and Mr. Hyde.*[19] Dr. Jekyll wants to devise a potion that will isolate the potential for evil that resides within himself, and when he drinks the potion, he transforms into a small, mean little man. You see, Dr. Jekyll on the whole was relatively good, and so the evil within him was relatively small. The effect doesn't last long. The more transgressions he commits, however, and the more often he lets his evil side on the loose, the taller and stronger his evil personality grows. Eventually he becomes the monstrous Mr. Hyde, tall and strong, while he can only remain Dr. Jekyll infrequently, who has become short and weak. Dr. Jekyll and Mr. Hyde, two sides of the same person, are very similar to the rabbinic notion of an impulse for good and an impulse for bad, and the more one is used, the stronger and more dominant it becomes. In the end, Mr. Hyde takes over completely, and it leads to the death of this man.

Unlike Stevenson's tragedy, however, the Torah is full of hope. The Torah is filled with imperfect people, people like Joseph and his brothers, who grow in moral stature. Even though they commit transgressions and sometimes fail each other, on the whole they learn from their mistakes and try to cultivate goodness within themselves. They understand that one *mitzvah* leads to another, and the more good they do, the better they become. At the end of the saga in the Bible, the family is reunited in joy. Good triumphs in the end.

The happy ending of the Torah should give us hope, just as the tragic ending of Stevenson's novel might serve as a warning. Joseph the *Tzaddik* leads the way for cultivating a path to virtue, and if he could do it after such a traumatic and trying childhood, then perhaps so can we.

The idea of cultivating virtue, however, faces serious challenges in today's culture. People often do not want to talk about ethics or integrity. It is unfashionable to be caught "moralizing," and often we risk a "holier-than-thou" attitude. However, there are thoughtful and respectful ways to discuss ethics, and the world would be a better

---

[19] Robert Louis Stevenson, *The Strange Case of Dr. Jekyll and Mr. Hyde* (1886).

place if we had these discussions, especially while getting an education. This should be especially important to Jewish people. We have a long tradition of discussing ethics, and we should continue to do so. In the past presidential elections, "moral values" was listed as a top reason why people voted, and it is incumbent upon the Jewish community to have a stake in defining what those values are.

It was reported two years ago in the Washington Post [August 4, 2002], during the height of several corporate scandals, that business schools, for instance, did not teach any ethics classes as their students studied for an MBA. In the 80s, only one-third of business schools in the United States had any ethics classes whatsoever. The idea that ethics should be a part of a business education was met with outright hostility at the Harvard Business School as reported by one professor named Amitai Etzioni. At one meeting, an economist argued, "We are here to teach science," and another faculty member said, "Whose ethics, whose values, are we going to teach?' These valid points notwithstanding, rather than face these challenges, the idea of teaching ethics was scrapped. The result was the creation of business men and women without appropriate boundaries, and the same professor witnessed certain discussions in class about how best to take advantage of employees by using verbal agreements and how much one can lie without getting caught. In addition to this, the professor who spoke out and wrote this editorial risked the anger of his colleagues, especially at such a prestigious institution, but he resisted the urge to be silent and spoke out anyway. Incidentally, Harvard now has a business ethicist as part of their faculty

Much like Joseph in ancient times, in today's world the right thing to do isn't very complicated, but it is hard to resist the temptation to make more of a profit, even if you had to betray a few anonymous employees, and it is hard to resist the desires of a crowd, even though you know it is wrong. It is hard to resist feeding our egos, or our desires and appetites, simply because we know that there are boundaries that must not be crossed.

In reaction to this disturbing report, Robert Harris, the Dean of the Darden School at the University of Virginia, wrote this reply [August 15, 2002], "There was much truth in what Amitai Etzioni had to say about the role of business schools in the development of ethical leaders… Too often, ethics is discussed as if it is to be bartered against other considerations in pursuit of a bigger bottom line. In fact, ethics is the bottom line."

Temptation can be resisted, and happily, many people do. The business man or woman who treats his or her employees honestly and fairly even though it might cut into some of the company's profit, the teacher who resists the temptation to appear as an infallible expert and admits in front of the class, "I do not know," the person who speaks out for something unpopular when it is easier to be silent, the friend who apologizes even though it is easier to pretend that nothing ever happened, these are choices that we all make in our daily lives about what kind of people we want to be.

Joseph was a *Tzaddik*, a righteous person, not because he was exceptional but because he took responsibility for his choices. Life is a series of choices. We cannot choose our circumstances, and we cannot choose what life throws in our path. But we can choose what kind of people we want to be. We have examples from our tradition of people resisting temptation and doing the right thing. We can cultivate virtue in our lives by letting one *mitzvah* lead to another. And we can take responsibility for ourselves by knowing that all moral decisions, for good or for bad, ultimately come from within each one of our hearts.

Let us pray that we go from strength to strength and that we use our strength for good.

## *Mikeitz* (Genesis 41:1-44:17)

### Dreaming of Cows, Corn, and Gratitude

We have an apparently strange Torah portion for Hanukkah. It is about Pharaoh having dreams, and Joseph interpreting them. I don't know how many people really dream of cows and corn. Farmers, probably. Kibbutzniks, even. But apparently Pharaohs do, or at least that is what the Torah says. And we will see that it actually does relate to this season, which brings up questions of abundance and generosity.

In this week's Torah portion, *Mikeitz*, Pharaoh has some dreams. Actually, they are nightmares. The first one is that he sees seven healthy cows come up out of the Nile. Then he sees seven scrawny, emaciated cows come out of the Nile and eat the healthy cows – which must have been pretty disgusting when you think about. And even though the seven skinny cows ate the fat ones, the skinny ones didn't get any healthier.

The second dream was the same, except it involved ears of corn. Seven healthy ears of corn grew, and then seven blighted ones grew up after and ate up the seven good ones (less disgusting), but the blighted ones didn't get any better.

The story then goes that Joseph interprets the dreams for Pharaoh and says it is a prophecy. There will be seven years of plenty followed by seven years of famine in Egypt. In order to plan for it, they must set aside twenty percent each year of the years of plenty, and that stored-up food will get them through the years of famine. Pharaoh thinks this is a great idea and puts Joseph in charge.

Today, psychologists tell us we are every person in our dream. If we dream something that means that everything in the dream came from somewhere deep inside us. So when Pharaoh is dreaming of cows and corn, he is really dreaming of his own worries and anxieties.

This is how the psychologically-astute Rabbi Nachman of Breslov understood this story. Rabbi Nachman thought the diseased cows and corn represented Pharaoh's insatiable greed. No matter how much money, animals, or land he had, it was never enough. It could devour everything and it was as if nothing happened. He was perpetually hungry and empty.

Joseph's advice, to set aside part of what he was consuming, therefore, was the medicine for disease of greed. According to Rabbi

Nachman, Joseph was telling Pharaoh to make sure every year he gave *tzedakah* that he set aside a portion of his wealth for others, and this would serve as an antidote for the bottomless pit in his soul. And who knows? As the wheel of fortune turns, and someone who has a great deal today winds up with little tomorrow, Pharaoh might need that kindness paid back to him in the future. This was the real "stored-up" wealth (*Likkutei Halakhot* II:79a).[20]

If we are every person in our dreams, and the Torah is the collective dream of the Jewish people, then this means there is a greedy Pharaoh in each of us. There is always parts of ourselves that want more, that are never satisfied, and that feel empty.

Each one of us also has a happiness meter inside of us. On an average day – not a bad day or a very good day, but just an average day – on a scale of one to ten, how happy are you? An eight or nine, meaning you are very happy? A five, which means you're just eh? A two or three, which means it is a real slog?

We have entered the time of great consumerism, and people are selling material happiness, stuff that is supposed to fill us up. Black Friday weekend, Hanukkah, and Christmas sales abound. We can buy and buy and buy. And what looked so amazing one week seems kind of empty the next. There are people who are enormously wealthy and are unhappy. And there are paraplegics who feel content. So how do we fill ourselves up?

Rabbi Nachman is teaching us that we paradoxically feel most full when we set aside a portion of what we have and give it away. Generosity and thankfulness fill us up, not more stuff, and the only thing we have some control over in life is our attitude we bring to the world around us.

So let us practice generosity of spirit and resources. Let make sure at least one night of Hanukkah is dedicated to charity. Let us volunteer. Let us do something good for someone else. After all, this is really about creating light and warmth during the darkest and coldest time of the year. Let us share our light, and in doing so, move from a culture of "gimme" to gratitude. One candle lights another, but is not diminished in itself. Our spirits are most full when we are generous and thankful.

---

[20] Chaim Kramer, *Rebbe Nachman's Torah: Genesis* (Israel: Breslov Research Institute, 2011), 294.

**The Family Circle**

Occasionally, we are all reminded about where happiness truly comes from. Sometimes we think that happiness comes from success, wealth, or fame. And those things do feed our ego. But true happiness, that is, a sense of fulfillment, contentment, and meaning, comes from other things.

For instance, if we look at this week's Torah portion, we know that Joseph, the son of Jacob and the brother of Jacob's other eleven sons, seems to have everything he needs to make him happy. His is the famous "rags to riches" story. Earlier, Joseph is a brat who angers his brothers one too many times, and they sell him into slavery in Egypt. As a slave, he becomes rather successful in that he is promoted to be the head of a rich man's household. When the man's wife flirts with him, however, he is sent to prison. He has hit "rock bottom," so to speak.

In our Torah portion this week, Joseph continues to defy the odds as he is promoted from being a slave in prison to being one of the most powerful men in Egypt. Because of his skill in interpreting dreams, Joseph predicts the success of his fellow inmate, Pharaoh's cupbearer, and the death of another prisoner, Pharaoh's baker. When Pharaoh has dreams that no one can interpret, the reinstated cup bearer remembers Joseph. Joseph is brought in to Pharaoh, and the rest is history. Joseph interprets Pharaoh's dreams to relate a prophecy that a famine is on its way, and he devises a strategy by which Egypt can outlast the famine. Pharaoh is so impressed that he makes him second only to himself. It is likely that his was a very young Pharaoh, for at one point Joseph claims that he is like the Pharaoh's father.

In any case, with the help of God, Joseph gains wealth and fame, and everyone in Egypt who approaches him must bow down. He could not be more successful, at least in the terms of an ancient society.

One would therefore think that Joseph would consider Egypt his adopted home and have fond feelings for the place where he has accomplished so much. One would think that with fame and fortune, he was fulfilled and happy. However, we read that Joseph marries and fathers two children, Manasseh and Ephraim. The Torah tells us the meaning of these two names. Manasseh, we are told, means,

"God has made me completely forget my hardship and my parental home" (Genesis 41:51). Now, with this name, that Joseph gives his son, he "protests too much." Why would he name a child to constantly remind himself of something that he claims he has completely forgotten, especially something as disturbing as the trauma of his brothers getting rid of him? And when his second son is born, Joseph names him Ephraim. Ephraim, we are told, means, "God has made me fertile in the land of my affliction" (Genesis 41:52). He may experience abundance and plenty, but he still feels afflicted.

It is revealing that, with the name given to his first child, Joseph refers to his birthplace, the Land of Israel, as a place of "hardship," and with the second child, he tells us that Egypt is the land of his "affliction." Joseph does not seem at home anywhere. He has all of the power and money that he wants, and he has even found favor in the eyes of God for saving hundreds of lives from famine. But he is not fulfilled. He is not happy. And he has yet to learn that he will not feel contentment until he deals with his feelings of estrangement from his family circle. He will not be at peace until he has made peace with his brothers and his father, and the rest of Genesis focuses on this struggle.

We, also, need to remember that the things that typically make us successful are fundamentally different from the things that bring us meaning. Wealth has little to no correlation to fulfillment. And we also know in our hearts that making peace with our family relations is often a life-long task, much like it was for Joseph in the Bible.

Families are strange things, and yet human beings simply cannot exist without them. Sometimes we are blessed to have loving, nurturing families, but sometimes there is at least someone in our family who always knows how to push our buttons. There is someone in our family, or maybe more than one person, with whom we find ourselves getting upset, even over little things. Families, as necessary and as natural as they are, sometimes seem built for conflict. After all, there does not seem to be a single completely conflict-free family in the entire Hebrew Bible much less here on earth.

What complicates this state of affairs is that we all belong to more than one family, and our families change as time goes by. When we are young, we belong to one family, and we struggle to relate to our parents. The problem with parents, of course, is that once they had parents. And as we grow we gradually extend our family circle. We gain circles of friends who are as close to us as family, and as people get married and have children, the circles of our families change. When extended family members are suddenly inherited, our roles shift, with or without our consent. And so on. What happens in one circle fundamentally affects what happens in all the others.

As a rabbi, I have the privilege of seeing many kinds of families, and let me tell you something: I gave up on the idea of "normal" a long time ago. There is no such thing.

But what I think the Torah keeps insisting on, whether for Joseph who is estranged from his family or for us today, is that isolation, no matter what, never leads to any kind of sense of peace. Joseph in the Bible is isolated from his family and so he experiences his home as a place of hardship and affliction. What the Torah seems to be telling us is that we may never heal, perfect, or even "normalize" some rifts that occur between family members, but it is part of our struggle nevertheless to attempt to find some kind of acceptance and a sense of peace.

There is a Hebrew term that seems to be at the essence of what Joseph and all of us are looking for, a value of which we should all be aware. It is *shalom bayit*, that is, "peace in the home." It does not mean a home that is quiet or free of conflict. It does not mean a family that is perfect. It certainly does not mean "normal."

*Shalom bayit* means family members who, no matter what their differences, are not isolated from one another and try to accept each other. To make peace with one's family is a constant demand, and sometimes it is a struggle that occurs entirely within oneself, trying to come to a sense of acceptance about another. Sometimes the struggle for *shalom bayit*, the effort to feel at home, takes place entirely within one's own heart. Or sometimes it takes the openness, honesty, and risk of two people to reach out to each other.

Let us, then, pray to break through isolation and search for *shalom bayit*. Let us seek to create family relationships for ourselves that bring us more meaningful lives. And let us accept within ourselves that, ultimately, we are all one human family, sharing this home, our community and our world.

## *Vayigash* (Genesis 44:18-47:27)

### Finally, a Brother's Keeper

Two stories: one from the beginning of the book of Genesis, and one from the end.

The first story begins with two brothers. They were very close, perhaps too close. Often they felt as if they had only each other in the whole world. But to differentiate themselves, one of them became a hunter, bringing in the game from the wild, and the other became a farmer, raising food from the field. And each would present an offering to God. The farmer, however, did not offer the very best of what he had, while his brother offered the most select of his bounty. God found favor in the one brother's sacrifice but not the other. And when the farmer's face fell in disappointment, God said to him, "Why has your face fallen? If you do well, then your offering will be accepted. If not, then sin lies crouched at the door. Even then, however, you may rule over it" (Genesis 4:6-7).

But then Cain went out into the field with his brother, Abel, and slew him. God confronted him and said, "Where is your brother?' Cain answered, "Am I my brother's keeper?'" (Genesis 4:9) God does not answer Cain's question, and we are left hanging, waiting for a response.

The book of Genesis thus begins with a tragedy. But now let us fast forward towards the end of the book of Genesis, to this week's Torah portion. Again, we are faced with a set of brothers. Judah, the leader of the brothers, comes forward and approaches the Pharaoh's prime minister of agriculture. He cannot believe what he is hearing. The Egyptian Prime Minister is a madman. There is a famine in the land, and Judah and his brothers have come down to Egypt to beg for food. All of the brothers have come to Egypt, including the youngest, Benjamin, their father's favorite. And the Egyptian Prime Minister has asked something insane of them. "Sell me your brother, Benjamin, and I will give you your food. Let your brother, Benjamin, your father's favorite, stay here with me and be my slave, and I will give you what you seek, enough for you and your families. Then you can bring back your bounty to your father and explain to him what happened."

To Judah, this is unacceptable. He cannot let his brother, Benjamin, become the property of this madman. Who does he think he is? And yet, in the darkest, guiltiest part of Judah's soul, Judah knows that once, during his childhood, he committed a crime. There was once another brother, Joseph, now dead, who he helped sell into slavery in Egypt. Joseph had been his father's favorite, and Judah had hated him. So Judah and his brother got rid of him in an act of spite. Not a day had gone by where he wasn't filled with regret. And underneath it all, hadn't he really been angry with their father for showing favoritism among them?

And so Judah steps forward and tells this Egyptian Prime Minister that he is not going to do that again, not ever. Benjamin is his responsibility, and he knows it. In so many words, Judah says that he **is** his brother's keeper.

Of course, much to his shock, the moment he takes responsibility for his brother, the Prime Minister reveals himself as Joseph, the lost brother from long ago. "I am Joseph, your brother," he tells them.

It takes the entire book of Genesis to answer Cain's question. The entire Book of Genesis could be read as a search for the answer to: Am I my brother's keeper? Through all of the family sagas of Isaac and Ishmael, Jacob and Esau, and then finally, Joseph, Judah, and the rest of the brothers, we are looking for someone who will finally stand up and take responsibility for the life of their brethren. It is only when Judah stands up and, accepting the fact that family love is often arbitrary and unfair, nevertheless comes forward to protect the life of his kin. It is Judah who finally responds affirmatively to the question of responsibility.

The name of this week's Torah portion, *Vayigash*, illustrates just how Judah made his stand. The verb, *vayigash*, means, "he approached," (Genesis 44:18) but it means to approach in a special sense, which is explored in the *Midrash* (Genesis Rabbah 93:6). First, one rabbi teaches that it means to approach to do battle, for this verb is used elsewhere in the Hebrew Bible when King David's army charged at the enemy. In this sense, Judah was ready to fight for Benjamin when he came forward.

In a different sense, Rabbi Nehemiah points out that this verb, *vayigash*, "to approach," can also mean the opposite: to approach for reconciliation. This very same verb is used later when Joshua is approached to make peace among his people. Perhaps Judah was coming forward to soothe and persuade.

Finally, some sages say that this verb, "to approach," means to come forward for prayer. The verb is used when Elijah steps forward to pray to God. Perhaps Judah was coming forward in a pious fashion, knowing that he needed God's help to save his brother.

But it is Rabbi Eleazar who offers the most insightful response. The verb means all three ways of approaching. Judah came forward, ready to do all three. He was ready to fight, to make peace, and to pray, all at once. "I come whether it be for battle, for conciliation, or for prayer," the rabbi teaches. Judah takes responsibility for his brother, no matter what it will take. (Genesis Rabbah 93:5)

Perhaps this is part of the reason why we all practice Judaism, named after Judah's tribe. We are to be the religion of our brother's keepers, the way Judah took responsibility for his brothers. Judaism is about being able to stand up for others, to take responsibility for the life of another. This is what it means to be a Jew.

Today, in modern times, we can expand the notion of family. We understand that, in addition to our own particular tribe, we are also all children of God, and thus all siblings in a way. To be our brother's keeper, therefore, means to assume responsibility for all of humanity. "You shall love your neighbor as yourself," stands side-by-side with the commandment, "You shall not stand idly by while your neighbor bleeds" (Leviticus 19:16, 18).

It was the great Rabbi Leo Baeck who taught that to be a Jew is to be humanity's keeper. He wrote: "The Jew is the great non-conformist, the great dissenter of history…[21] It may well be [Judaism's] historic task to offer this image of the dissenter, who dissents for humanity's sake."[22] Rabbi Baeck, who understood ethics to be at the essence of Judaism, also understands what Judah understood, that our role is to be a moral example, the one who stands up and is willing to fight, make peace, or pray for the sake of humanity, no matter what it takes.

Today's generation has begun to understand this. Today, people understand how interconnected we all are. More than a family taking responsibility for each other or even the Jewish people standing in

---

[21] Leo Baeck, *The Essence of Judaism* (New York: Schocken Books) 261.

[22] Leo Baeck, "Mystery and Commandment" in *Judaism and Christianity* (Philadelphia: Jewish Publication Society 1958) 184-185.

solidarity for one another, we know that we are our sisters and brothers' keepers, whether we like it or not. There is not a single action that happens on this world that does not eventually affect us, and there is not a single thing that we do that does not affect others. Pollution in one place will damage those at the far end of the globe. A message broadcast in one country can affect the outcome of elections in another. War fought here affects the economy over there. The global network, represented by such things as the Internet, cell phones, and the quickness of travel, makes us all part of one family on this world, to say nothing of our common humanity. And we Jewish people, we who live to be examples of and teach ethical monotheism, are duty-bound to be ready to fight, make peace, and pray each day to take responsibility for our common fate.

The story of being our brother's keeper began with the first family of creation. It continues to the present day. In this new understanding of what it means to be a keeper for another, perhaps we can now better comprehend the famous meditation of John Donne:

> "All mankind is of one author, and is one volume; when one man dies, one chapter is not torn out of the book, but translated into a better language; and every chapter must be so translated...As therefore the bell that rings to a sermon, calls not upon the preacher only, but upon the congregation to come: so this bell calls us all...No man is an island, entire of itself...any man's death diminishes me, because I am involved in mankind; and therefore never send to know for whom the bell tolls; it tolls for thee."[23]

[23] John Donne, "Meditation 17," *The Works of John Donne,* vol. III, Henry Alford, ed. (London: John W. Parker, 1839), 574-575.

## *Vayechi* (Genesis 47:28-50:26)

### Truth, Kindness, and the Unity of God

It seems to me every family has its dirty laundry. There are things that people do not like to talk about and would prefer to keep private or even hide from outsiders. This can be a real challenge, however, when a family has a life-cycle event like a wedding or a funeral and they are put on display. Everyone can see so-and-so are not speaking, or this person has a drinking problem, unless they can put on a good show.

I often encounter this reality when I meet with people to prepare for a funeral. The information I receive for the eulogy comes from the family. While this is usually a cathartic affair, and then we present as truthfully as possible the best parts of a person's life, sometimes people keep their secrets and blatantly lie. I find this out when I am giving the eulogy, and people are looking at me quizzically. If people do not recognize the person I am eulogizing, I know I have been sold a bill of goods. "He was generous to all," I say. That's when I hear the woman in the second row, whose hearing aid is off, "whisper" to the person next to her, "He was the cheapest *shtunk* [jerk] on this side of the Mississippi!"

It seems, however, that in this week's Torah portion, our patriarch Jacob tries to air some harsh truths, and he is unafraid as to who will hear. Before he dies, he blesses each one of his children. Some might say that he has gone over into TMI – "too much information." He lays out everyone's faults out on the table, much, I imagine, to everyone's dismay. Listen to some of the things Jacob has to say about his children. If you think our family secrets are something, just listen to this:

> Reuben, you are my first-born,
> My might and first fruit of my vigor,
> Exceeding in rank
> And exceeding in honor.
> Unstable as water, you shall excel no longer;
> For when you mounted your father's bed,
> You brought disgrace—my couch he mounted!
> Simeon and Levi are a pair;
> Their weapons are tools of lawlessness.

> Let not my person be included in their council,
> Let not my being be counted in their assembly.
> For when angry they slay men,
> And when pleased they maim oxen.
> Cursed be their anger so fierce,
> And their wrath so relentless. (Genesis 49:3-7)

And that's just the first three sons! He has nine more to go!

It is always hard to tell the truth kindly. If we don't tell the truth, then we become co-conspirators and perpetrators of falsehoods. We can become accomplices to foolishness. If we do tell the truth, but without kindness, then our criticism is not constructive, and we often offer a skewed, negative version of reality. Revealing negative truths unnecessarily is considered *lashon hara*, a wicked tongue. But telling the truth kindly, especially within our families, is what we ought to do.

Later Jewish tradition tried to teach this lesson this way. In the Talmud (*Sotah* 47a), it says that "in dealing with one's own nature, one's child, and one's [spouse]: one pushes with the left hand and pulls with the right." In all of our interactions, there is a balancing act. We strive to be honest and open, and we push our loved ones and ourselves to be the best that we can be. On the other hand, we must be compassionate, forgiving, understanding, and accepting. There is a push and pull with all of our relationships, even with how we look at ourselves. This is perhaps why it says in the Psalms 25:10: "All the paths of the Eternal are loving kindness and truth to those who keep God's covenant and testimonies." We must bring kindness and truth together.

This balancing act is difficult. The sages of antiquity even imagine God struggling with it. On the one hand, God has a *midat din,* an attribute of honest judgment with which God looks at the world. On the other, God has a *midat rachamim*, an attribute of compassion, for if God were only to look at the world with unforgiving truth, the rabbis say, the world could not stand. Ultimately, this balancing act is essential to being human. If we treat each other with both truth and kindness, then that is what human decency is all about. One without the other will not do.

Even though Jacob may have offered harsh assessment in our Torah portion, it seems he had enough of a relationship with his sons that they were able to stick together and show him loyalty, even if he did give them a good tongue lashing. Jacob's other name is Israel. In one interpretation of the *Shema*, the sons are gathered around Jacob's deathbed. When he asks them if they will keep the covenant of the One God, they answer and reassure him, "*Shema Yisrael*: Hear, our father Israel, the Eternal is our God, the Eternal is one!" (Deuteronomy 6:4)

Perhaps in their answer about the unity of God is the secret to human wholeness. They were able to balance out his criticism with love. Martin Buber, who wrote a great deal about dialogue, believed that it is not just in study and in prayer that we find God but in our speech with one another. Our open, vulnerable, honest dialogue with each other, our mutual meeting and responding to the humanity in one another, is a place where the spiritual can be found. But these meetings are always a mix of emotions, all coming at once. Buber wrote, "The unity of the contraries is the mystery at the innermost core of the dialogue."[24] Or, as our Bible might put it, where is God? When "loving kindness and truth meet together; righteousness and peace kiss each other" (Psalms 85:11).

Let us pray to learn from those around us. Let us pray that we always speak the truth and are known for our integrity. But let us also do so with kindness and compassion. Let us speak to each other with softness and understanding. In the wholeness and unity of our relationships with one another, our family and friends, there may we find God.

## A Jewish Last Will and Testament

The Torah depicts the death-bed scene of Jacob in this week's Torah portion. He has his twelve sons gathered around him. He pronounces blessings over each of them as well as instruction. In this passage, Jacob is referred to by his higher name, Israel, in this moment, for he is giving his sons sacred teaching, or Torah.

A *midrash*, or rabbinic legend, says that the *Shema* prayer actually comes from this moment (Genesis Rabbah 96). Jacob is worried that his sons will not keep God's covenant. But as the sons stand around his bed, they reassure him, "*Shema Yisrael* – Listen, our father Israel,

---

[24] Martin Buber, "The Faith of Judaism," *Israel and the World: Essays in a Time of Crisis* (New York: Schocken Books, 1948), 17.

we know that '*Adonai Eloheinu Adonai Echad*' – the Eternal is our God, the Eternal One alone." With these words of testimony, Israel's mind is at ease, and he passes away. It is a perhaps fanciful but touching understanding of the *Shema* prayer.

About a month ago (November 11, 2013), a nurse named Sina Anvari shared something profound on her blog. This nurse worked in palliative care for many years and spent her career being with people during the last three to twelve weeks of their lives. She wrote what she felt were the "top five regrets people shared on their deathbed." She wrote:[25]

"People grow a lot when faced with their own mortality. I learnt never to underestimate someone's capacity for growth. Some changes were phenomenal. Each experienced a variety of emotions, as expected, denial, fear, anger, remorse, more denial, and eventually acceptance. Every single patient found their peace before they departed though, every one of them.

"When questioned about any regrets they had or anything they would do differently, common themes surfaced again and again. Here are the most common five:

"I wish I'd had the courage to live a life true to myself, not the life others expected of me....

"I wish I didn't work so hard.... This came from every male patient....

"I wish I'd had the courage to express my feelings....

"I wish I had stayed in touch with my friends....

"I wish that I had let myself be happier."

Nurse Anvari closes with this bit of wisdom: "Life is a choice. It is YOUR life. Choose consciously, choose wisely, choose honestly. Choose happiness."

Why should we dwell on something so maudlin? Why talk about deathbed scenes, just because they happen to be in this week's Torah portion? Because as the psychologist Carl Jung said, "To confront a person with his own shadow is to show him his own light." We learn and grow by talking about things that we may not want to. And very few things in this world become worse just because we tell the truth about them.

There is a practice in Judaism that when someone makes out

---

25 bbncommunity.com/nurse-reveals-top-5-regrets-people-make-deathbed/

their will, they also write something called an ethical will. There is a long history of ethical wills in Judaism, beginning with Jacob talking to his sons in our Torah portion and going through the Middle Ages to modern times. An ethical will is a letter to family and friends about the things that you learned in life. It is completely free-form, in any way you want to write it. If you were to leave behind some truth, some kind of life lessons, what would they be?

An ethical will is not an easy thing to write, nor is it an easy thing to read. No one wants to be remembered as preachy, guilt-inducing, or scolding, and no one wants to read something like that. Instead, however, an ethical will can be a love letter to your family. In a non-judgmental tone, written over time, it can be a powerful way to think of your life and to pass on your values.

Rabbi Bruce Kadden explains it this way: "Think about those values that are important to pass on and what you would say to your loved ones if you only had one more opportunity to speak to them." There are no formal writing requirements for this kind of thing. But writing everything down makes it tangible. "It can be done at any age. It helps a person think about what is important in their life, what they want to teach their children [or friends] and how they want to go about living their life."[26] It's also okay to review, edit and make additions to the will as time passes. And even though you might say that people have heard enough lectures from you, and people already know what you think, you would be surprised how writing down your values can change how you see yourself and what people actually remember.

If anything, writing down your values forces you to confront the question, is my life now a reflection of what is most important to me? I think Father Jacob would tell us that in confronting your own shadow, you can see your own light.

[26] jweekly.com/article/full/14056/giving-children-your-blessing-a-rabbi-s-tips-for-ethical-wills/

# *SHEMOT* - EXODUS

## *Shemot* (Exodus 1:1-6:1)

### Looking For a Human Being

"Who? Me?' How many times have we found ourselves asking that question? There have been many times when we feel put on the spot, and often we would rather retreat to be part of the anonymous group. There is comfort in being a part of a crowd. It is hard, sometimes uncomfortable, to stand out.

Moses, as he is described in the Torah, must have felt the same way. When we think of Moses, we think of a great leader, often with a flowing beard and a staff, who split the Red Sea and carried stone tablets. We think of a man who confronted Pharaoh and who decided the law for the Israelites. All of these are scenes where Moses led by standing out in front of the crowd.

In this week's Torah portion, however, we find a different kind of Moses, one who is younger and a bit more timid. As spectacular as these other events were, there was an earlier event in Moses' life that was, perhaps, even more of a defining moment than the Red Sea or Sinai. It is the moment when Moses learned to step forward and take a stand.

Moses grew up in the palace of the Pharaoh, raised by Pharaoh's daughter. As he grew into adulthood, the Torah says, he "went out to his kinsfolk," that is, he realized he was Jewish and saw the suffering of his fellow Israelites. It was at this time that Moses, "saw an Egyptian beating a Hebrew, one of his kinsmen. He looked this way and that way and saw no one, so he struck down the Egyptian and hid him in the sand" (Exodus 2:11-12).

In this episode, we find that our young patriarch Moses kills a man and then hides the body. We wonder about the morality of his actions: Moses wanted to stop his kinsman from being beaten, possibly to death, but to take a man's life is a weighty matter. Being a Jew, he knows that the consequences will be grave if his act is discovered. The narrative continues that his killing of the Egyptian does become known, and this is what causes Moses to flee for his life, setting him on a course to encounter God in the wilderness.

The most telling phrase of the story is it says that Moses "looked this way and that and saw no one." In the plain sense of the phrase, it means that Moses looked around to see if anyone was watching him to see what he was about to do. He wanted to kill the brutal Egyptian in secret, and he hid the body so as not to be found out. Moses was afraid of being caught.

There is, however, another way to read the very same phrase. Moses looked this way and that and saw no one. We might imagine that Moses was watching the scene of a brutal Egyptian taskmaster beating an Israelite slave, possibly to death. He identifies with the plight of his kinsman, and he asks himself: Isn't someone going to come and stop this? And so he looks this way and that, looking for someone to intervene. Isn't there some officer of the law that is going to intervene? Who is going to help this person? Perhaps he saw people calmly walking by with averted eyes, going about their business. It was then that he realized that it was up to him, that he was the person who could do something. He was the person he was looking for.

Moses looking around, from this perspective, is not part of premeditated murder. In fact, it is just the opposite. Not only does Moses witness the crime of the beating, but he most likely saw other people's inaction, the crime of the by-stander who does nothing, who assumes someone else is going to take care of the problem. The Hebrew literally says that Moses saw no one, that is "saw no *ish*," no human being. No one was human enough, or feeling enough, to act on behalf of another. At some point, Moses must have realized that it was up to him, and him alone, to put a stop to the crime. He may have asked himself, "Who, me?' But in his conscience the answer came back: "Yes, you. Now do something!"

This defining moment in Moses' life was not when he stepped forward on behalf of another but also when he realized how desperately the people needed a leader, needed someone to shake others out of their complacency. He must have felt called by God to act when no one else was willing to do so. The *Midrash* states: "He saw that there was no one" meaning he saw that there was no one who was impassioned by God to strike back at the Egyptian (Exodus Rabbah 1:28-29). Moses, at that moment, felt singled out and empowered to do what needed to be done.

Just as we might understand the feeling of safety that we get in a crowd, so also do we know its dangers. In psychology, there is something called the bystander effect or more technically, Genovese syndrome. On March 13, 1964 in New York City, Kitty Genovese was murdered in the plain sight of thirty-eight people, and not one of them called the police.[27] That attack, which included rape and robbing, took approximately a half-hour. The reporting of this event, as some here may remember, caused shock at the callousness of Kitty Genovese's neighbors, one of whom summarized their attitude when she said, "I didn't want to get involved."

While the reporting of the crime was sensationalized, the incident begged a question, a question that was raised by Moses in the book of Exodus and follows us into modern days: Why is it that people do not want to get involved? Why do we assume that, if we are standing in a crowd, someone else is always going to take care of a problem? Whenever one receives training in first aid or CPR, we are taught to never say: "Someone call an ambulance," because most of the time, people will simply stand there. Instead, we are supposed to point directly to someone, look at them and say, "You, call an ambulance." Our first instinct is to hold back rather than step forward, even when another's life is on the line.

Thankfully, we are not faced with life and death situations on a regular basis. More commonly, at most we are asked to help someone carry something or to pull over to help change a flat tire. Even in these mundane instances, however, our instinct for selfishness often has to be overcome to help with these inconvenient good deeds. It is telling, therefore, that many of God's commandments in the Torah are addressed to us in the second person singular: You should not stand by while your neighbor bleeds. You shall leave food for the poor. You shall love your neighbor as yourself. Each of these is as if God is pointing a finger at us and saying, "You, yes, you sitting right there, this is the right thing to do."

In *Pirkei Avot* 2:6, Hillel says when no one else acts like a human being, we should still strive to be human. Moses did not see anyone human enough around him to act, and so, after a moment of asking himself, "Why me?" stepped into the fray. It was certainly inconvenient, and he also paid a price. But he also was at peace with his God and his conscience. We should also pray that, from the simplest, everyday acts of decency and respect to the larger deeds of

[27] newyorker.com/magazine/2014/03/10/a-call-for-help

social action and responsibility, we are able to follow his example. May we be human enough to step forward when life's challenges come to us.

## The Truth of the Book of Exodus

The Torah is a book of truth, but it is not a book of facts. By that I mean that the Torah attempts to communicate in human language events that are beyond words and what God demands of us, but hardly anything in the Torah can be verified as factual. Facts are things we can demonstrate and prove. We can demonstrate certain laws of physics or statistics attained through reliable methods. Dates and places can be proven with evidence. But there is very little factual evidence to either confirm or deny the events found in the Bible. And the narrators of the Bible seemed to want it that way. The Bible seeks to tell the truth about our relationship with God and our morality, but it is decidedly disinterested in recording facts for posterity.

For instance, in this week's Torah portion, what might seem like a very important and obvious fact is left out by the Torah portion. We are told that the former Pharaoh died, and a new Pharaoh arose "who did not know Joseph," (Exodus 1:8) that is, who was not hospitable to the Israelite people. An obvious factual question is: who were these Pharaohs? The Bible does not name them. If we had their names, we could place the events of the Exodus in a neat historical framework. As it stands, we only have our best guess. Many scholars believe that the story makes the most sense if the new Pharaoh is Seti I and the Pharaoh after him is Raamses II. But this is our best guess, far from factual proof.

How amazing it is, then, that our Torah portion does give the names for the two midwives who play a key role in the beginning of our story. The new Pharaoh, whatever his name is, makes a decree that all of the Hebrew boys who are born are to be killed. The midwives of Egypt, however, who revere God, refuse to obey Pharaoh's decree, and they save the lives of the Hebrew children. The Torah reads, "The midwives, revering God, did not do as the king of Egypt had told them. They let the boys live" (Exodus 1:17). And the Torah also tells us their names: Shifra and Puah.

It is no coincidence that the Torah does not give us the names of the wicked Pharaoh but does tell us the names of two humble midwives of Egypt. The Torah is not interested in relating the historical facts of the dynasties of Egypt and recording which king came after which. But the Torah is interested in the moral acts of those people, Shifra and Puah, who may have been part of the lowest class of society but whose acts were noble. Those are names worth remembering, whereas Pharaoh's name, due to his wickedness, deserves to be obliterated.

This highlights a major difference between the Egyptians and the Israelites. Each culture had different answers to the question: what is worth remembering? The Pharaohs of Egypt are remembered and listed in their dynasties. And when the Pharaohs die, they are encased in grand tombs, pyramids that are to last for all eternity. Everything is focused on memorializing the dead kings of Egypt.

And yet, our Torah states that Moses, our most famous leader, was a humble man. Rather than be buried in a grand tomb like a pyramid, the Torah simply states that Moses was buried, and we do not know where his burial place is to this day. The moral lesson of humility of Moses, like the bravery of Shifra and Puah, is of much more interest in our tradition than recording the facts of history.

The act of Shifra and Puah, the saving of Israelite children, may call to mind the acts of many other people who we have come to call, "righteous gentiles." Perhaps we might think of the people of Denmark who resisted Nazi power and smuggled out Jewish children to Sweden. At great risk to themselves, they hid Jewish children in boats and in homes, revering God and letting our children live. When it was decreed that all Jews should wear a yellow star on their sleeve to label themselves as Jews, all the people of Denmark, including the king, put on stars the next morning so that the Nazis could not tell the difference between Jew and Gentile.

And so when we recall the lives and actions of righteous people, we have a saying: may the memory of the righteous be a blessing. Another one goes: a good name endures beyond the grave. And the opposite is also said in Jewish folklore. When someone is wicked, it is a custom to say: may so-and-so's name be forgotten.

So what is worth remembering? We may have trouble recalling all of the facts of the story. The dates and places may have been lost, waiting for an archeologist or a historian to find. But the moral deeds upon which our lives are built, the truths taught to us by the daring acts of both Jew and Gentile who have given us our freedom, and the humility of those who revere God are not to be forgotten.

The title of this week's Torah portion is *Shemot*. It means, "Names." May these names, linked with our own if we prove worthy enough, be an abiding blessing. Let us pray for the strength to make them so.

## *Vaeira* (Exodus 6:2-9:35)

### Plagues or Miracles?

We do not read about all Ten Plagues in this week's portion but only the first six. Frankly, I do not know what Pharaoh must have been thinking, for six should have been enough. Moses begins by turning the Nile into blood. It is fitting that this is the first plague, for it recalls Pharaoh's most heinous crime of drowning the first born sons of the Israelites in the Nile, and thus the first and tenth plagues serve as a kind of frame alluding to this murderous decree. As one Chasidic source puts it, the Egyptians had all-too-much experience drowning humankind in bloody rivers (*Itturei Torah* III:66-67).

The second plague of frogs illustrates the lack of control that the Egyptians experienced, for, as Samson Raphael Hirsch has written, they could not "enjoy one's house, bed, and board without constantly being molested." Lice, beasts, cattle disease and boils follow. Time and again, we see that in the midst of the affliction, Pharaoh wavers and considers letting the people go, but after the danger has passed, Pharaoh's heart stiffens. A *midrash* explains that such is the way of all transgressors: when in trouble we cry to God; when we have relief we return to our destructive ways (Exodus Rabbah 10:6).

One of the most disturbing elements in the story that we read is that it is God who stiffens Pharaoh's heart, increasing the suffering upon the Egyptians in order to display God's wonders. Such a depiction of God seems rather cruel, for it seems intolerable for us to think of our loving and compassionate God to ever want to increase suffering in any way. And yet there we have it, and we realize that what was from the Egyptians' point of view a plague was a miracle from the point of view of the Israelites. To the Israelites, the plagues were the miraculous intervention of justice on the Egyptian populace who stood by and benefited from the atrocity of slavery, a humbling of the mighty Pharaoh who considered himself a god, and proof of the existence of the One God above all of the Egyptian deities. What was affliction and strife to one group was fair dealing for years of slavery and murder to the other.

We might ask ourselves: what is the real difference between a plague and a miracle? A miracle, as defined by Martin Buber and

Emil Fackenheim,[28] is something so wondrous, it become more astonishing the more you try to explain it. Even understanding how it happened does not take away the "abiding astonishment" at the event. A plague is almost like an anti-miracle. It also is astonishing, but it brings about catastrophe. It is endlessly fascinating in its horror. And the same event can be a plague or a miracle, depending upon one's point of view.

I was once privileged to hear the actor Michael J. Fox address a large audience on the subject of stem cell research. He was pleading for the expansion of such research, and he did so speaking from his own experience as someone who suffers from Parkinson's disease. He did not know then that this week the House of Representatives would pass HR 3, 253-174, a bill that would greatly expand the number of stem cell lines available for federally funded research. The vote is still 30 short of what would be needed to override a Presidential veto. At the gathering, Fox talked about his family, his life with Parkinson's, and his experience trying to pack up his kids to get them to arrive at Hebrew School on time. Fox described his living with Parkinson's as the "gift that keeps on taking." His movements had become more uncontrollable, and every day he felt that he had lost something more. And yet, he still was able to see past his disease to live life with deeper appreciation, to use his time for goodness in the world, and to transcend himself by creating the Michael J. Fox Foundation. For sure, he would rather be less wise and not have the disease, but he has nevertheless responded to his situation by living his life as fully as possible and giving to others. What is a plague for him has become a miracle for other people in that he has been able to provide much needed comfort and support to those around him.

The question that seems to address us today from the Torah is to reconsider the plagues in our own lives, to think of the lessons we might learn or the opportunities to give that they might have in store. If we can expand our minds, not to diminish or minimize the difficulties we all face or the tragedies we have endured, but to include with the bad also the good - the friendships we have discovered, the love that we share, the community that surrounds us - then we have learned to appreciate the miraculous. Someone once said that if we all went around the room and were given the

---

[28] Emil Fackenheim, *What is Judaism?* (New York: Collier Books, 1987), 230.

opportunity to put our *tzures* on the table and swap with someone, we would all inevitably take back our own. I suspect it is because with our hardship also comes our love and devotion to one another, and we dare not give that up.

We need to have the strength and insight to see the good along with the bad, to have the wisdom to see life from a variety of perspectives, and to appreciate the miracles that are around us every single day - in the beauties of nature, in the touch of a loved one - if but open our minds to them. There is a blessing found in the Talmud upon the occasion of realizing that a miracle has occurred in one's life, no matter how everyday it might seem: *Baruch sh'asah li nes b'makom hazeh…* Blessed is the One who made a miracle for me in this place (*Berachot* 54a).

## *Bo* (Exodus 10:1-13:16)

### What is the Real Torah?

This past weekend, I had the privilege of having our 11th and 12th graders to our house. We always have great discussions, and this one centered on what one's future roommate might ask you about Judaism. What is that crooked thing on the doorpost? Why don't Jews accept Jesus? And, are most Jews rich? These are just some of the questions our young people will inevitably be asked by someone on a college campus or while at a job after they leave the bubble that is Sharon, Massachusetts. We practiced what some of our answers might be.

One of the questions that a curious roommate might ask is what is the Torah? Aside from simply answering, "The Five Books of Moses," there is a deeper question behind this one. The question is, "Do you believe that what the Torah says is true?" Some of our political candidates have been asked a similar question, especially during the caucus in Iowa. During the Republican CNN-YouTube debate, one gentleman held up a bible and asked the candidates, "Do you believe every word of this book?" Aside from the appropriateness of the question, it is clear that religion is constantly in the public sphere.

This week's Torah portion asks a similar kind of question, albeit in a different way. In this week's portion, we get the first extensive halakhic discourse in the Torah. Chapter twelve begins with the commandments regarding Pesach. "This month shall be the beginning…" (Exodus12:1) the section begins, and it gives the details of the Passover sacrifice. The rabbis who interpreted the Torah wondered why the Torah did not begin here. After all, this is where the Torah has some kind of practical significance. If we are supposed to read the Torah as a "how to" manual for living, then all of the stuff before is simply irrelevant. This is the first part that actually tells us what God wants us to do.

The sages' answer comes in the form of a parable. If a king were to come to a land and give out all kinds of laws, even if they made sense and were very good laws, the people would still probably respond with, "Who are you to tell me what to do?" That seems to be an especially Jewish question.

But, if the king introduced himself and explained that he was the one who created the world, guided their ancestors through the wilderness, and set them free out of Egypt, then the people would be more receptive to his laws. This is why the Torah begins with the stories of creation, Abraham, and the Exodus. The stories give meaning and force to the laws. *Halakha*, the practical part of the Torah, is complemented by the *aggadah*, the stories.

In this spirit, I told our students my definition of what the Torah is. I told them that I believe the Torah is the divinely-inspired autobiography of the Jewish people. Unlike an Orthodox perspective, I do not believe that the Torah was given "as is" at Mount Sinai and that every word of the Torah is literally true in a factual sense. There is too much evidence from studies of literature, history, and archeology for me to accept such a belief, for to do so would constitute blind faith, and I believe God meant us to keep our eyes open. I am sure that I would not have done well at the Iowa caucus.

Rather, by saying that the Torah is the divine-inspired autobiography of the Jewish people, I join the community of critical thinkers who believe that the Jewish people as a whole wrote the Torah over a long period of time. It was eventually edited together in the time of Ezra, and it recorded people's first-hand experiences of how they encountered God in their lives. One of these stories tells of someone who experienced God when he saw a sky in the desert full of stars and envisioned a future of descendants. Another tells of experiencing a sense of the divine in crossing a sea and feeling liberated. Sometimes, as often happens in any game of generational "telephone," some details become altered, but the force of the memory remains. All of these threads were woven together in a mixture of memory, tradition, and teaching, always with the commanding "thou shalt" as the goal. The stories tell us who we are and the commandments tell us how to be in this world, revolving around a central axis, our covenant with God.

One of the ways we might think of our Torah is through two tales I once heard about the same event. When the State of Israel liberated the Jewish community of Ethiopia and brought them to Israel, two different stories emerged. One told of how the Israeli government sent airplanes to neighboring Sudan to airlift the Jews out of that hostile country. The people's experiences were very primitive, and many of them had never seen a plane before. They were brought to Israel and housed in absorption camps until they could be acclimated to modern life. This was a matter of saving a precious part of the Jewish people whose beautiful traditions have become part of the fabric of the Jewish state.

When asking an Ethiopian Jew, however, about the experience, some of the older refugees initially told of how they met with spies from the Land of Israel who told them of their future liberation. They walked many days, some dying along the way. Eventually, large silver birds came from the sky. They climbed into the belly of these silver birds and were flown, as it says in the Torah, "on eagles' wings" (Deuteronomy 32:11) to the Land of Israel. In this way, God beautifully redeemed them with a mighty miracle.

Which version of the story is true? The answer, of course, is that both of them are true, each from a different perspective. One may tell us more details of the facts, but another tells us of the emotions and meaning of the events. The most important part is to pass down the enormity of the miracle of freedom and the preciousness of life.

When we read our stories of burning bushes and splitting seas, we are reading the divinely-inspired autobiography of the Jewish people. We are relating something sacred to be passed down, parables of what it means to be human in the presence of infinity and transcendence.

Such a reading of our sacred Scriptures requires a tolerance for nuance and ambiguity. In the realm of religion, these can be hard to come by in today's world. Nevertheless, we can recommit ourselves to a pursuit of our Judaism that includes intellectual honesty along with spiritual feeling. As a prayer by O. Eugene Pickett claims, we thank God "for high hopes and noble causes, for faith without fanaticism."[29] Let us embrace our Torah as one of many paths to God, and hold it close as our personal parable for living.

## Come Be With Me

The name of this week's Torah portion, *Bo*, is a lesson all in itself. The name comes from the opening line: *Yayomeir Adonai el Moshe, Bo el Paro....* "God said to Moses, "Come to Pharaoh…" (Exodus 10:1)

We read here the story of Moses confronting Pharaoh and the showdown that results in plagues and the ultimate liberation of the

---

29 worldprayers.org/archive/prayers/celebrations/for_the_expanding_grandeur.html

Israelites. Moses must go into Pharaoh's chamber and declare, "Let My people go" in God's name. Moses was very reluctant to do so, but God's word is insistent: *Bo el Paro…* "Come to Pharaoh."

It was Rabbi Menachem Mendel of Kotzk who noticed the strange use of the word *Bo* that gives the portion its name.[30] Grammatically, you would think that the word should be *Lech*, as it, "Go to Pharaoh." We see this happen with other people in the Torah, such as Abraham. Abraham is told *Lech Lecha*, "Go forth to the place that I will show you." Similarly, we might expect that God should tell Moses, "Go forth." But instead the word is "Come."

The Kotzker explains that when we use the word "Go," it means we are standing with a person and we are sending them away from us. But if we use the word "Come," it means that we are in a room and we are calling someone to join us, as in "Come be with me," "Come here," or "Come into this room."

By using the word *Bo*, therefore, the Torah is teaching us that God is already in the room with Pharaoh, and God is calling Moses to come and join God with Pharaoh. According to this interpretation, the opening sentence means God is saying, "You may think that in this place of Pharaoh's cruelty and hard-heartedness that there is no God, but I am everywhere. Come be with Me because believe it or not, I am here, too."

Building upon this interpretation, Rabbi Nachman of Breslov understands Pharaoh to symbolize any supposedly Godless place (*Likkutei Moharan* I:64). Pharaoh is a *bechinah* or manifestation of the *challal hapanui*, a space that appears vacated by God. But "the hardening of the heart is simply the inability to sense or understand Godliness. Moses must enter the paradox of the Vacated Space and answer the questions that arise from there."

There have been times in my life when I have felt distant from God or questioned God's presence. I think there are spaces, rooms, and moments that feel absent of the Divine in all of our lives. We feel very alone, lost, or afraid. There are times of panic, stress, and anxiety where we lack trust in ourselves, others, or the future. This is the room of Pharaoh. It is very hard to be in that place in our lives.

But this Torah portion is saying, "Do not panic. God is in that place with you, even if it is very hard to feel. Greet the truth of this

---

30 Cohen, 105.

experience with honesty and compassion. Even in this difficult moment," God is saying, "come be with Me."

To illustrate this, I can only ask you to look into your own life's experience, to the moments when you felt the rebirth of hope, the triumph of justice, the overwhelming feeling of unexpected kindness.

And I can tell you about a student in his second year of rabbinical school in Cincinnati who was called out of the Hebrew class he was teaching by one of his professors at Hebrew Union College and told to go visit a man in the hospital who was dying. This was a man whose end was long, painful, and unjust. He was a war veteran and deserved better. My teacher asked me to go to him and say the *Shema* with him and his family in a final act of faith before he died, despite all he had been through.

With fear and trembling, I climbed into the car, and I was near panic. Who was I to stand by this person's bedside? Why was my teacher picking on me?

So I drove to the hospital, and I was shocked that they let me in and led me right to the man's room even though I did not feel I belonged there at all. I stood by this man's bedside, and I took his hand, and I stroked his knuckles with my thumb, and I recited the *Shema* prayer, and I told him that everything would be okay. I do not know what made me say that last part, but I did.

And ever since that night, I have had to believe that, whatever room I find myself, God is in that room with me. I cannot prove it. I cannot explain it. I just believe it to be true.

I have been in that situation many, many times since. I was just in that situation this past Wednesday late afternoon. It doesn't get easier, but it is also unambiguously meaningful and heartfelt.

The commandment is, "Come be with Me here in this hard place and affirm the Divine attributes of truth and loving kindness." And so that is what we try to do. Sometimes we succeed. Sometimes not.

But whenever we are in a moment of panic, whenever we feel overwhelmed by stress and anxiety, we can always take a breath and say, "I greet the truth of this experience with compassion." In this way, we affirm that place of God in our world, both for our own sakes and for others.

*Bo el Paro*. "Come be with Me."

## *Beshalach* (Exodus 13:17-17:6)

### Looking Up

I remember very clearly when we were wandering in the desert. It was a long and hot day, and the ground was rocky. Our hiking boots were laced up tightly, and our necks were sunburned. Our water bottles had performed an immense magic trick: the more we drank from them, the heavier and heavier they got as the day wore on and as our strength waned.

And we always had to keep an eye on where we were stepping. We had all heard horror stories of twisted, sprained, or broken ankles and hikers having to have been left behind until someone with a jeep could come and get them. No one wanted to be left behind. Then our guide had to tell us the story of rattlesnakes found in the area, and that didn't relieve our anxiety any. We kept our eyes glued to the ground.

And no one wanted to touch anyone. We were all hot and sweaty. Any sense of deodorant was a joke by now. Even our appetite had disappeared. And if someone tripped, and we all tripped, and fell into someone else, the event was followed by profuse apologies. God forbid we should touch each other. We would say, Hey, why don't you watch where you're stepping?

When the guide showed us the map, none of us cared to look. It was a relatively meaningless piece of paper. It was just a bunch of colorful squiggles in a sea of the unknown, and even thinking about a map brought up the thought that we might get lost, and that would be the worst thing possible, or so we thought.

And then something amazing happened. Up ahead, someone whispered, just loud enough for the rest of us to hear, "My God, it's beautiful." And for the first time all day, we looked up, leaving our feet to the ground. And we realized that we were in a beautiful canyon. We had been traveling all day, and for the first time, we forgot our water bottles, our feet, and the map, and we saw the beautiful terrain laid out in front of us. Names and geography didn't matter. It was just beautiful, and that's it. Suddenly, I felt a hand on my shoulder. I didn't mind it. It was a squeeze that said, "Isn't this why we paid for this hike in the first place?' We were all just happy to have someone with whom to share the moment.

We are traveling in a desert still. *Va'yasev Elohim et haAm derech bamidbar Yam Suf...* "God led the people roundabout by way of the desert at the Sea of Reeds" (Exodus 13:18). In our Torah portion, we read of the first wandering of our ancestors when they came out of Egypt. In their memory was the wanderings of their ancestors as well. They traveled, and they continue to travel, for forty, four hundred, or even four thousand years. And while the immediate scenery has changed, the essence of humanity has not...

When we get up in the morning, we begin our routines. Around the kitchens we go, getting our breakfast, making our tea, busying ourselves with the hurried process of not being late. Out of the house, into our cars, spinning wheels and tires, taking us to work and school, we head out on our roundabout paths. We sit at our desks, we run our errands, entering one door and exiting another.

And at home, too, we wander. The laundry goes in and comes out, the dishes travel from cupboard to table to sink to cupboard. The carpet gets worn out, the door knobs turn back and forth, and the cat runs underneath our feet, pacing in its enclosed path.

In which direction are we going? Do we even have time to ask? How much time do we spend doing things designed to save us time? Are we actually just sitting, stirring a big pot of something we don't understand and calling it our lives? Do we have the time to catch our breath and to stop running in circles? Where is the meaning, the direction, and the sense of contentment that gives us a sense of purpose?

The plague of our modern time is that we are overwhelmed by the minutiae of our lives, the toothpaste and tomorrow's dinner and the phone ringing. We are overcome by too much information coming too quickly in the form of gadgets we don't know how to use. All of these things are built to take care of us and save us time, and instead, we spend all of our time taking care of them, filling the car with gas and calling the person from Sears to come out and fix the washer. We are stuck self-consciously looking at our feet lest we sprain an ankle and somehow get left behind, get lost, get left alone.

We go roundabout by way of the desert... but then someone says, "My God, it's beautiful." We look up. Can we hear their voice speak to us? Their voice is a faint whisper... Can we hear it? How can we spot the clues and the hints that tell us to leave our feet behind for just a moment?

Our lives are indeed made of roundabout paths. Why must they be roundabout? We will probably never know. But even in our darkest moments, let us listen for the whispering voice. The leaves that change color. The passing of the seasons. The miraculously thin balance of health and healing or of comfort and care. Our world is made of grandiose terrain, if we look up for but a moment.

Can we hear God's voice speaking to us through the world around us? It is only a whisper, but what a powerful whisper it can be! It can change and transform us. It might be an awe-inspiring display of power, where the sky burns its lightning and clouds explode in booms. It might be the most delicate loveliness, where a flower opens just for a day, and then drops its petals in the evening. Or it might be the still grandeur of a canyon, the crust of centuries in which our lives are only a few inches of sedimentary rock.

In all of these cases, the thinker Abraham Joshua Heschel would call this an encounter with the Ineffable. There are some things for which there are no descriptions or expressions. There is only prayer. Our symbolic words, our *berachot*, are just that, symbols to express things beyond words. There are things for which our vocabulary fails us. We can only listen to God's voice speak to us through the moment.

No less grandiose is the terrain of the human soul. The touch on the shoulder. God didn't just lead Moses through the desert. God led the people. All of them, together. The journey was meant to be shared.

But we Americans especially don't like to be touched. We are perpetually hot and sweaty from our journey. If we trip and bump into each other, we are expected to apologize profusely, even to strangers. Sociologists call it, "the American two-foot bubble." There is a two-foot bubble that surrounds every person. Only our intimate loved ones can invade that space, but we don't touch in public.

If the person is a person of authority, the bubble grows in size. The lecturer sits or stands alone up on a stage or behind a big desk. If you want to speak, you must raise your hand and take your turn. It seems that part of becoming "important" means also becoming "unapproachable."

But the journey was meant to be shared. To travel as a people, each on our roundabout paths. Perhaps we can hear God's voice in nature, but what about each other? What of God's intimate touch?

Can we take off the child's headphones long enough to let her hear us say, "I love you?' Can we listen to each other, not waiting for the next opportunity to talk about ourselves, but to hear the other person? Even more difficult, can we hear what others mean to say, the feelings that are driving their words, the ideas, emotions, and silences that motivate them?

And what of the voices in our memory? There are those voices, too, the voices of parents and teachers and loved ones and friends and children, all speaking to us in a tremendous multitude of 600,000 or more. What are they trying to say to us? Do we have the time to listen?

Can we hear God's words and feel God's touch here, in this synagogue? Isn't that why synagogues are built? To build a community is to share the journey. I once heard what I believe is the loveliest description of a synagogue. It was during an appeal for a fundraiser on behalf of a synagogue, and the person said, "Here, life is a little less lonely."

*Va'yasev Elohim et haAm derech bamidbar Yam Suf...* "God led the people roundabout by way of the desert at the Sea of Reeds." We wander from detail to detail, wasting time while we try to save time. We are stuck in ourselves, just trying to see where we should put our next foot. We are driven by the fear of being lost or alone.

But there are voices to guide us. There are the prayers of our ancestors and the wind through the buildings and trees. There are those ineffable moments of grandeur and awe. And there are also the people about us, in our memory and in our community. There, too, are moments of holiness.

Shall we listen to them, these sacred places of the mind? They are telling us, "Let us be led by God through this wilderness, in our roundabout paths. Let us not do it by ourselves, but let us do it together. It is a journey meant to be shared."

## *Yitro* (Exodus 18:1-20:23)

### The Compelling Presence of Sinai

When we think back to childhood, we can all think of role models that changed our lives. There were people in our lives who made us change our behavior or inspired us to do something new. Role models are people who, when we watch them, we say to ourselves, "I want to be more like that." Perhaps we don't need to think back too far. Perhaps our role models are in our homes or are our friends right now. But the point is that there are people whose presence we find to be compelling, and long after they are gone, they shape our decisions.

I, personally, can think of a few of my own role models. My parents are role models, and so are my teachers. As a rabbi, I think of Rabbi Leo Baeck, a great Reform rabbi from Germany, who inspired many to live through the Holocaust. He not only wrote about ethics, but he lived them out publicly. Even though I never met him, he is still a role model to me. But did you know that, according to Jewish tradition, not only people can be role models, but even God is a role model in a certain way?

In the Torah this week we discover a new dimension to God's existence and relationship to the Jewish people. In this week's Torah portion, God serves as a role model. The Torah portion begins, "Be holy, for I, the Eternal One, am holy" (Leviticus 19:2). We are supposed to follow God's example and be holy just the way that God is holy. God is our role model for holiness.

In the Talmud (*Sotah* 14a), we read that God is a role model for some of the most important *mitzvot* in the Torah. Rabbi Chama ben Rabbi Chanina taught that the Torah teaches: You shall walk after the Eternal One, your God, meaning, you shall imitate God and what God does. But how is it possible to imitate God? Isn't God above and beyond anything we can imagine, burning like an eternal fire? How can we humans imitate the holy God?

Rabbi Chama explained: We should do the things that God did in the Torah. It says in Genesis that God made garments for Adam and Eve, and so should we clothe the naked and save the homeless from exposure. It says that God appeared to Abraham after his circumcision, and so should we visit the sick and relieve the ill of their loneliness. It says that God blessed Isaac after the death of his father, and so should we give comfort to the bereaved. And it says that God Godself humbly buried Moses, and so should we take care of our dead with dignity and respect. From clothing our children to taking care of the vulnerable to burying the dead, throughout our entire lives, we should imitate these actions that God did and thus bring meaning and holiness to our community.

In Judaism, we are more accustomed to thinking of God as a commanding voice, not a role model. Usually we understand that God issues commands, *mitzvot*, orders that we are to follow. We feel that God tells us to do things. And telling people to do things is a valuable form of leadership. We need those who are wiser than we are to help us and tell us what to do. We need the commanding voice of Sinai informing our conscience.

But another kind of leadership is leadership-by-example. Often, this inspires us more than being told what to do. We see something so compelling that we are inspired to follow suit. Just as there is a commanding voice at Sinai telling us what to do, there is also God's compelling presence, inspiring us to acts of goodness. We want to be holy the way God is holy.

Indeed, some Jewish thinkers understand that there are two ways to serve God in this world. One is out of fear, and the other is out of love. When we serve out of fear, we are commanded to do what we should, and we obey because we fear the consequences. But when we serve out of love, we do so because we want to draw closer to that which inspires us, to become better and more worthy people.

The Ten Commandments are *mitzvot* that some of us may obey out of fear: fear of disappointing others or ourselves or of the consequences and inevitable punishments that will follow. If we show disrespect and disregard for others, the same will be done to us. If we emotionally sabotage our families, we will reap sorrow for generations. If we spiritually corrupt our family and friends, we will pay for a long time. And so we obey God's commandments with appropriate fear for what might happen otherwise.

But in this portion, we are told to serve out of love. "Be holy the way I am holy," God compels us. We serve because we want to, not because we are told to. We want to transcend to a higher plane of behavior. In addition, all of the Ten Commandments are repeated in this Torah portion in one form or another, but the context is different. Now, the commandments are compelled from us with God as a role model.

The commandment to love only appears in two different modes in the Torah. The first we know from our prayer books: *v'ahavta et Adonai eloheicha.* You shall love the Eternal One your God (Deuteronomy 6:5). The other place that love is commanded is here in this Torah portion: *v'ahavta l'rei'echa kamocha* (Leviticus 19:18). You shall love your neighbor as yourself. Jewish tradition has understood these commandments to actually be one and the same: to love God is to love your neighbor. We cannot separate the two. If you want to love God, you must serve your fellow human beings and see the divine image in each of them. You cannot walk to synagogue, ignore the homeless on the way, and pray at services and think that you love God. It is only through the love and service of one's neighbor that we draw close to the Eternal.

And so we come full circle. God is our role model for how to be as people, and in order to serve God we must serve humankind. So let us pray to imitate God by performing *mitzvot*, not out of fear, but out of love. And let us also remember to take heed of our actions, because, who knows? Someone just might be imitating us, and we might have the privilege of showing them the compelling presence of Sinai.

## Some Unsolicited Advice

Our Torah portion this week focuses on great events. This week we hear of the Israelites' encamping at Mount Sinai and their vision of God. We read about Moses receiving the Ten Commandments. We hear the thunder, and we see the lightning of revelation. I would like to turn our attention, however, to a much quieter event that happens at the very beginning of this week's Torah reading, an event in the life of a family, the details of which the Torah leaves out, only hinting at what might be happening.

When we begin this week's Torah portion, Moses and the Israelites have escaped Egypt. It is at this moment that we read that Jethro, Moses' father-in-law, meets up with Moses, and he brings Moses' wife Zipporah and two sons Gershom and Eliezer with him. Apparently, while Moses was off doing terribly important stuff with God, plagues and Pharaoh in Egypt, he had left his family behind. Jethro was left taking care of his daughter and his two grandsons while his son-in-law was off at work. They reunited, and then, the Torah says, "They went into the tent" (Exodus 18:7). We do not know the exact content of what was said in that tent. We are left standing outside. But can you imagine what kind of conversation went on there? Perhaps I am reading too much into the story, but we might guess that Jethro probably gave Moses a piece of his mind for leaving his family.

I also imagine that this might have come as a bit of a shock to Moses. After all, Moses' father is entirely absent in the Torah, and the only father figure that Moses has ever known has been Pharaoh himself. Not exactly kind and nurturing. Suddenly there is this man who is full of expectations and advice, telling him about his responsibility to his family.

Jethro continues to give Moses advice. Later in the Torah, it is Jethro who takes Moses aside because he feels that he is spending too much time at work again. He tells him that, "The thing you are doing is not right; you will surely wear yourself out, and these people as well. For the task is too heavy for you; you cannot do it alone. Now listen to me. I will give you counsel" (Exodus 18:17-19). Jethro convinces Moses to appoint elders to help Moses lead the people so Moses isn't the only one in charge and can spend more time at home. This is certainly timeless advice given from countless fathers-in-law.

While it is a bit of a soap opera that we see acted out in front of us between Moses and Jethro, it does raise a few issues for all of us. Jethro feels the need to intervene in his son-in-law's life and, acting for his family's best interest, give some unsolicited advice. But all of us know that no one really listens to unsolicited advice unless they absolutely have to. None of us like to be told what to do. We want to figure things out for ourselves.

At the same time, however, perhaps the Torah is trying to teach us that we should learn a certain kind of humility and honesty. Moses benefits from his father-in-law's wise counsel, even though I am sure he didn't want to hear it at first. And it must also have been difficult for Jethro to confront his son-in-law and tell him the truth, to give him his opinion without holding back. Perhaps what we can learn from this story is that we should try to be humble enough to ask for advice and help, even when we think we don't need it, and when we are asked, we should be as truthful as possible to the other person. Telling the truth about something never made it any worse than it already is.

Often, today, just like human beings long ago, we think we can convince people with our unsolicited advice about things they don't want to hear. And we also think that we don't need anyone's help, that we can do it all ourselves. In the words of Rabbi Edwin Friedman:

"The colossal misunderstanding of our time is the assumption that insight will work with people who are unmotivated to change. Communication does not depend on syntax, or eloquence, or rhetoric, or articulation but on the emotional context in which the message is being heard. People can only hear you when they are moving toward you, and they are not likely to when your words are pursuing them. Even the choicest words lose their power when they are used to overpower. Attitudes are the real figures of speech."[31]

We have to be ready to hear the advice of others, and when asked, we have to be ready to tell the truth. It all depends on our attitude, either in our giving or our receiving. If we are closed and full of our own ego, we cannot hear the words of others and our words are empty. If we are humble and truthful, however, we have the potential to grow as human beings. We might even call this a "prayerful" attitude, one that is open and sensitive to the words of God that come to us.

There is a story about the Hasidic master and rabbi, the Baal Shem Tov,[32] who once traveled a long way to join a small village for Shabbat. He arrived in the town on Friday, and everyone was getting ready. However, everyone seemed to be preoccupied with what they were doing, and no one seemed very concerned about the other. By the time Shabbat descended and the candles were lit, everyone had crowded into the synagogue. All the people were dressed in their finest, and as the Baal Shem Tov began his sermon, he noticed that the people were busier comparing what everyone was wearing than listening to his words that he had worked hard on and prepared for so long. And when they sang their prayers, people were trying to outdo each other, trying to show that they had the most beautiful voice.

Finally, the Baal Shem Tov got off of the *bimah*, walked down

---

[31] Edwin Friedman, *Friedman's Fables* (NY: The Guilford Press, 1990), 5.

[32] oztorah.com/2013/09/penitence-prayer-charity-an-anthology-for-rosh-hashanah-yom-kippur/

the aisle, and turned to the door. To everyone's shock, he walked right out, before the service was over. And then the people heard him continue to conduct the service, standing outside of the building. When the people followed him outside to ask the famous rabbi what he was doing, he told them, "I can't lead the services in there. It is too full of egos, and it weighs down the prayers."

The people of the story couldn't hear the words of the Baal Shem Tov because they lacked an attitude of humility. And it was only when the Baal Shem Tov did something shocking that his words of truth were heard. Without a prayerful attitude, without humility and honesty, then people cannot grow. Words of persuasion are useless if we are wrapped up in ourselves. Our egos weigh down our potential.

But if we open ourselves to the possibilities and perspectives of others, then miracles can happen. "Who is wise?" it says in *Pirkei Avot*. "The one who learns from all people" (*Avot* 4:1). Moses eventually heeded his father-in-law, and we have the potential to do the same, learning and growing. While I am risking giving unsolicited advice myself, instead, let us join in a prayer. Let us pray to be humble enough to ask for advice, strong enough to tell the truth when asked, and wise enough to help each other as members of a community and a family, each responsible for the other.

## *Mishpatim* (Exodus 21:1-24:18)

### Biblical Masters and the Slaves Who Love Them

At the beginning of *Mishpatim* we meet a strange person. He is a slave in biblical times. Really he's not so much a slave but an indentured servant, someone who has sold his services for a certain period of time to some master. After years of sweat and toil, perhaps working off a debt or jail time, he is finally able to go free. More than that, he is entitled to some benefits and perks. He and his family can finally go out on their own. But... what's this? He doesn't want to go free! He wants to stay with his master! That's right! On this week's episode... "Biblical masters and the slaves who love them!"

At first look, it seems strange to begin this week's Torah portion with a subject like slaves who want to remain with their masters. Who is this guy? Why would he want to remain a slave? What's his problem?

Our portion shows deep disapproval of the individual who wants to remain a slave. The slave is given every incentive to leave, for the master is required to give the slave gifts and secure his family. If the slave insists on staying with his master, a painful ceremony follows. The slave is taken to the doorpost of the house, in front of everyone, and his ear is pierced through. He is literally installed into the household.

Why is the slave pierced through the ear? Rashi explains it for us.[33] This was the ear that heard God's voice at Sinai. This was ear that heard God declare, "You are servants of God," but this person has found a human master for himself! Even today we recite the *Shema*, we "hear," and we realize that this slave just didn't get it. God didn't redeem the Israelites from slavery in Egypt so that someone would choose to remain a slave. Somehow the message went in one ear and out the other.

Why is the slave pierced into the door post of the house? First of all, it is a public ceremony. Everyone will see what choice this person is making with his life, and no one can accuse the owner of any wrong-doing. But Rashi again explains the deeper meaning. The door posts were the witnesses to God passing over the homes of the

---

[33] Rashi on Exodus 21:6.

Israelites in Egypt. The door posts were the symbol of the Jewish people's redemption. And yet this slave refuses to leave his subservient condition.

Despite the obvious disapproval in this week's Torah portion of this individual, we must ask ourselves to look at the situation from the slave's point of view. Why won't he or she go free?

Perhaps the slave is comforted by the life he knows. He has job security. He knows where his next meal is coming from. He doesn't have to take care of anyone else. He only needs to be taken care of. And there will be no surprises. Tomorrow will be much like today and much like yesterday. It is a very safe world with clear boundaries and clear expectations.

Even more powerful is the fact that a slave does not need to think. All of her decisions are made for her. She doesn't have to agonize over right and wrong, and she doesn't have to worry about being consistent or setting an example for others. It's all taken care of for her.

It's a very enticing world, isn't it? We know, somewhere inside, that part of us craves the life of the slave. We have all been to Egypt. It is a place of apathy, of letting others do the work for us. It is a place where we avoid thinking about what really needs to be done, about the people we should be taking care of, of the obligations left neglected by our complacency. Egypt, most of all, is a state of mind.

We are in Egypt when we are enslaved to a routine at work or an unhealthy dynamic at home. We are in Egypt when we expect others to make decisions for us. We are in Egypt when we assume others will volunteer to take care of the details of running our community with compassion and fairness.

Then a Moses comes around and whispers in our ear: pssst, you're a slave. "A slave!" we protest. "Who, me? I'm an important Egyptian citizen! See that pyramid over there? I built that!"

But God's voice is very loud in our text. You are not to be slaves to other people. You are not to worship things. The only thing you are to serve and worship is God. And that is, in the words of Jewish thinker Emmanuel Levinas, a difficult kind of freedom.

It is difficult to serve God, to go on a quest after an ideal, often changing direction. It is difficult to constantly question authority, to have to discover the truth for ourselves. It is difficult to be disciplined in our service to an ultimate good, to shed our petty concerns for things of ultimate importance.

To be a Jew means to leave the Egypt of complacency, thoughtlessness, and apathy behind and to live in the difficult freedom of serving God alone. To do anything less would be to choose slavery, to nail ourselves to the door and reject one of our greatest gifts, our independence.

Out there is a wilderness, a desert in which we may wander. It is full of uncertainty and ambiguity. Behind us is Egypt. We are standing next to a mountain, and a Voice is telling us, "*Shema*... Listen. You are servants of God and God alone. God passed over your door posts to redeem you. Now you may go forth. If you really want to, I'm sure that the Egyptians will be glad to take you back. But there is another direction, and, with a little hope, I think we can find our way."

## They Beheld God

It has long been a mystery to those who are not Jewish why theology is only a minor topic of conversation among Jewish people. In other words, many cannot understand why it is that there are many people who are practicing Jews but who do not necessarily believe in God or who doubt God's existence. How is it possible that the religion that gave the world monotheism, the belief in one God, can have adherents that deny God's reality? Yet the fact is that even if one does not believe in God, one can still be Jewish. While belief is a major part of Jewish identity, it is not a prerequisite.

Perhaps the source of confusion is the word, "God." In this week's Torah portion, it says that Moses, Joshua, and seventy elders looked up on Mount Sinai, and "they beheld God" (Exodus 24:10). This sentence is rather bizarre. It is strange because everywhere else in the Torah, it says that we cannot see God face to face, for no one can see God face to face and live. Moses had to hide in a cave and could only see the trail that God left behind. Jacob wrestled an angel of God and escaped that encounter wounded, wondering how he got off so lucky. And Jewish philosophers like Moses Maimonides emphasized that human beings cannot know God's essence at all. Nevertheless, according to the Hebrew Bible, God paradoxically says, "Seek My face" (Psalm 27:8). Seek God's face even though we can never see it? How, then, is it possible that the elders in this week's Torah portion could be so certain of their clarity of vision? Or perhaps we have to ask: what did they mean by the word, God?

I personally believe very deeply in God, but what I mean by the word "God" might be very different than what someone else means. If you mean an all-controlling king who singles some people out for disease while blesses others with health, who sends hurricanes on some cities while gives moderate summers to others, than this is not the vision of God I believe in. If we are talking about the Soure and Soul of the Universe, then we are getting closer to what I think of when I use the word God.

Not only that, but if we think about it, we all know that each one of us has different spiritual needs at different times of our lives. When we were children, we might have thought of God as a large man with a beard. During our teenage years, we may have questioned the existence of God a great deal. Upon becoming an empty nester, we might find ourselves more drawn to Friday night services and thinking through things a bit differently. Our faith changes along with our life cycle. It is far from static. Before we judge another, we ought to be respectful about where he or she is on their journey.

The word God, therefore, can mean many things. It might be a comfort to some that one need not memorize any kind of creed or singular definition of God, for theology is far more subtle than that. Judaism has always placed a far greater emphasis on deeds than creeds; it is of ultimate importance to follow the commandments, examine one's ethics, and create a responsible community. Whether one believes in the theology of Martin Buber versus Joseph Soloveitchik is of less importance. Rationalists, mystics, and humanists all have long histories of coexisting within Judaism.

I think that there are several reasons why Judaism has been so flexible concerning belief. The first is that Judaism has never shied away from skepticism. Judaism is a religion where it is not only acceptable but encouraged to ask questions. The Talmud has far more questions than answers, and some debates are left with no real resolution. The rabbis say that some topics are left up to the spirit of Elijah the Prophet to eventually resolve, not us human beings. Skepticism, that is, thinking critically and working something through in a rational manner, only adds to and enhances knowledge and faith.

Modern Judaism has learned to embrace skepticism as a part of faith. It does so by not only reading our Scriptures through the lenses of medieval commentators and religious believers but also with the tool of historical criticism. How did the time and place influence something that was written? How does the Torah compare, for instance, to the Hammurabi Code of Babylonia or other Ancient Near Eastern literature? Rather than be afraid of what we might find, we might be struck by even a greater sense of awe concerning our heritage. It is the difference between looking at a painting of a bowl of fruit and either saying: it is a bowl of fruit, praise it but don't examine it too closely, and saying: it is a beautiful painting from a given era, and appreciate the brushwork, the materials, and the effort that it took to create it. We might believe that all things, no matter how they came to be, were ultimately inspired by God, and certainly God would want us to examine everything closely and to ask deep questions.

The second aspect of Judaism that provides latitude with theology is not only encouraging skepticism but allowing for doubt. There have been many famous agnostics, and even outright atheists, among the Jewish people. For them, the word God was simply too difficult to become meaningful. Some, especially after the Holocaust, simply could not use the word. Ahad Ha'am, the great Zionist, Sigmund Freud and Erich Fromm in the field of psychology, and some say Albert Einstein were avowedly agnostics. This may be that their personal use of the word God was simply unrecognizable. Others, who have seen the word God misused by violent religious fanatics, cannot bring themselves to employ the same vocabulary as the people they reject. The word God has become too tarnished for them to use. Some may prefer the word spirituality instead of religion for that very same reason. In light of these realities, doubt has been institutionally allowed and even appreciated in Judaism.

A section from the prayer book in our pews reads as follows: "Cherish your doubts, for doubt is the handmaiden of truth. Doubt is the key to the door of knowledge; it is the servant of discovery. A belief which may not be questioned binds us to error, for there is incompleteness and imperfection in every belief… Therefore, let us not fear doubt, but let us rejoice in its help."[34]

This leads us to a third and final value that we might take away from the idea that the elders beheld God as they gazed up at Mount

---

[34] Robert T. Weston, *Hymns for the Celebration of Life* (Boston: The Beacon Press, 1964), No. 421.

Sinai. One of the most important parts of this section of the Torah is where the people are situated. It says that the people beheld God, but that they stood at the foot of the mountain and could only see the very bottom of God's throne. The positioning of God being incomprehensibly far above while the people are down below gives us a picture of humility. Before we announce the certainty of our faith, before we state a belief as it if it is the absolute truth, we should remember the perspective with which we are blessed. We are on the bottom, craning our necks to look upward. We ought to be humble about what our minds perceive.

One of the greatest articulations of this sense of humility is found in the book of Job. When Job calls God to account for the evils that have befallen him, God gives him a truthful if not comforting response. God says to the small man in front of him:

"Where were you when I laid the earth's foundations? Tell me if you have understanding. Who settled its dimensions? Surely you know? Who laid its cornerstone, when the morning stars came together, and all the children of God shouted for joy? Who watched over the birth of the sea when it burst in flood from the womb, when I wrapped it in a blanket of cloud and cradled it in fog, when I established its bounds…? Have the gates of death been revealed to you? Have you comprehended the vast expanse of the world? …Did you proclaim the rules that govern the heavens, or determine the laws of nature on earth?" (Job 38:4-10, 17, 33).

The book of Job tells us that we are so tiny in the greater scheme of things that we ought to be humble enough to accept the limits of what we cannot know. And if we are humble enough before God, perhaps we will also be humble before each other as each person tries to live a life filled with meaning.

Skepticism, doubt, and humility are not the enemies of faith but its necessary companions. If we use them wisely, not as weapons but as tools, not as swords but as plowshares, then we will be on a better path to coming to our own personal definition of the word God. Let us pray to seek out God's face, knowing that it is ultimately far above us.

## *Terumah* (Exodus 25:1-27:19)

### Building a Temple

The buildings and monuments of a place often reflect the values of the community. This is certainly true of the memorials and buildings in Washington, DC. White marble buildings with columns in front and over-sized statues of men speak of power and grandeur. Some have famous speeches carved into stone, hinting at divine wisdom. The twists and turns of the Holocaust Memorial Museum, with exposed bolts and dark gray metal, point to a more ominous part of history.

If this is true of our nation's landscape, it is also true of the one we find in our Bible. This week's Torah portion, *Terumah*, could also be called the Building and Development Shabbat. The Torah portion speaks of the construction of the Tabernacle, and the Haftarah portion (I Kings 5:26-6:13) tells us of the construction of the Temple in Jerusalem by King Solomon. This latter monument, the Temple in Jerusalem, has especially occupied the imagination of Jews for the last two thousand years. The orientation of our prayers, the subject of many of our holidays, and the basis of much of our literature goes back to the worship that took place in King Solomon's Temple. So we must ask ourselves, what values does this structure represent? If we were to walk around it in when it was in its full glory two thousand years ago, how would we feel?

Actually, our tradition has conflicted feelings about the Temple in Jerusalem. On the one hand, the Temple was the focal point of all religiosity for hundreds of years. It marked the location of the Ark, the point on which Abraham almost sacrificed Isaac, and the place where heaven touched the earth.

In addition, legends surround the event of its construction. One source has it that, while the Temple was being built, no one could hear the sound of a chisel or a hammer. It was supposed to have been erected in complete silence. Another legend elaborates that King Solomon found a magic worm, called the Shamir, that ate through the rock and did all of the necessary cutting. Quietly and quickly, the Temple was supposed to have been erected in complete tranquility.

If we were able to walk around the ancient Temple in Jerusalem, then, we might come away with the feeling of peace. Iron, often used in war, was not to touch a single stone of the altar. In peaceful silence, without any banging or clanging, God's sanctuary was built. When King David, who was Solomon's father, desired to build the Temple, God forbid him from doing so. God said "no" to David because God considered David a man of war. Regardless of how necessary any of the wars the David waged may have been, God did not want the Temple built by someone with blood on his hands. The peace that the Temple symbolized was not to be blemished in any way.

However, there are completely different stories that come to us from our Bible that say quite the opposite from these legends. One account has it that Solomon used forced labor from his people to erect the Temple. In other words, the Temple was not a product of peace, but of slavery. As a place of sacrifice, it was a bloody affair. Another rabbinic idea elaborates that Solomon must have had an Egyptian uncle who was descended from the taskmasters of Pharaoh and that is where Solomon received the idea to use forced labor in the first place. And it is quite certain that, as history moved on, greedy administrators and power-hungry kings corrupted Jerusalem. Instead of being a place of offering our hearts to heaven, it became a symbol of fraudulence and iniquity. It is for this reason that the prophets condemned the Temple to eventual destruction.

Isaiah speaks to this point about Judaism's central monument:

> "What need have I of all your sacrifices?"
> Says the ETERNAL.
> "I am sated with burnt offerings of rams,
> And suet of fatlings,
> And blood of bulls;
> And I have no delight
> In lambs and he-goats.
> That you come to appear before Me—
> Who asked that of you?
> Trample My courts
> no more;
> Bringing oblations is futile,
> Incense is offensive to Me.
> New moon and sabbath,
> Proclaiming of solemnities,

Assemblies with iniquity,
I cannot abide. (Isaiah 1:11-13)

So which is it? Do we have a Temple of peace or do we have a Temple of strife? Which values do we find as we read through this sacred literature?

Perhaps God is teaching us through our Bible that we have a choice. Perhaps, indeed, this was the same structure, but it just depended upon how and when it was used. Different people can look at the same monument, and we can see different things, depending upon our experience. The human element makes all the difference.

And we who build homes and synagogues, who expand buildings and lay foundations all are forced to make a decision. What kind of structure do we want to build? Are our institutions going to be ones of peace or ones of trouble? Whenever we come into our sanctuary, what kind of community do we build that sets up the real pillars and ceilings?

We build our congregation every time we step into it. We build it with the words that we say, with the expressions on our faces, and with the openness of our embraces. We color the perspective of what a place means by our actions. When we are in a room designated as sacred space, everything that takes place there speaks of the values we possess.

A prayer by Sydney Greenberg illustrates these sentiments, and it is a prayer I read every time we formally welcome new members into our midst:

"May the door of this synagogue be wide enough to receive all who hunger for love, all who are lonely for fellowship. May it welcome all who have cares to unburden, thanks to express, hopes to nurture. May the door of this synagogue be narrow enough to shut out pettiness and pride, envy and enmity. May its threshold be no stumbling block to young or straying feet. May it be too high to admit complacency, selfishness, and harshness. May this synagogue be, for all who enter, the doorway to a richer and more meaningful life. Amen."[35]

[35] *Mishkan T'filah: A Reform Siddur Shabbat* (New York: CCAR), 6.

**Behind the Veil**

The expression "behind the veil" is a phrase commonly used in English to refer to life after death. Recently, one of the Harry Potter novels literally has a veil of death that divides this world from the hereafter. In the movie made from the book, one can see ghosts cross over on this one-way trip. John Taylor, the third president of the Church of Latter Day Saints, used the phrase as it is commonly known when he said, "While we are mourning the loss of our friend, others are rejoicing to meet him behind the veil."

This metaphor of a veil dividing the living from the dead comes from this week's Torah portion. We read in Exodus 26 that the Israelites are to create a sanctuary for God to carry around with them as they travel through the wilderness. This portable and elaborate tent, called the Mishkan or "God's Dwelling Place" contained an innermost chamber where the Ark of the Covenant was kept. The Ark also served as a throne for God, and it was the focal point of the Israelites' prayers and sacrifices. But the most sacred chamber, called "the holiest of holies," was curtained off. The Torah reads, "You shall make a *parochet* – curtain – of blue, purple, and crimson yarns, and fine twisted linen; it shall have the sign of the cherubim [guardian angels] worked into it. Hang it upon four posts of acacia wood overlaid with gold and having hooks of gold, set in four sockets of silver. Hang the curtain under the clasps, and carry the Ark of the Pact there, behind the curtain, so that the curtain shall serve you as a partition between the Holy and the Holy of Holies" (Exodus 26:31-34).

Protestant scholar William Tyndale of early 16th century England translated *parochet* as "veil," and the holy of holies, filled with power and danger in the imagination of readers of the Bible, became life beyond death.[36] Read in the original Hebrew, the curtain has little to do with afterlife, but nonetheless, it has now taken on that meaning. In Jewish experience, we have kept the *parochet* as part of our synagogue architecture. Often in arks in synagogues, there will be synagogue doors and then behind them a curtain, dividing the Torah scrolls from the rest of the room. Opening the ark doors and *parochet* is an honor given out in traditional Torah services on Torah reading mornings and afternoons. Our synagogue has an unusual structure in

[36] Tyndale Bible on Exodus 26.

that we have two sets of doors: wooden doors for the ark, and then instead of a curtain, glass doors that reveal the Torah for all to see.

While a history of the words and architecture might be interesting, the real question for us in this prayer service is what do these things mean? What is holiness? Is it something scary and powerful from which we need to be protected, like death? Is it something open, accessible, and beautiful, like the glass doors to the ark? Why do we need a *parochet*, a veil or a curtain, to maintain sanctity in our lives?

In Judaism, holiness is both something other-worldly and even dangerous, and paradoxically also something a part of this world in the everyday. Holiness – symbolizing powerful, secret knowledge of God's universe – was something to be revered but also something around which you had to be careful. In the TaNaKh, when someone isn't careful carrying the Ark and it slips, he reaches up and tries to catch the Ark with his bare hands. It is like someone who curiously, with no evil intent, sticks a screwdriver in an electrical outlet just to see how the house really works. He gets zapped, and the Bible says that a fire of God obliterates him. The message is clear: when dealing with the inner secrets of the universe, be careful.

Similarly, we can think of all sorts of things that we have done as human beings where we may have meant well, but we now have to live with the consequences. For instance, we have unlocked the secrets of the atom, the innermost chamber, so to speak, of the universe, but should we have trespassed there? Should we have pulled back the veil and tampered with power that we have yet to control? With the capacity for weapons of mass destruction falling into the wrong hands and nuclear waste that destroys the environment and is beyond our control, should we have entered that kind of holy of holies of power?

On the other hand, we also see examples of holiness that are of the everyday variety, open and accessible to everyone. *Kedoshim t'hiyu* – Be holy, our Torah says (Leviticus 19:2). It then lists the ethical commandments which are at the heart of Judaism. You shall share your food with the poor. You shall not but a stumbling block before the blind. You shall not hate another in your heart. You shall love your neighbor as yourself. There is great holiness is raising up society to be a community set apart, answering to a higher standard.

The *parochet*, then, really seems to symbolize appropriate

boundaries and balance. We all need boundaries. We need to know that there is a certain amount of God's divinity that we share and enable us to thrive. There is a higher calling that is at the center of our existence and gives our lives meaning. This is the holiness of the Torah in our Ark.

But beware lest we think we can play God, that, like Daedalus, we can fly too close to the sun and arrogantly trespass wherever we want. Just because we can, doesn't mean that we should. That curtain that is drawn is there for our protection, to keep us in our humble bounds.

I would like to conclude with by teaching of a piece of Talmud that speaks of what it means to follow God. The book of Deuteronomy tells us to be holy by walking in God's ways. But is this really possible? Can we really follow in God's footsteps, for isn't God "a consuming fire"? Trying to follow God literally or play God is like trying to follow a rocket. You will get burned.

Rather, teach the Sages, following God means to respect the divine but to strive to be the best you can be. It means imitating the commandments that God performed for us. For, the Talmud elaborates, just as God clothes the naked, so shall you clothe the naked. Just as God visits the sick, so should you visit the sick. Just as God comforts mourners, so should you comfort mourners (*Sotah* 14a).

We should be content with trying to achieve this level of holiness, if we can. It is enough for us.

## *Tetzaveh* (Exodus 27:20-30:10)

### The Power of the Uniform

Recently, I saw a documentary on a school in South Carolina that was being cited for its excellence in teaching science. What immediately struck any viewer of this documentary was the fact that all of the teachers wore uniforms. The senior staff wore white lab coats, and the rest of the teachers wore red shirts. All of them had a NASA symbol on their coat or shirt, representing the award they had received.

People have always had mixed reactions to uniforms. On the one hand, these teachers had a great deal of pride in their work and their achievement. Their coats and shirts were badges of honor. Not only that, but to be able to wear the uniform, you had to live up to a certain level of excellence. To put on the shirt was to commit to reaching a high standard. And it also removed any social or financial distinctions. You couldn't tell how much money people had because they all looked the same. Everyone was equal and there to do their job, part of a team.

On the other hand, people can find uniforms stifling. There is a certain level of conformity that comes with putting on a uniform. Spontaneity and creativity can be squelched. Worse, sometimes people feel the cover of anonymity that they can get away with some things if they are part of a group that they wouldn't be able to if they stood out as individuals.

In our Torah portion, the priests or *cohenim* are described as wearing uniforms. The priests wore tunics and sashes, headdresses and robes. Their uniforms were to be made of the finest linen, and they were also to be colorful. Gold, blue, purple, and crimson are some of the colors that are described for us.

These wonderful uniforms, however, might seem strange when one realizes that the main vocation of the priests was the slaughter and sacrifice of animals. Unfortunately, people today tremendously misunderstand what sacrifices really were in biblical times. Just like we have barbecues on holidays in modern times, so too did our ancient ancestors. They would take their animal to the butcher stand and have the animal slaughtered. Then they would go to the altar, which was really a glorious grill, and the priests would cook the festival meal. The fat and other inedible parts were burnt up of as portions for God while the people ate the meat. In this way, the mysterious taking of life and shedding of blood for food was to be controlled and sanctified by the priests while at the same time people could celebrate the holiday.

But were the priests to perform their job dressed in their finest outfits? An apron seems more appropriate, or at least an old pair of jeans. The priests were to take the blood from the animal and dash it upon the altar. The blood was the perceived "life-force" of the animal, and it was held in holy awe. Sacrifice was a messy business. It just doesn't make any sense that the priests were supposed to be all spiffed up in their gold jewelry and blue sashes while doing this. This is especially true on holidays when there were even more offerings than usual, and the priests would be very busy doing their job next to the barbecue.

So perhaps, we may wonder, the priests were supposed to get dirty, even in their nice uniforms. Perhaps, lest they feel too important in their gold, blue, purple, and crimson tunics and sashes, they were supposed to walk away from a day's work a little messy. Just in case they forgot themselves in their roles as being the so-called holiest people of the Israelites, a little mess on their uniform might do their ego and identity some good.

We, too, wear hats, uniforms, or even masks. These costumes help us make sense of our world and ourselves. We dress up to mark important occasions. We dress casually to make ourselves more approachable. And we don the uniforms of makeup or ties to help us feel more professional and perhaps a little more important.

But we, too, can get lost in the feelings of eminence and or inflated self-worth depending on how we look. As part of basic social interaction, we act differently depending on how we are dressed. A badge at work with our name on it makes us feel like we belong to an institution, something larger than ourselves. Getting dressed in suits and other nice clothes makes us feel more professional and more empowered to take charge. And soldiers in uniform act differently than when they are wearing civilian clothes. A uniform gives soldiers feelings of power that enable them to be able to do things that they would ordinarily be unable to do.

Unfortunately, as we all know, these feelings of empowerment can backfire. People, lost in the drama of their costume, can get lost in the roles they are playing and do some very terrible things. Badges, suits, and battle-dress often empower people in the wrong ways.

Perhaps this is why the Talmud says that the uniform of the priests is so supposed to make them humble, not haughty. Each piece was supposed to atone for a past sin of the Israelites and serve as a reminder of our fallibility. The robe atoned for the Joseph's coat when he was sold into Egypt. The turban, now become a *kippah*, to atone for arrogance, so we do not walk with an upright posture but remember that God is above us. The sash was worn across their chest for immoral thoughts of the heart. And the breastplate to remind them that they we are supposed to be keepers of the laws. And so on. Rather than elevate the wearers, they are supposed to remind them of their humanity.

Underneath each of our uniforms is a person that must not get lost role-playing in acts of power. Underneath our badges of office is a person of mere flesh and blood. We can learn from our priestly ancestors that we may indeed wear uniforms, for they can help us in marvelous ways. They help us order our world, dramatize the significance of going to important places, and proclaim something of who we are. But we may also learn from them that some visible stains on the hem of our garments might help us remember that we are only people who are responsible for our actions. In the different roles that we must play, let us remember the common blood that runs in our veins and the divine image in which all of humanity shares.

## *Ki Tisa* (Exodus 30:11-34:35)

### Twelve versus One

It is an odd fact that the number thirteen is considered to be a lucky number in Judaism and an unlucky number in the world at large. I remember the first time I went into a building in which the number thirteen was skipped in the engravings for the elevator floors and was surprised that our so-called enlightened society could be so superstitious. In Judaism, the number thirteen represents, among other things, the number of years at which one comes of age, which is usually celebrated on Shabbat, which begins on a Friday night. Friday the thirteenth, then, would seem to be a fantastically lucky day in Judaism, and not the inspiration for a series of horror movies.

In this week's Torah portion, the number thirteen figures prominently. Moses is on top of Mount Sinai, asking for forgiveness on behalf of the people Israel for making the Golden Calf. God forgives the people and reveals to Moses thirteen attributes that Jewish sages have interpreted to be divine. You may recall them from a song in the Passover Haggadah, *Echad Mi Yodea*, "Who knows one?" which culminates with thirteen attributes of God.[37]

The thirteen attributes of God are derived from a verse in Exodus chapter 34, where God's forgiveness for the Israelites' sin is greeted with: "*Adonai*! *Adonai*! A God compassionate and gracious, slow to anger, abounding in kindness and faithfulness, extending kindness to the thousandth generation, forgiving iniquity, transgression, and sin; yet not remitting all punishment" (Exodus 34:6-7). If one kept track of all of the Hebrew phrases in that line, there are thirteen of them. Of course, this takes a bit of creative math, counting "*Adonai*" twice and cutting off a phrase about visiting iniquity onto the third and fourth generations, but the rabbis of antiquity were never shy about selective reading. Regardless of the literal meaning, Judaism founded a tradition based on this phrase that there are thirteen attributes of God, and this phrase is pronounced during services as the Torah is taken from the ark on such holidays as Yom Kippur, Sukkot, Passover, and Shavuot.

If one looks even more closely, a better description of these

---

[37] Shoshana Silberman, A Family Haggadah II (Minneapolis: Karben Publishing, 1987), 57.

thirteen attributes might be explained as "twelve versus one." The first twelve, according to the rabbis' counting, are all ones of mercy: The repetition of God's name, Adonai, is supposed to denote that God is merciful both before and after we have sinned. God's rule, compassion, graciousness, being slow to anger, abounding in kindness, truthfulness, kindness to the thousandth generation, and forgiveness of iniquity, transgression and sin all fall within this general, positive idea of mercy and comfort. The thirteenth attribute, not remitting all punishment, counterbalances these, representing the idea that there are consequences to our actions and that justice is due. Nevertheless, the rabbis were projecting a picture of a just God who is overwhelmingly inclined to compassion. On a scale of twelve to one, the Jewish view of God is far more loving than harsh.

It is instructive that rabbinic theology continuously describes God as being more compassionately loving than the Judge of all of our deeds, as true as the latter may be. Rosh Hashanah and Yom Kippur continuously invoke God as the one who watches everything we do, and nothing goes unnoticed. We know in our heart of hearts that, as one *midrash* teaches, if humanity were judged by the standard of strict justice, humanity would fall considerably short, and we would not merit existence. Nevertheless, even though we have little merit, we still ask God to "be gracious and answer us; treat us generously and with kindness and be our help."

There is a beautiful passage in the Talmud that illustrates this idea. The phrase is used of the synagogue is a *beit t'filati*, the place of the worship of God. The worship of God is commonly understood to mean our prayers to God, and yet, read hyper-literally, it can also mean God's worship (the worship of God). But what does God worship? What could God possibly pray for? The Talmud puts words, so to speak, in God's mouth: "May it be My will before Me that my attribute of mercy always overwhelms my attribute of judgment" (*Berachot* 7a). In other words, God prays to always be loving, even when we do not deserve it.

What does all of this really mean for us today? Descriptions of God are often projections, of aspirations for the best in humanity. When we say that God is merciful, we might be really saying that we hope we can be merciful.

Dr. Ron Wolfson points out,[38] the stories in the Torah tells us what God does: God creates, blesses, rests, calls, comforts, cares, repairs, wrestles, gives and forgives. But these stories are supposed to serve as inspiration for what we ought to be like. In imitating God, we strive for the best within us that we label divine.

Can we, as individuals, be more loving, more merciful, and more compassionate than judgmental toward others on a scale of twelve to one? Can we truly give everyone the benefit of the doubt and judge others favorably? Can we try to actualize in our lives that our attribute of mercy continually overwhelms our desire for punishment?

When life is unfair and difficult, it is easy to be angry and bitter. It is easy, and justified, to complain and feel resentment. But to be so makes us short-tempered and harsh towards others when often the situation calls for exactly the opposite. Precisely in hard times, we need to be more loving, more selfless, and more giving. When tested, we can strive to be gentler.

And so, let us pray to God to remove any urge to be judgmental or bitter from our hearts, to let our love and generosity overwhelm our lives. If we can do so, we will bring God's blessings to each other.

---

[38] Ron Wolfson, *God's To-Do List* (Woodstock: Jewish Lights Publishing, 2007), 117.

## *Vayakhel-Pekudei* (Exodus 35:1-40:38)

### Worth Its Weight in Gold

Think back to the last time you took a written exam. Perhaps it was in college or in graduate school. Actually, think back even earlier than that. Think back to elementary school, when you held one of those thick number two pencils without an eraser and were not allowed to use a pen. When the teacher handed out the pieces of paper for your spelling test or simple arithmetic, a sentence or two was usually at the top of the page, underneath the title. It said, "Please follow the instructions. Read all of the instructions before taking the test."

One of the first skills that we learned as children was how to follow instructions. Whether in a classroom or during that famous game called "Simon Says," we learned that listening and following instructions exactly was important. Sometime later we would learn that there are also times when we might need to rebel and buck the system, but first we learned to say, "Mother May I…" By following instructions, we learned that there were those who knew more than we did. We had to show some humility and that we were ready to learn.

This week's Torah portion, *Vayakhel-Pekudei*, contains a great deal about following instructions. In previous passages in the Torah, the Israelites received all of the directions in minute detail about how to build the Tabernacle which was the Tent of Meeting where they could encounter God's presence in the wilderness. In this week's portion, they actually build the Tabernacle, being careful to read the instructions first and follow them carefully. We see them bring gold to be melted down and all kinds of precious contributions and give of themselves.

To us, reading the instructions and then the verbatim fulfillment of those instructions appears tedious. If the world was created in six days and takes up only one chapter in the Torah, how come the instructions for and the building of the Tabernacle takes up many times more that space? We become impatient and our attention wanders. "Can't we get to something a little more exciting?" we might ask. What's all this about golden coins melted into a golden ark?

Ours is a society that does not want to be able to slow down and follow instructions. We want excitement and instant gratification. We want things prepackaged and ready to go. In this day and age, things should be "user friendly." No tedious repetition, please. It's just not our style. Otherwise, frankly, we will just get bored.

But there is a place for slowing down and doing things over and over again. There is a place for developing patience. By learning to listen carefully to the instructions of the world around us, we might be able to build our own Tabernacle in which we can encounter God.

Instructions from our Teachers

One of the most obvious places from which we might receive instruction is from the people who could be our teachers. There are so many people around us who have so much to teach us that all we need to do is be able to slow down, pay attention, and listen to the instruction that they have to give. As we rush along, we all need to be able to take the time to recognize that there are teachers at our every side, waiting for us to have the patience to learn.

I will not easily forget when I accidentally encountered a man who became my teacher. It came in what I felt was one of the most unlikely of places. I was on the bus going from long-term parking to the airport in Cincinnati. Here I was, a young man in graduate school, full of essays to write and places to be. And as always, I was in a rush. I needed to catch my plane. So as I watched the bus driver whistling as he stopped at a stop sign and then rounded a certain corner for perhaps the hundredth time that day, I felt that I had to ask him a question.

"Excuse me," I said, gathering up my *chutzpah*, "don't you ever get bored just driving around in the same circles all day?' I realized only afterwards that it was probably a rude question, but these things usually occur to me only when it is too late. But the man just smiled back at me and he even winked.

"Son," he said, "we all drive around in circles. It's just that some are little bigger than others, that's all."

After he said that, I slowed down a bit and took in something of my surroundings. I looked out the window of the bus, and I noticed things about the people and places that I normally would have just rushed by. This bus driver became my teacher in that moment, teaching a lesson about taking the time to notice the patterns we all run in and the things that surround us. If I hadn't taken the time to ask the question, I wouldn't have noticed that here was a man with great patience, ready to teach those who watched him. As our rabbinic sage, Ben Zoma, once taught, "Who is wise? The one who learns from every person" (*Avot* 4:1).

Instructions from our Tradition

And just as we might learn instruction from all the teachers around us of whom we may be oblivious, so may we also learn some valuable lessons from our tradition that we might all too easily ignore. Our synagogues and our services are always here, week in and week out, ready to teach us if only we have the patience to listen to their instructions.

When I ask people what they are doing on Friday night and whether or not they keep Shabbat, sometimes I get an answer that makes me sad. "Oh, we're just too rushed. Our family is just too busy." What they don't realize is that Shabbat, the centerpiece of Jewish tradition, is precisely the cure for too much rushing and busyness. We keep Shabbat precisely because we are rushed and busy. Every Friday night, no matter what, a huge difference can occur in our lives if we take the time to light our candles, say a blessing over a cup of wine, and give thanks over a loaf of bread. If we do so vicariously or irregularly, we miss the beauty of Shabbat. Ritual demands discipline and patience. It demands that slow down and follow instructions carefully by doing a meditative act over and over. The beauty of Shabbat comes when Friday night and Saturday until sundown establishes its own rhythm. Our weeks get a new sense of time, and our family life gains a set of sacred expectations. We know that it is time to get together and get our priorities in order.

I once heard the tradition of keeping the instructions of Shabbat this way. Someone once asked a rabbi if he ever got bored doing the same thing every Friday night, saying the same prayers, lighting the same candles, drinking the same wine, and eating the same challah. He answered simply, "No," and then he explained the process this way: "I do not get tired of it for the same reason that no gets tired of saying or hearing the words 'I love you.'"

Keeping Shabbat can be an expression of love. It can be the ritual that gives our family life sacred time. But that requires the discipline of slowing down and the patience to make the time to be together.

Instructions from our Hearts

And while our teachers and our tradition have constant instructions that we could benefit from by slowing down in order to pay attention, it is our hearts that have the most instruction to give us. All too often, we race along, oblivious and hurrying, ignoring what our hearts have to say. There is internal wisdom that we know to be true in the deepest and most profound parts of ourselves, but often we do not take the time to listen to what we know to be true. Despite our intuition or our conscience, we can take life for granted, running off to the next accomplishment or extra-curricular activity. Why is it that we don't take the time for what we know in our hearts is important until we discover, too late, that we are out of time?

There is a young woman in college who taught me the true meaning of following the instructions of the heart, although through a very upsetting way. She was a busy undergraduate, going from one club to the next, running around, and, well, just running. Then, a great tragedy occurred. She was diagnosed with a very rare form of lung cancer that strikes regardless of whether one smokes or anything else. As she faced her illness and as she faced a barrage of medication, she would attend services at the local Hillel house to gain solace from Shabbat and her community. One week, she gave the sermon during the Friday night service.

What she talked about was the value of following directions. She talked about all of the instructions in building the Tabernacle, and then she compared those to the instructions she had to take for her medication. She needed to take a certain amount of this three times a day, some of that five times a day for pain, something else altogether as needed for nausea. She was in an unexpected wilderness, and she found herself following instructions for her very survival.

But as she went on, she also talked about the gifts of the heart that she discovered in others. She found them in the people who stopped by, just to keep her company. The boss who let her stay at her job so she could feel useful. The community of her fellow Jewish students who shared Shabbat with her each and every week so that she was never alone. She knew that soon she was going to lose her beautiful, long brown hair to chemotherapy, but she also discovered that there were people who still thought she was beautiful nonetheless. Just as she followed the instructions of her doctors in erecting her Tabernacle of safety, her friends followed the instructions of their hearts, and they built a Tabernacle of love. No one was able to take her presence for granted, and everyone breathed a little deeper and cherished life a little more.

Conclusion: *Shabbat Shekalim*

It says in our Torah portion that everyone contributed to the construction of the Tabernacle, either by lending their talents or giving something of value. It goes on to say that everyone gave at least a shekel of gold, and some gave more than was needed. Our Torah even says that the people were "generous in heart," *Nadav libam*, and Moses had to tell the people to stop giving because he was overwhelmed by the quantity of donations. It is for this reason that this Shabbat is called Shabbat Shekalim, the Sabbath of golden gifts, for the people gave of themselves generously while faithfully following God's instructions. Whether these instructions came from Moses or a bus driver, whether they came from the tradition of Sinai or the Friday night ceremony at our modern dinner tables, or whether they appeared in the hearts of the gifts of people ancient or contemporary, a Tabernacle came together. It is a place of encountering God's presence. It is made of gifts both physical and spiritual. It is assembled by following life's all-too-easily-skipped instructions.

Let us learn to follow such instructions ourselves, in our generation. Let us learn to slow down and discover teachers around us, a tradition waiting to help us, and the empathy of our hearts, waiting to be *Nadav libam*, vehicles of holy giving. And when we do, we will find that we, too, have shekels to give, and that our gifts of patience and kindness are worth their weight in gold.

# *VAYIKRA* - LEVITICUS

## *Vayikra* (Leviticus 1:1-5:26)

### Having a Small *Aleph*

Judaism is a religion that works on a variety of levels. On the social level, it helps to build community and seeks to transform the world into a more just and compassionate place. Judaism also works on an individual level, inspiring reflection and growth in moral characteristics. One of the characteristics that Judaism emphasizes is the quality of humility.

What is humility? According to Maimonides, humility is the midway point between arrogance and self-abasement. Arrogance was repugnant to the rabbis. To be full of yourself allows no room for others or God. But self-abasement, to have no self-esteem or self-worth, was also seen as detrimental to a healthy life. It was in this spirit that Rabbi Simcha Bunem famously said[39] you should have two notes that you keep with you. One should read, "I am but dust and ashes" (Genesis 18:17). The other should read, "The world was created for my sake" (*Sanhedrin* 37a). If your ego has gotten too big, you take out and read the first, but if you feel like nothing, you should take out and read the second.

This week's Torah portion gives us a lesson in humility. When we read the opening verse of Leviticus, we notice two strange things. The verse reads, "He called to Moses." The first thing we notice is that the text doesn't say explicitly who "He" is. We assume it is God. The second thing we notice is that, in the Hebrew, the letter aleph of "*vayikra* – He called" is written smaller than all the other letters. This is a tradition in writing Torah scrolls. It is as if that letter alone was written in a much smaller font, without any reason given.

### The Significance of *Kiddush*

After every Shabbat service, we gather in the foyer or we simply stand before the bimah for *Kiddush*. It is one of the prayers that our *Bat* and *Bar Mitzvah* students learn. Most Jewish kids in Hebrew

---

[39] Martin Buber, *Tales of the Hasidim: Later Masters*. (New York: Schocken Books, 1948), 249–250.

school at least learn to say *borei p'ri hagafen* in an early grade. Not only for Shabbat but also for most Jewish holidays, we say *Kiddush* to sanctify a moment in time.

While we may be familiar with the prayer, most of us probably do not know the reason behind it. Of all things, why do we listen to a prayer said over a cup of wine or grape juice? Why, of all things, is this called *Kiddush* or "holiness"?

The practice of offering a libation to God goes back to the ancient times when we offered sacrifices. Most sacrifices were offered with some kind of libation offering poured onto the altar along with animal offered for the sacred meal. The Torah describes the recipe in detail:

"When you enter the land that I am giving you to settle in and you would present an offering by fire to Adonai from the herd or the flock, be it a burnt offering or sacrifice...producing an aroma pleasing to the Eternal: the person who presents the offering to the Eternal shall bring...a quarter of a *hin* of wine as a libation for each sheep" (Numbers 15:2-10). And so forth.

The *Kiddush* that we say today, therefore, recalls the holiness of the sacrifices of our ancestors. The contents of our *Kiddush* cups remind us the libation offerings that were given at the altar of the Mishkan or Tent of God by the priests in the wilderness and then later in the Temple in Jerusalem. Just as today prayer has replaced sacrifice, so too has *Kiddush* replaced the libation offering. (Of course, there is also a long tradition of wine be associated with song and joy, but that probably has to do with it being an inebriant. *Kiddush*, however, can be legitimately said over grape juice, independent of those factors.)

There is a deeper lesson here relevant today for our lives. Rabbi Levi Yitzhak of Berdichev points out in his commentary to this week's Torah portion, *Vayikra*, (*Kedushat Levi*, *Vayikra*) that the sacrifice of an animal and a libation were offered together, but whereas animal sacrifice is no more, we still keep the practice of a prayer over wine. Why is this so? Why wasn't *Kiddush* disposed of along with the animal sacrifices?

He teaches that animal sacrifices represent blessings from God that come to us without any effort on our part. Miracles like manna from heaven or springs of water from a rock have nothing to do with human endeavor. Like the birth and existence of animals, they exist independently from us through nature's creation. But whereas an animal is born naturally, wine is man-made. Wine, therefore, represents the blessings we make ourselves, in partnership with God. Wine is a product that comes through human effort and ingenuity.

In our reality today, we do not experience the miracles represented by animal sacrifices. We do not see splitting seas or other supernatural events. Accordingly, says Rabbi Levi Yitzhak, we do not offer animal sacrifices that represent these kinds of miracles independent of human endeavor. We do, however, see miracles that come through human effort, and so we still say *Kiddush* representing this combination of the human and divine that can transform the world.

Rabbi Jonathan Slater explains: "[Wine] symbolizes our role in transforming creation for the good.... Hidden behind this teaching is Levi Yitzhak's preference for the good that results from our actions that please God, that bring joy to God. Blessing that results from our endeavors is greater still than that which flows spontaneously from God."[40]

A Shabbat meditation teaches this lesson as well: "When the world was created, God made everything a little bit incomplete. Rather than making bread grow out of the earth, God made wheat grow so that we might bake it into bread. Rather than making the earth of bricks, God made it of clay so that we might bake the clay into bricks. Why? So that we might become partners in completing the work of creation."[41]

*Kiddush*, therefore, represents a human and divine partnership. Animal sacrifices in the Temple and the supernatural miracles they represent are no more, but the miracles we make together with the inspiration and materials God has given us are part of our daily lives.

On a rather mundane level, I see this lesson played out in our kitchen at home. Like I am sure many of you have experienced, my children can be picky eaters. "I'm hungry," they complain.

"What would you like to eat?"

---

[40] Jonathan Slater, *A Partner in Holiness Vol. 2: Leviticus, Numbers, Deuteronomy* (Woodstock: Jewish Lights Publishing, 2014), 8-9.

[41] Mark Dov Shapiro, *Gates of Shabbat* (New York: The CCAR Press, 1991), 27.

"I don't know."

"Would you like some scrambled eggs?"

"No."

However, we have learned that instead of having this conversation that goes nowhere, Julie and I can ask, "Who would like to help me make scrambled eggs?" Usually both hands shoot up. And if our children help make them, they also will eat them like they are manna from heaven. Things seem to taste better when you are involved in the process and are able to benefit from your own effort.

I can't help but think that we are all fickle children living in God's kitchen. Somewhere along the line God stopped handing miracles to us. Instead, God seems to be saying, "Come be partners with Me. I have given you intelligent minds, sharp senses, beautiful natural resources, commandments, and the ability to cooperate. Now make some miracles!"

*Kiddush,* then, is about the blessings we make together. God has done God's part; the rest is up to us.

## *Tzav* (Leviticus 6:1-8:36)

### "C" is for Commandment

The name of this week's Torah portion goes to the heart of Jewish identity: *Tzav*. It is the root of the word *mitzvah*. God tells Moses to "Command Aaron and his sons thus…" (Leviticus 6:2) We are commanded. We do some things because we feel we should or even must. There are certain things we feel we have to do just because we are Jews.

Let me offer an illustration from this past summer. While the conflict in Gaza was going on, Israel continued to treat Palestinians in Israeli hospitals for free. Over 180,000 Palestinians were treated in Israeli hospitals this past year. They were treated, even though we know that if the situation were reversed, no such regard for common humanity would have been shown by Hamas. Why did the Israelis continue to treat them, paid for by Israeli taxes? I think the answer is both simple and complex: because we are Jews.

Judaism is a religion of *mitzvot*. Judaism is not necessarily a religion of doctrine or creeds. Judaism does have basic beliefs: there is only one God, we are made in God's image, and we shouldn't make idols out of things or ideas. But mostly Judaism is a religion of doing. We fast on Yom Kippur. We light Shabbat candles. We give *tzedakah*. And we make meaning as we do. To quote the rock band Boston, "It's more than a feeling." (Now I am showing my generation.)

Personally, in my definition of the concept of *mitzvah*, I offer you three "Cs." I know you learned from Sesame Street that C is for Cookie, and frankly, that is good enough for me, but I suggest a different spin on the letter C for a *mitzvah*: a *mitzvah* is a commandment, it's an act of conscience, and it's a connection. These are the three Cs of mitzvot.

A *mitzvah* is a commandment. Usually people understand the word *mitzvah* to mean, "good deed." But that is the softer, Yiddish meaning of the term. "Do a *mitzvah* for someone!" But the Hebrew is much more direct and demanding. *Mitzvah* is in the command form. "Do I have to?" "It's a *mitzvah*. Yes, you do."

Technically, if someone orders you to do something, it is not a *mitzvah*. If a sergeant tells a soldier to do push-ups, they have to do them. It may be an order, but this isn't a *mitzvah*. There can be only one commander for a *mitzvah*, and that is God. So a *mitzvah*, technically, is a divine commandment. It is something we believe God wants us to do.

You shall not murder. You shall not steal. You shall not stand idly by while your neighbor bleeds. You shall open your hand and give to the needy. You shall repent. You shall return. You shall rest. You shall create light on Shabbat. You shall offer gratitude. These are just some of the commandments Judaism teaches. You shall and you shall not. This is the law.

People today, however, flinch at being commanded to do anything. In America and in Western societies generally, we stress independence, rights, and liberties. We are a nation of freedom. Commandments - precisely - limit our freedom. As Moses Maimonides taught, "I want to steal, I want to cheat, and I can get away with it. No one will know. But what can I do? God will know, and *Avinu Malkeinu* forbids it."[42]

Many of us rebel against this kind of religion. It has been abused too often, and countless atrocities have been done in the name of religious authority. But what also makes Judaism different, which brings us to the second letter C, is that a *mitzvah* is not only a commandment but also an act of conscience.

Judaism has a long-standing tradition of asking questions and challenging authority. At the beginning of the book of Exodus, before even Moses has entered the scene, we find this understanding of *mitzvah*-as-conscience. Pharaoh orders all the Israelite boys to be drowned in the Nile River. Two midwives, Shifra and Puah, refuse to obey the order. They defy Pharaoh. Why? Because they had *yirah* - which is conscience, an inner feeling of awe for the Divine. The midwives respected God's love of life over Pharaoh's command of death, and they followed their conscience, even at great risk to themselves.

And this concept of *mitzvah*-as-conscience even has people challenging God in the Torah (or more accurately the prevailing perception of God at the time). When God tells Abraham that God is going to destroy the cities of Sodom and Gomorrah because they are so wicked, Abraham talks back: "What if there are fifty righteous

---

[42] A paraphrase of *Shemoneh Perkaim* 6.

people in the cities? Shall not the Judge of all the earth do justly?" (Genesis 18:25). Abraham challenges God because of his conscience.

Even more radically, when Moses gets the Ten Commandments, Moses read a line we often skip today, "You shall not bow down to idols, for I am an impassioned God, visiting the guilt of the parents upon the children, upon the third and fourth generations of those who reject Me, but showing kindness to the thousandth generation of those who love Me and keep My commandments" (Exodus 20:5-6) According to a *midrash*, a Rabbinic interpretation, Moses said to God, "Is this fair? Wasn't Abraham the son of an idol-maker? How can You punish the children for the sins of their parents?" Some even teach that this is the real reason Moses smashed the tablets, because he didn't like this line. The rabbinic story continues as God says, "You are right. I will change My words" (Numbers Rabbah 19:33). And so it is written later in Deuteronomy, changing the previous wording, "Children shall not be put to death for their parents, and parents will not be put to death for their children" (Deuteronomy 24:16).

This idea of *mitzvah*-as-both-commandment-and-conscience challenges us. There are times when we need to obey, and there are times when we need to disobey. Abraham himself was rewarded for both obeying God by offering up his son but also when challenging God before Sodom and Gomorrah. And we, too, are caught in that tension. There are times when obeying a higher authority, and not doing whatever we feel like, is the higher moral path, and there are times when our conscience dictates that we must object. Both have deep roots in Judaism. Rabbi Harold Schulweis details these many instances in his book entitled *Conscience: the Duty to Obey and the Duty to Disobey*, where he writes: "I view the Jewish tradition as a pendulum swinging from the duty to obey to the duty to disobey and back.... It requires wisdom to embrace both duties: both the law and conscience, both the external commands and the internal moral imperatives."[43]

But, in addition to commandment and conscience, there is a third C to the definition of a *mitzvah*. Hasidic teaching, such as in *Sefat*

[43] Rabbi Harold Schulweis, *Conscience: the Duty to Obey and the Duty to Disobey* (Woodstock: Jewish Lights Publishing, 2008) 126.

*Emet* and other sources, reads the Hebrew word *mitzvah* in light of the Aramaic *tazvta*, which means "connection."[44]

When we do a *mitzvah*, we make a connection with God and people. When we fast on Yom Kippur, we are doing something Jews all over the world are doing together, as well as generations past and future. When we create light on Shabbat by kindling Shabbat candles, we are connecting ourselves to a deeper rhythm of time. When we give tzedakah, we are hopefully also giving dignity to another human being. Judaism is about belonging, and spirituality is an intangible connection to something greater than yourself. And I believe that if you feel connected, to a melody with a prayer, or to the words of Torah, or to the community you create, then the Connection behind all of the connections, the deepest connection, is God.

That is what I think we are really saying when we say the *Shema*. When we say there is One God, we are saying everyone and everything is interconnected. We are interdependent with other people and nature, whether we realize it at the time or not: the people who grow your food, who deliver and package it, and who put it on your table and you who bless and consume it; the electricity that comes into your home, and the impulses that run through your nerves; the water that comes through the pipes, and the blood in your arteries, the tree breathing through its leaves, and you breathing through your lungs; the doctor and nurses on the hospital staff in a country at war and the patient who could be seen as an enemy but in that moment is just a human being coming in through the door - we are tied to and affect one another.

But this Connection is deeper than even than what we experience at present. We are also connected through time, to the people who came before us and those who will come after us. We all go back to one common ancestor (whom we can call Adam, if we want), and even before that to a single point of extraordinary light that exploded in a Big Bang (for which the Torah says, "Let there be light"). And we are making a future.

To live a life of mitzvot is to be aware of these connections and the obligations that come with them, to be responsible. As the metaphor of the Book of Life teaches us: what we do and say matters.

---

[44] *Sefat Emet* on *Tetzaveh.*

And Jewish people and their families are connected to each other in a heritage that nurtures and enables a life of mitzvot. Many people say that you do not have to belong to a synagogue in order to be Jewish or to feel Jewish. This is absolutely true. But in order to **do** Jewish, to participate and be connected to the Jewish world and ongoing Jewish activities, the synagogue is essential. The synagogue is a *mitzvah*-making machine, if you take advantage of it. Learning, celebrating, being connected to Israel, organizing and working together, hearing Jewish music, and most of all, simply standing up and being counted - all of this takes place only with the mitzvot made possible by the synagogue.

C is for cookie. We have them every Friday night at the oneg. C is also a helpful letter for the definition of a *mitzvah*: commandment, conscience, and connection.

Let us pray: God, you have created a staggeringly beautiful world and given us commandments and a conscience by which we may live our lives. You have done Your part of the covenant. You have upheld Your part of the deal, giving us the tools and resources we need to choose wisely and to act with kindness and justice. But we need to maintain our connection. That is up to us. Help us to be in relationship with You and each other and make a future that leads to redemption.

## *Shemini* (Leviticus 9:1-11:47)

### Incensed

*Avinu Malkeinu* – "Our Father, our King." *Melech Haolam* – "Ruler of the Universe." *HaRachaman* – "The Compassionate One."

When we read the Bible or the prayer book, there are many names for God. Most of these names are rather anthropomorphic. They label God in uniquely human terms: God as a father, a king, or as a being capable of compassion and mercy. These are the main images of God conjured up by the words of our sacred literature.

Such names, however, are instantly problematic. These names describe God in human terms, but God is not human. We put God in human terms because that is what we know, but God is much bigger than we are and beyond our comprehension. As science has progressed, we have also discovered that human beings aren't necessarily the main characters in God's story: It must have been both thrilling and disconcerting to find out that not everything revolved around us. We learned our planet revolved around the sun, and not vice versa, and not only that, but our sun is merely a star among an infinite number of similar balls of gas aflame in space. In other words, we human beings are not the center of the universe. We learned that we needed to cope and survive in a universe that may be indifferent to our survival, a challenging message to our Hebrew Bible that says the opposite!

It is precisely for this reason that this week's Torah portion is so interesting. In the portion, two priests named Nadab and Abihu, sons of the High Priest Aaron, Moses' brother, are serving at the Tabernacle. They are mixing together incense to be put in front of the altar.

Now, a word has to be said about incense in ancient times. In the Ancient Near East, many people had incense altars not only in their places of worship but also in their homes. It was a way of perfuming the house with spice and also having a warm, smoldering flame. The spices from Havdalah come from this ancient use of incense. In the Temple, the incense was viewed as especially powerful because the smoke literally traveled up to heaven, farther than any tower or pyramid could reach. People reached God in heaven most directly by burning up sacrifices into smoke or using incense. It traveled through the air into heaven.

In other words, incense was a big deal. To mess up the recipe for the incense was to tamper with how one communicated with God. The Mishnah (*Keritot* 1:1) teaches that compounding the incense that was used in the Temple for one's personal use at home was an indulgence punishable by exile.

Back to Nadab and Abihu. The Torah says that they offered incense before God, but that this offering was "a strange fire before the Eternal which God had not commanded them to offer." Because of this transgression, "fire came out from the Eternal and devoured them." In other words, their new chemical mixture blew up in their faces. "They died before the Eternal" (Leviticus 10:1-2).

This tragedy challenges us as modern readers on many levels. First of all, Moses tries to console Aaron with some pious words. Aaron's two sons were just killed doing nothing less than making an offering to God. In response to his brother's words, the Torah says that Aaron is silent. What we read into that silence is up to us. It could be anger. It could be protest. It could be acceptance. We do not know. It is interesting that the Torah goes out of its way to say that Aaron was silent. Perhaps silence in the face of a tragedy is the only appropriate response.

But this passage challenges us on another level. God as depicted in this part of Leviticus in neither a Father nor a Ruler nor a Compassionate listener who makes us human beings the center of divine attention. Instead, two people messed with things divine, transgressed, and were blown up. Rabbi Judith Abrams likens this incident[45] to a time when she was looking at the fuse box with her contractor. There were some cobwebs in the middle of the fuses, and she was about the brush them away with her house key. The contractor grabbed her hand right before she would have completed an electrical circuit that would have certainly killed her.

This Torah portion enables us to think of God not in terms of a Person but as a Power. In this part of the Torah, God is much more like electricity than like a king, and those who transgress, saint or sinner alike, can get zapped. Aaron's sons offered a strange fire. The Torah also hints that they were intoxicated when doing so, which certainly couldn't have helped. In any case, Nadab and Abihu

---

[45] Judith Z. Abrams, *Torah & Company* (Teaneck: Ben Yehuda Press, 2006), 53).

tampered with a force much greater than they, and in their lack of caution they were killed.

For some reason, the Sages in the Gemara (*Keritot* 6a) decided to actually list all of the ingredients for the incense that was used in the Temple. One wonders what they were thinking. It might strike us as equivalent to explaining how to make a homemade bomb on the Internet. But the Sages must have thought that educating people about what to do and what not to do was the safer route.

Is it helpful to think of God as more like a Power and not a Person? I don't know; maybe in certain times and places. Religion itself can be used for great good or evil. If this fire of God is true to our experience, then our goal as worshipers is to relate to that Power that creates and sustains the universe and live in harmony with it for life and peace. The same Divine Force that gives us gentle rain, sunsets, and mountains also gives us thunderstorms and avalanches. It is all One. We are also to remind ourselves of our boundaries, moral and physical, and consequences for transgressing them.

Let us pray to realize our boundaries and our limits as human beings. Let us try to live in harmony with God and nature, cultivating strength, insight, and patience. And let us use our sweet-smelling fire for the right and the good. In doing so, perhaps we can shed some light and warmth on our small corner of the universe.

## *Tazria-Metzorah* (Leviticus 12:1-15:33)

### Mysteries of Life and Blood

There are certain stories that people love to tell, and among these are the personal stories of how their children were born. People tell stories about how they drove through snowstorms to get to the hospital, who was out of town or sick and couldn't make it, or some other narrative about the arrival of a child. The birth of a child, especially the birth of a first child, is a life-changing moment. It fills us with awe and wonder and alters how we see the world.

This week's Torah portion, Tazria, explores the subject of childbirth as a sacred event. Women who gave birth were isolated from the community in a state of impurity due to the blood that came with the birth, similar to the period of impurity that accompanies menstruation. For the ancients, blood was a symbol of life. It was powerful stuff that could somehow mean the difference between life and death. Our ancestors looked upon birth and blood with awe and even fear. This was not unusual. Most ancient cultures isolated a woman about to give birth and then performed purification rituals after the child was delivered before reintroducing her to society.

If birth is a miraculous mystery for all, it is especially true for men who are biologically outside of the process. Cantor Klepper wrote an article on this subject in *The Modern Men's Torah Commentary*.[46] The writers of the Torah were men, and they seem to have looked upon the event of birth with shock and awe. In this regard, not too much has changed. For many years, men did not come to the hospital for the birth of a child. A friend of mine related a family story that when her mother gave birth to her sibling, their father went out fishing, waiting to be told when it was all over. Today, however, men are expected to be the number one coach. Men are invited into the delivery room, and they even have mirrors set up so that you can be sure to see the whole thing – if you want to. Being there for the event, however, does not diminish the mystery of it. Martin Buber once wrote that a miracle is something that the more

[46] Jeffrey K. Salkin, ed. *The Modern Men's Torah Commentary* (Woodstock: Jewish Lights Publishing, 2009), 98-102.

you explain it, the more amazing it gets.[47] There is an "abiding astonishment" that accompanies the event. It does not matter how many books you read or how much science you understand. Birth is accompanied by "abiding astonishment."

It is only in this sense that we can understand this week's Torah portion. A woman gives birth, and she is quarantined for a week if it is a boy and two weeks if it is a girl. The birth of the boy cuts short the woman's state of impurity because of his *brit milah* or circumcision. Then comes a second stage of lesser impurity that is again twice as long for a girl than for a boy. The Torah offers no explanation for this. Anthropologists have many theories but no definite conclusions. One is that the birth of a girl is also the birth of a potential menstruant and therefore a future source of impurity. Another is that the ancients believed that male embryos were fully formed at forty-one days and female embryos at eighty-two, so this reflects an ancient misunderstanding of biology. This idea of a slower development of females was shared by Greeks such as Aristotle and Hippocrates. But the fact is that the earliest rabbis were deeply puzzled by this rule. Ultimately, they took it as a mystery of the Torah without a clear rational explanation. For them, the end of the matter was that "there are three partners in the procreation of a person: the mother, the father, and the Holy One of Blessing" (*Niddah* 31a).

Regardless of how views of birth and biology have changed, the main idea that we should take away from this week's Torah portion is how even the most skeptical of philosophers is moved to awe, often spiritually, when it comes to birth. I wish I still had a copy of an article that I read years ago that I have not forgotten. A man reflected on the birth of his daughter. He had considered himself an atheist his whole life. He did not attend any religious institution, nor had he prayed in any recent or long ago memory. Yet the day after his daughter came into the world, he found himself driving around, floundering, wondering what to do with himself. He felt as if some kind of loud gun had gone off right behind him, and he was in a state of shock. Faced with the beauty of his child and the amazement of witnessing the birth, he asked himself: Whom shall I thank for this wonderful gift? He found himself praying despite everything. Thank

---

[47] Fackenheim, *What is Judaism?*, 230.

you for this child.

The Torah portion *Tazria* asks profound questions about life, birth, healing, and recovery. These are existential questions about the human condition. They will always be with us. And we will always feel mystery and awe, the abiding astonishment that tells us we have witnessed a miracle. We come to this moment with anxiety, humor, and joy.

## *Acharei Mot-Kedoshim* (Leviticus 16:1-20:27)

### Practical Holiness

As a student studying in Jerusalem, occasionally I would go walking in the streets of the Old City. Being surrounded by stone walls, many of them built in the Middle Ages, and walking past ruins from antiquity and earlier, one's imagination can run wild. One cannot help but think of all of the people throughout history who made pilgrimage to this city from many different faiths seeking a sense of holiness.

Today, Jerusalem is no different. There are more religious faiths crammed into the streets than perhaps any place else on earth. The Israeli poet Yehuda Amichai once wrote that there are so many kinds of prayer rising into the air above Jerusalem that if we could see them it would look like smog.[48]

On one particular walk, I found myself going across the roof of the Church of the Holy Sepulcher. Inadvertently, I walked under an archway and found myself surrounded by regal looking men of dark skin in magnificent robes of blue. Because there was no door, I had accidentally wandered into a cloister of Coptic monks. After apologizing and scurrying out as fast as I could, I saw one of the monks put a wooden cross under the archway to block the path.

What does it mean to be holy? On the one hand, solitude (such as on a rooftop) enables us to pray in a way that is different from congregational prayer. By and large, however, Judaism is a communal religion. What does holiness mean in a Jewish context as opposed to the asceticism of some other faiths?

In this week's Torah portion, we read Leviticus 19, which scholars refer to as the Holiness Code. It begins with the words, "*Be holy, for I the Eternal your God am holy*" (Leviticus 19:2). In Hebrew, the word for holiness is "*kadosh.*" We say the *Kiddush*, from the same root, to sanctify time for Shabbat. We recite the *Kaddish* in memory of those who have died. And in the morning we echo the angels of Isaiah when we say, "*Kadosh, kadosh, kadosh… Holy, holy, holy is the God of hosts!*" (Isaiah 6:3) At a traditional Jewish wedding, we give a ring

---

[48] Chana Bloch and Stephen Mitchell, "The Ecology of Jerusalem," *The Selected Poetry of Yehuda Amichai* (Berkeley: University of California Press, 1986), 136.

and say that the other person is *mekudash* and *mekudeshet*, holy to us.

If the Holiness Code in this week's Torah portion teaches us anything, it is that Judaism understands holiness to be a part of our everyday lives. It is not reserved for the clergy on a mountaintop. It is part of our daily existence and is invoked regularly in our *prayers.*

The Hebrew word *kadosh* literally means, "to be set apart." We "set apart" Shabbat from the other days of the week. We "set apart" an anniversary to remember our dead. We set apart another and set ourselves apart in an exclusive relationship that we call marriage. And God is "set apart" from our world as a source of transcendent authority.

But the Torah this week teaches an even more radical understanding of what it means to be "set apart." "*Be holy for I the Eternal your God am holy*," it says. We are supposed to be holy not only at these special times but also when we are out on the street. In many ways, being *kadosh* means not so much setting ourselves apart but rising above behavior that is beneath us.

Rising above hurtful language and disrespect

Consider the following commandments that are included in the Holiness Code and part and parcel of what it means to be holy. The first one we can focus on is: *You shall not go about as a talebearer among your people* (Leviticus 19:16).

Now, we might be accustomed to thinking of gossip as something so serious that it impacts upon holiness. For the sages, however, the words we use, for good or ill, are of tremendous importance. Words can be used to slander another or can be used for prayer. The chief commandment of *shmirat halashon*, guarding one's tongue, therefore, is found in the Holiness Code.

Jewish law describes three categories of what it means to guard our tongues. The least serious offense but the most common is gossip. Sharing information that may or may not be true about another can do great damage. The second degree offense is slander. Telling a lie about someone to hurt him or her is an outrageous form of attack. But it is not as bad as *lashon hara*, the wicked tongue, which is sharing some kind of negative truth about someone against their will. Breaking a confidence or digging out the dirt on someone is seen as the ultimate transgression of this commandment. At least with slander, a lie can be proven wrong. With *lashon hara*, however, what recourse does the damaged party have?

And so the Torah includes a commandment about speech in its definition of holiness. We cannot be holy if our words do not enable us to rise above such things as gossip, slander, and breaking a confidence.

Rising above greed

Similarly, to be holy in Judaism also means to rise above another evil inclination. Being holy means to set ourselves apart from greed. The Holiness Code states: "When you reap the harvest of the land, you shall not reap all the way to the edges of your field, or gather the gleanings of your harvest. You shall not pick your vineyard bare, or gather the fallen fruit of your vineyard; you shall leave them for the poor and the stranger: I the Eternal am your God." (Leviticus 19:9-10)

This commandment is the basis of the Jewish practice of *tzedakah*, or philanthropy. Whether it is passing around the *pushka* [charity box] before lighting Shabbat candles, giving annually to various charities, or stopping to give a dollar on the street, the commandments about giving are rooted in what the Torah commands an Israelite farmer to do with his field.

If we look at the passage carefully we see that holiness does not begin with giving. It is first found in an act of restraint. It might be tempting to reap one's entire field, or glean everything in our path, or to pick a field bare. We could, after all, get more of a profit this way. But rather than vacuum up all of the food on our property, God asks us to show restraint. We are supposed to leave a little where it falls. Giving begins with rising above greed. Scrounging for every dollar is something that God tells us is beneath us.

Similarly, we, too, can show acts of restraint when it comes to our money. People's relationship with money is ultimately not about the money itself. Some people are afraid of money, others find it a burden, and others are wasteful. But there is the potential for spirituality in how we relate to our money, especially considering the fact that it a symbol of value.

Money is supposed to move. It is supposed to make things happen. It is not supposed to be hoarded and held still and protected. One fundraiser recently likened it to the Sea of Galilee versus the Dead Sea in Israel. The Sea of Galilee takes water from the mountains and channels it out into the Jordan River. The water moves and therefore lives thrives. When it reaches the Dead Sea, however, it stops. Nothing moves, and no life can be found in its waters.

Holiness can be found in the restraint we feel towards greed that allows life-giving generosity to take place. To rise above hoarding and feeling alive by giving freely enables us to share our resources and bring us closer to what the Torah understands to be *kadosh*.

Rising above common immorality

There is still a third commandment that illustrates Judaism's definition of holiness that is found in this week's Torah portion. In addition to rising above hurtful words and greed, we are also supposed to hold ourselves to accountable to a higher moral standard in general. Much of what today is taken for normal or the cost of doing business is simply unacceptable according to Jewish tradition. Just because hatred, prejudice, or discrimination are common and therefore acceptable as normal, our Torah teaches, it does not make them right. Instead, we read this week, "You shall not hate your kinsfolk in your heart. Reprove your kin but incur no guilt on their account" (Leviticus 19:17).

Jewish tradition has taken this passage to mean that we must rise above what the newspaper presents as normal and instead ask ourselves what is right in God's eyes. We are even supposed to be unafraid to offer reproof. Going out and marching on the Mall in front of the Capitol in an act of protest, writing letters and editorials, or sending emails to Congress can be nothing less than acts of holiness if they demand that we raise the bar on our moral behavior. We are commanded to engage in acts of constructive criticism for the sake of our world. We are not to confuse what is commonplace for what is right.

Rabbi Abraham Joshua Heschel, when he was marching with the Reverend Martin Luther King Jr., illustrated this idea when he remarked that he felt "as though my legs were praying."[49] Rising

[49] Susannah Heschel, "Theological Affinities in the Writings of Heschel and King," in *Black Zion: African American Religious Encounters with Judaism*, ed. Yvonne Chireau and Nathaniel Deutsch (Oxford: Oxford University Press, 2000), 175.

above the mundane is precisely what holiness is about, and we are supposed to not only lift ourselves up to a higher plane of behavior but also to reprove our fellow citizens when we see our community going astray. It is perhaps one of the greatest acts of patriotism to risk our country's wrath by pointing out its faults.

Practical holiness: transcendence through morality

At the end of the matter, we see through this Torah portion that Judaism has a unique understanding of holiness. Rather than escaping our world, Judaism asks that we rise above immoral behavior and do our best to make our world a better place. Holiness, for Judaism, is not found so much in a monk's hideaway or on a mountaintop but on the streets, in everyday respect for and treatment of others. Judaism asks that we engage with our world actively for what is ultimately good and right. Judaism demands a practical sort of holiness, a sense of transcendence through morality.

"Be holy, for I the Eternal your God am holy." Holiness, in Judaism, is ultimately a question of ethics. The Holiness Code is filled with ethical commandments. And in striving after a greater moral good, we are striving after God.

## *Emor* (Leviticus 21:1-24:23)

### A Hierarchy of Heart

When you walk into a Jewish funeral home, you may notice that to the side of the building is a small room with couches and a television set. This room is set apart from the chapel and the family greeting room. It is a special room off to the side that is reminiscent of something from this week's Torah portion. It is a room set aside for *cohenim* or people of priestly descent.

Our Torah portion begins with rules for a special class of people, the *cohenim* or priests, who originally served in the Tabernacle in the wilderness and then later in the Temple in Jerusalem. As the elite class among the Israelite tribes who facilitated the worship of God, the *cohenim* needed to abide by special ritual rules. One of these was to avoid contact with the dead, for they felt that contact with the dead would bring impurity into God's sanctuary. However, if the person who died was part of the *cohen*'s immediate family, the priest was allowed to participate in the funeral. To this day, some people who consider themselves descended from cohenim still will not be in the same room as a dead body, and so many Jewish funeral homes have a special room set aside for them. Descendants of *cohenim* are able to watch the funeral on close-captioned television while sitting on a couch just a room away. Try as I might, however, I cannot find the close-captioned T.V. part anywhere in the Torah.

To many of us, I imagine this idea of an elite class of people determined by birth may feel a bit alien. One is a *cohen* if one's father was a *cohen*. Yet for a majority of human history, much of one's status was determined by birth. Royalty passed down their power through heirs, and landowners bequeathed their holdings to their children. It is only with the birth of democracy that the idea of electing people from humble backgrounds to power became commonplace. Nevertheless, the medieval concept of inherited power is still with us. The sons of presidents become presidents, Kennedy, Clinton, and Bush families have claims to power, and while we live in a nation with great social mobility, class systems are slow to die.

Judaism had its own internal class system which was founded in the Bible. The *cohenim* were at the top, part of the tribe of Levi, which served as God's direct functionaries. To this day, in many traditional synagogues, the first *aliyah* to the Torah was given to a *cohen*, the second aliyah is given to a levite, and the third could then be given to an Israelite or regular Jew. Reform Judaism did away with these distinctions entirely so the idea may be unfamiliar, but originally – before Reform Judaism - homage was paid to the old caste system. We find in the laws of *tzedakah* in Maimonides' *Mishneh Torah* from the 12th century that when you had a limited supply of food to give to the poor or had to decide which hostages you could redeem from captivity, a cohen took precedence over a levite, a levite over a regular Jew, a regular Jew over an illegitimate child of a priest, an illegitimate child of a priest over an illegitimate child of a regular Jew, an illegitimate child of regular Jew over a foundling, a foundling over a mamzer (who was a child born of a union forbidden by the Torah), and so on down the line of people of questionable or what was perceived of as lower birth. *Yichus*, or "lineage," mattered.

And yet, as much as the rabbis were conscious of this hierarchy of birth status, they also legislated something revolutionary. In Maimonides' *Mishneh Torah*, right after it lists this hierarchy, it turns it completely on its head with these words, "But if there is a High Priest who is an ignoramus and a mamzer who is a wise student, the wise student takes precedence, for anyone who is great in wisdom takes precedence over another" (*Hilchot Matnot Aniyim* 8:18). In other words, as much as the rabbis honored their past and the caste system that went back to biblical times, they felt that merit in learning trumped all. Wisdom was the real measure of one's status in society.

This rule that Maimonides codified into law actually goes back to the 2nd century in the Mishnah. One's status was determined by one's merit in learning, not by how much money you had or who your father was. We know that certain rabbis of the Mishnah, such as Rabbi Joshua ben Hananya, were very poor. Rabbi Joshua was an impoverished blacksmith. Yet when he walked into the academy, he was given the front chair of honor because of his wisdom. For a period of time he was head of the Sanhedrin or rabbinic Supreme Court. Some 2000 years before the French Revolution or our Western universities, Jews had decided that how one got ahead in life was through education. Even the poorest of the poor could be grand leaders among the rabbis if they were great in learning.

This week's Torah portion, then, begs a question. How do we confer status on people? Is it if they come from a good family? Is it by their profession? Is it by a title that they have or a certain diploma from a certain school that hangs in their office?

I hopefully will never forget a lesson that a certain teacher told me. We were running a program together on prejudice where African American and Jewish teenagers were interacting with each other. Of course, coming from different backgrounds, they immediately began sizing each other up, and they had to confront their own stereotypes about race. He told the group, "People are like icebergs. What you see on the surface is very little compared to who the person really is underneath."

I try to instill this lesson each time our Religious School students come into this sanctuary for morning prayers. On the front of our learning siddur is a phrase from the book of I Samuel 16:7, "A human being sees only what is visible, but God sees into the heart." If we look with the heart, we can see past all hierarchies and status symbols. We can honor our traditions, culture, and histories, for education and family do matter. But ultimately, it is the spirit that counts.

The playwright S. Ansky said it best, although where he says "man" I would say "person": "Every spot where a man raises his eyes to the heavens is the Holy of Holies. Each moment of life is Yom Kippur, the Day of Judgment. Every Jew is a High Priest. Every word that a man utters piously is the Name of the Lord."[50]

This is a hierarchy that is based upon the heart. We should expand this understanding of radical equality and opportunity from Judaism to the entire world, for we are all made in God's image.

---

[50] S. Ansky, *The Dybbuk* (Washington, DC: Regnery Gateway, Inc., 1974) 114.

## *Behar-Bechukotai* (Leviticus 25:1-27:34)

### On the Mountaintop

This week's Torah portion is a double portion called *Behar-Bechukotai.* The name of the first portion, *Behar,* literally means, "on the mountaintop" (Leviticus 25:1). It is especially relevant for us to think about mountaintops this morning because we are approaching the holiday of Shavuot, the holiday that commemorates the Israelites receiving the Torah at Mount Sinai. As we see in this week's portion, our ancestors gathered at the foot of the mountain while Moses went up and received the laws that give meaning to our lives today.

I am sure many of us have, on vacations or simply weekend trips, been to the tops of mountains. There is something mystical about standing on the peaks of these high places that has captured the imagination for thousands of years. Perhaps you have gone skiing and looked at the blue sky and the valley below. Perhaps you have been to Switzerland and seemed as if you were able to touch the clouds. Or perhaps you have simply taken the walk up a local hill and taken in the view of the surrounding area with a deep breath of satisfaction.

But climbing to a mountaintop is not just a pleasant activity. It is also one of the most popular metaphors of human history. There is the great effort that is required to reach the top of the mountain that we identify with striving and working toward a goal. And there is the ability to see far into the distance, further than we could see before, that makes reaching the zenith a symbol of wisdom and revelation.

How odd, therefore, it might seem to us that the rabbis of the Talmud tell us that Mount Sinai was the lowest of the mountains in the desert (*Midrash Tehillim* Psalm 68:17) Mount Sinai, they inform us, was the smallest mountain, surrounded by much larger mountains on all sides. When Moses climbed Mount Sinai and the people gathered at the foot of the mountain, they were surrounded by much more majestic peaks. Clearly, the greater effort and the better view would have been elsewhere.

And yet we are taught that this lowly mountain was the mountain of God. Not only that, but when God's presence entered the Tabernacle and was carried by the Israelites through the wilderness, Mount Sinai ceased to be special. It became just another lowly hill in the desert, available for hiking by tourists with no particularly spectacular scenery.

Why would this be the case? Why would our tradition teach us that the peak of revelation, the receiving of the Torah on Mount Sinai, took place on a relatively low-lying area? What is the lesson here?

Our sages elaborate that Mount Sinai was chosen because it was the humblest of all mountains. Yes, it was a mountain, and it carries with it all of the metaphors of peaks and distance and effort and wisdom. But it was also a low, humble place, teaching us that we should be humble. Our knowledge of the divine is miniscule, and our wisdom is tiny.

And so it is with each one of us. We are all at one time or another convinced of our greatness and hold ourselves up with enormous pride. But the rabbis teach us that is only the one who makes him or herself small who is made great. Only by diminishing our haughtiness do we make room for God. We are a small mountain in the scheme of things, a small dot on the map of the universe for a blink of an eye, and we only transcend our lives when remember our smallness.

The Torah teaches that Moses was the humblest of all men. It does not say that he was the wisest, or the best looking, or had the highest standardized test scores. It does not say he had the most charisma or was the most charming public speaker. It says he was the humblest, and for that reason he was able to receive the Torah and give it to the people. God needed someone who had enough space in his soul, who was humble enough, to make room for the Torah to fill him up and give to others.

Indeed, Moses is so humble that the Torah tells us that no one knows where he is buried. In contrast to the great tombs and pyramids of the Pharaohs with whom Moses did battle, the very enemies who though themselves gods, Moses does not even have a tombstone which we can visit. He is simply a man who once stood on a low mountain and transmitted the learning that was given to him. Perhaps this is why Heinrich Heine once wrote, "How small Sinai appears when Moses stands upon it."[51] Moses' moral stature overshadowed all else. His smallness was his greatness.

---

[51] As quoted in Martin Buber, *Moses: the Revelation and the Covenant* (Amherst: Humanity Books, 1998), 4.

I am personally convinced that most of the evils that beset our world today are the results of humanity's arrogance. We truly act as if we can get away with anything. We pollute the earth as if someone will come along and clean up after us. We infiltrate other people's homes or refuse to live with those who are different from us because we think we have some God-given claim on our real estate. And we collect a heap of material wealth, when we already have enough resources to feed the whole world if we would only use them correctly, and put bumper stickers on our cars that say, "Whoever dies with the most toys wins." These are the results of arrogance, of putting ourselves at the center of the world, of assuming that what we want this moment is of the most importance. It took humanity centuries to realize that planet earth was not the center of the solar system, but we still have not realized that perhaps human beings are not the central part of God's creation.

But, if we remember Moses, on a small, little mountain called Sinai, then we can remember our potential for true greatness. Yes, we have much of which to be proud. But we are filled with wisdom when we lower ourselves in our own sight. We are able to be receiving vessels when we empty ourselves of grandiose fantasies of self-importance. What does height matter when what counts is the depth of the soul?

We are humble when we share our world. We are humble when we give of ourselves freely and joyously. We are humble when we remember that the things that give us wealth and fame are categorically different from the things that give us peace and dignity.

So let us pray for the strength of conscience to be humble. Let us admit our smallness, our weakness, and our shortcomings. Let us reverently be partners with God, nothing more and nothing less. In so doing, we will stand on our little mountains and see to the ends of time and space.

**What Freedom Means**

We think about the Land of Israel this week for two reasons. First, last Tuesday was Yom Ha'Atzmaut or Israeli Independence Day. The preceding day was Yom HaZikaron, or the Israeli Memorial Day. It is an emotional transition to go from one to the other. Every generation of Israelis has known war, and a siren sounds across the country as a nation-wide commemoration. During the time of the siren, people stop whatever they are doing, even if they are in the middle of the highway. They pull over, come out of their stores, stop at their desks, and stand at attention for the duration of the siren. They remember those who have been killed in the Israeli Defense Force defending their freedom and existence. And it should be noted that every family has lost someone at some time.

But then a few minutes after sundown, Israel celebrates its independence. There are parties in the streets, picnics and barbecues during the day, and at the end of the day, the Israel Prize is awarded to individuals for their contribution to the country's culture, art, or science.

The second reason we think of the land of Israel this week is because it is the main theme of this week's Torah portion. The portion *Behar* talks about ownership of land, the obligations of landowners to their servants, and the practices of the Sabbatical or *Sh'mittah* year and the Jubilee or *Yovel* year. During the *Sh'mittah* year, which occurs every seven years, the land was to be let lie fallow so that it too might observe a Shabbat. During the 50th or *Yovel* year, land ownership was to return to the original tribal owners, debts were supposed to be forgiven, and indentured servants were to be set free. It is clear from these rules that God is really the only Land Lord, and we are merely renters. "The land is Mine," God says in this portion (25:23), "you are but strangers resident with me." It also says a line that has been made famous in our culture by being inscribed on the Liberty Bell (25:10): "Proclaim LIBERTY throughout all the land unto all the inhabitants thereof." Bells were rung to mark the reading of the Declaration of Independence on July 8, 1776, and this was reportedly one of the bells that was sounded. It became a symbol for abolitionist states during the Civil War as well, and they were the ones who named it "the Liberty Bell."

Considering the themes of Israeli and American Independence that are linked so closely with the land we live upon, we should ask ourselves on Shabbat what freedom really means. One American dictionary understands freedom to mean, "the power to act, speak, or think without externally imposed restraints; immunity from obligation."[52] This is an understanding based upon how we can express ourselves.

---

52 The Free Dictionary by Farlex: http://www.thefreedictionary.com/freedom

In Hebrew, however, there are two different words for freedom. One is *chofesh*, which is similar to the American understanding. When a slave no longer has a master, he is *chofshi* or free. It refers back to the Israelites escaping Egypt. Egypt was *Mitzraim* or the narrow, constricting place. To escape slavery was to flee constriction and oppression. Rabbi Bradley Artson cites Rashi in supporting this understanding when he says that freedom means "the ability to reside anywhere. [Rashi] adds that freedom precludes living under the authority of others."[53]

But the second Hebrew word also demands our attention. It is the word *cheirut*. The rabbis say in *Pirkei Avot* 6:2, "*Ein lekha ben chorin ela mi she-osek ba-Torah*" - only the one who labors in Torah is truly liberated. This can best be understood by revocalizing the word: *charut* means "engraved." The Torah says the words of the commandments were "engraved" in stone. Yet it is that very engraving that allows us to experience *cherut*: true freedom. Freedom comes from service to God and others. Rabbi Moshe Taragin calls it the "freedom to transcend."[54]

This may seem contradictory at first. How can submitting yourself to a law be an act of freedom? It might be helpful to think of *cherut* as getting into a car. At first, it seems as if you are limiting your freedom. You are restricting your movements to a confined space. You are even strapping yourself in. But with that discipline, you are able to travel much further than you ever would on foot.

Similarly, if we think of freedom as solely about individual expression, than we are centered completely on the self without any real purpose. However, if we see freedom as the ability to serve God and others, then we live a life of purpose and accomplishment. Our moral or spiritual reach transcends our selfish desires. We can do much more when we are disciplined and purposeful with our actions.

I like to think of freedom as the ability to imagine and become whatever you wish. We should imagine who we want to be and then pursue the opportunity to become that vision. However, in order for that vision to be meaningful, it ought to serve a purpose.

---

[53] Rabbi Bradley Shavit Artson, *The Bedside Torah* (New York: McGraw Hill, 2001), 212.

[54] vbm-torah.org/alei/2-7freed.htm

Israel serves a purpose of being the Jewish homeland. It is its reason for being, and we celebrate that on Yom Ha'Atzmaut. America serves as a beacon of democracy. We will celebrate that on the 4th of July. But on an individual level, the Haggadah tells us that we should each see ourselves has having personally been freed from Egypt.[55]

What is your freedom being used for?

---

[55] Silberman, 36.

# *BEMIDBAR* - NUMBERS

## *Bemidbar* (Numbers 1:1-4:20)

### Numbers: The Million Moses March

On a certain day in Washington, DC, I was with a great number of people gathered in front of the Capitol building. I was joining in a march for gun control which had occurred right after a rash of school shootings and other atrocities. Joining the crowd, I had to wade through families sitting on picnic blankets and special interest groups with megaphones. As I carefully placed my feet, I hoped that I wasn't stepping on anyone. And as we stood sweating in the sun, a plane flew overhead to take a photograph so that someone somewhere could try to make an estimate as to the number of people who had gathered. Someone was going to try to count the number of people without wading through them like I was. Last I heard, the number was something like 700,000, but I'm not sure whether or not that counts children.

Counting. We do a lot of it. This week, we begin the fourth book of the Bible, which in English we call the book of Numbers, and it is full of counting. It begins with a census, and it continues to count people, donations to the sanctuary, and the generations of Israelites. This week's Torah portion features one such census. Page after page is filled with counting. It is truly a book of numbers as the Israelites are counted as they march through the wilderness. One might call it, "the Million Moses March."

And the question one might wonder is, why? Why all the numbers and the counting? Who cares about all these different kinds of numbers?

I would like to suggest that what and how we count signifies who we are. Counting is a way of paying attention, of saying something is meaningful. If we bother to count it, it must count, that is, it must be important in some way.

The way we use numbers differs according to our culture. In American English, we have cardinal and ordinal numbers. We either count one, two, and three or first, second, and third. It says that we are a society that thinks in a linear fashion and values order. We like to have all of our ducks in a row. We do not like ambiguity; we would much rather round up to the nearest set of ten.

And we do this kind of counting every day.

In the twenty-first of the Julian calendar, we like to count so many things that our lives books of numbers. We count how many pounds we would like to lose. We count calories and grams of fat and blood pressure. We count how old we are and continuously strive toward youth while we count the years to retirement. We also count how much time it is going to take us to get from one place to another going at how many miles per hour with often the goal of trying to get to someplace as quickly as possible. We count how many people die in accidents and tragedies and, when the number is too high, we round it off to the nearest zero. We also count how much money we have, how much someone else has, and then how much we don't have.

In Japan, I am given to understand, one counts entirely differently. One counts according to the shape of what one is counting. A Japanese person would use one set of numbers to count a set of cylindrical objects, for instance, and a different set of numbers to count something flat, like a stack of paper. Form and shape are very important in Japanese society, and it shows in how they count things.

In Hebrew, we have a very different way of counting things. We do not have different symbols for numbers and letters. The same set of symbols works for both. The letter *aleph* is also the number one, *bet* is two, *gimmel* is three, and so on. In a system called gematria, we add up the numerical value of a Hebrew word to help explain its meaning. For instance, the word for "mighty," *g'vura*, has the numerical value of 216, which is equal to that of the word for "lion," *aryeh*. Hence the aspect of being mighty is like the strength of a lion. We count our words. How many words do we use to say something? Is a long prayer better than a short prayer or vice versa?

And there are other ways that numbers are important in Judaism. The number seven has a great deal to do with why we are here today. The seventh day is a holy day called Shabbat. Interestingly enough, one theory proposes that there are seven planets visible with the naked eye from the earth's surface, giving the number seven a magical quality in a variety of cultures. We also have Ten Commandments, matching the number of our fingers. The number forty in Judaism signifies "a lot," and hence Moses stayed on Mount

Sinai for forty days and nights, Noah's flood rained for forty days and nights, and the Israelites wandered in the wilderness for forty years.

The book of Numbers itself counts people and families. It counts daughters and sons. More importantly, it counts generations. If one is a member of an older generation, one automatically gets more respect, which is the exact opposite of our culture today.

And as far as counting money goes, how much money one makes is not nearly as important as what percentage of one's income one gives as *tzedakah* to charitable causes. The Jewish legal standard is a whopping ten percent.

Even God is supposed to participate in this counting. On Rosh Hashanah, for instance, we read that "as the shepherd seeks out the flock and makes the sheep pass under the staff, so do You muster and number and consider every soul."[56]

Perhaps most importantly, however, we are asked to count our days. "Days are scrolls; write on them what you would have remembered."[57] What have we done with our day? What will we do tomorrow? One rabbi suggests that we should say one hundred blessings every day, and in that way, our days will most certainly count.

The act of counting as a way of paying attention and as a symbol of what is important to us can best be illustrated by a story by the Israeli poet Yehuda Amichai. This is a story that I shared with the group that traveled to Israel this past February, and I was reminded of it reading this week's Torah portion. I will take a few liberties in the retelling of it, but the point will remain the same.

Once a man in Jerusalem sat on the stairs at the gate of David's Tower in the Old City, and he put down the two heavy baskets he had been carrying. A group of tourists stood nearby around their guide, and inadvertently the man became their orientation point.

"You see that man with the baskets? A bit to the right of his head, there's an arch from the Roman period. A bit to the right of his head. But he's moving! He's moving!"

---

[56] *Gates of Repentance: The New Union Prayerbook for the Days of Awe* (New York: The CCAR Press, 1978), 108.

[57] Jacob Philip Rudin in *Gates of Prayer for Weekdays and at a House of Mourning* (New York: The CCAR Press, 1992), 36.

While they were calculating the time period of the Roman arch and its distance from them, the man did a different kind of counting. He thought to himself, "Redemption will come only when they are told: You see that arch from the Roman period? Never mind: but next to it, a bit to the left and lower, sits a man who bought fruit and vegetables for his three children at home."[58]

Amichai was teaching that the counting of souls and making our days on this earth count is more important than any other kind of numbering. We are challenged to count our children more than our calories. We should treasure the number of generations we know more than rounding off people to the nearest set of ten. And we are obligated to number our days more than our ambitions.

So now I ask all of us to take a moment and to think about what we number. What do we count, and why? Indeed, what counts, and why? By thinking and feeling in this fashion, we will make our way through that larger book of Numbers that we call, "Life."

---

[58] Bloch and Mitchell, 137.

## *Naso* (Numbers 4:21-7:89)

### Lifting Our Heads, Hearts, and Faces

I come from a family of bad backs. On both sides of my family, vertebrae wear out at the same rate that shocks do on cars. This concerns me because if I were to have to literally follow through on this week's Torah portion, "*Naso*," which means "lifting," I would not be of much help. The Torah portion is filled with all kinds of raising, lifting, and carrying. In this week's Torah portion, God instructs the Levites to lift up all of the components of the sanctuary and carry it through the wilderness. The sanctuary was portable, but it needed people to act as beasts of burden to get it from place to place as the Israelites wandered for forty years. I think it is safe to say that this is the biblical origin of lower back pain.

Rabbi Susan Einbinder comments that our portion sounds like "a technical instruction manual…from a faraway land." But raising, lifting, and carrying must have been important acts because this Hebrew verb, "*yisa*," is used eleven times in twenty-seven verses. Not only that, but the Torah instructs us that each person is to do this lifting and carrying "each one according to his or her burden": *ish ish al avadato v'al masa'o* (Numbers 4:49). Every person had something to carry and a burden to bear, and we can imagine that this was true in an emotional sense as well as physically schlepping around the Ark to the Promised Land. The Torah makes it clear: They had to lift. They had to carry. They had to raise up.

Today, we are involved in just as much lifting, carrying, and raising up as our ancestors were, although fortunately for us it involves less direct weight on our spines. When we gather into a room such as this one, there are invisible weights that each one of us carries in our minds. Each one of us, unbeknownst to onlookers, comes in dragging something behind them, our brows furrowed with worries or anxieties, and often we have no idea what the person next to us might be carrying because we are so preoccupied with keeping ourselves upright. We carry a lot on our shoulders, and chances are that next to us is another, although very different, kind of crushing weight.

I once knew a man who was near the end of his life and who I had the privilege of visiting as he battled what seemed to be endless illness and all sorts of other challenges. But more worrisome to Izzy than any of his physical ailments were questions about whether or not he was a good father, grandfather, and a good husband. No amount of reassurance would console him. Each one of us spoke in his respective accent, his in his toothless Polish-accented English, and me in my East Coast inflection. And when the conversation would die down into silence, he would often break it and out of the blue, say, "*Oy govult!*" I tried not to take it personally. One day, I asked him why he liked to say, "*Oy govult*," all the time. He turned his face to me and said with a wave of his hand, "It makes the heart lighter."

Now, I don't believe the traditional teaching that God only gives us what we already have the strength to carry. There are too many people with too many unfair burdens. Nor is Nietzsche correct in that what does not kill us makes us stronger. My exercise philosophy has always been, "No pain, no pain." But if we turn to our Torah portion, we can perhaps also see a few secrets as to how we are supposed to carry our burdens and manage with what life throws at us. If we look carefully at the way the verb, "*yisa*," to lift, carry, or raise up, is used, we might learn how to make our hearts a bit lighter.

The first clue is that the verb is used at the beginning of the portion when the Israelites are taking a census of their community. To stand up and be counted as a member of the group, one needed to *naso*, "lift up one's head" (Numbers 4:21) so that all could see you. Before picking up any excess baggage, we need to be sure to be among others who could share our burdens with us. There is a simple magic to sharing our burden by keeping our heads held high in the face of our community, and we are fools if we think that we can get through life alone or tackle our problems without asking for help.

This is perhaps why part of the Jewish wedding ceremony is called, "*nisuin*," using the same word from our Torah portion, *Naso*. *Nisuin*, "uplifting," is when we recite the traditional seven wedding blessings under the *chuppah*, the wedding canopy. Perhaps the idea is that, together, they will share each other's joys as well as challenges. Just as the couple shares a cup at that moment, surrounded by their community, so do they pledge to magnify their happiness and also to lighten each other's loads by lifting them together. With their family and community around them, they are lifted up out of isolation.

A second clue that Judaism teaches us in how to bear our burdens comes from the Talmud. There is a scene in tractate Ta'anit where disaster has struck a community in the Land of Israel in the form of a drought. Even together, with the burden shared and rationed among all of them, it seemed too much to bear. The instructions that the Talmud teaches in that situation were that the community was to gather together and declare a fast, symbolizing their shared pain and worry. And a respected member of the community was to lead them in prayer, as Rabbi Ammi explained (*Ta'anit* 8a) with words from Lamentations, "Let us lift up our hearts with our hands to God in heaven" (Lamentations 3:41).

In addition to lifting up our heads and being counted as a member of our community, we, too, can lift up our hearts in prayer. We should never doubt the power that prayer can have in our lives. I don't mean the belief that we send a prayer out and God, like a great big vending machine, gives us back what we ordered. But prayer has a remarkable ability to lift our spirits, to give us hope, and most of all, to help us find strength and courage when we thought we had run out. To raise up our hearts to God in heaven is to humble ourselves and, by making ourselves small, we make room to be filled up from the outside by an encouraging word, a thoughtful voice, or the discovery of strength we never knew we had. Perhaps this is why Rabbi Nachman of Breslov teaches us that in life, each one of us reaches in three directions: inward, to oneself, out, to others, and up, to God. The miracle of life, he said, is that in truly reaching in any one direction, we embrace all three.

But, in addition to our community's coming together to share our pain and our ability to pray for strength and courage, there is a third way that the verb, "to lift up," is used in our Torah portion that might teach us how to better carry our burdens. They come from words that we all know. In this week's Torah portion, we find a blessing that is in three parts that the priests, the *cohenim*, were supposed to use to bless and encourage the people. And just as each one of us must carry our own individual tasks, so is the blessing addressed to us in the singular, using the word "you" to indicate each one of us. This blessing is perhaps the oldest one that we have in Judaism. At the Israel Museum in Jerusalem, an amulet from the First Temple period is on display, and inscribed on it in ancient Hebrew characters were these three lines:

> *Yivarechecha Adonai v'yishmerecha.* May God bless you and keep you.
>
> *Yaer Adonai panav eilecha v'chuneka.* May the light of God's face shine upon you and be gracious to you.
>
> ***Yisa*** *Adonai panav eilecha v'yasem lecha shalom.* May God **lift up** His face to you and give you peace. (Numbers 6:24-26)

We may lift up our heads, our hearts, and our hands, but the Torah assures us with this blessing that God also does some lifting as well. God lifts up God's face. That face is out there, waiting for us to see it, eyes raised toward our own. This is not just merely an expression that God should watch over each one of us. It teaches that we should look for God in the face of all those who come before us and count the blessings that we have, each and every day. This is a blessing about light and peace, but most of all, God's face. We must look for that face and never take for granted the blessings that have been given us.

The blessing does not mention how well known we will become or how much money we will earn. The blessing does describe an upturned face, in that combination of dignity and peace that we call *shalom*. It is a hard lesson to learn that the things that give us fame, happiness, and wealth are categorically different than the ones that give us peace and dignity, but if we can separate those things in our lives, our burdens will be much lighter.

Let us then take a moment to put down some of the loads that we all are carrying. Let us lift up our heads and turn to our friends and family that make up our community and share our problems, using other people's strengths to help us. Let us lift up our hearts in our hands to God in heaven by humbling ourselves in a moment of prayer. And let us look to the Face that is lifted up to each one of us in the divine image of our loved ones, and never take our blessings for granted.

May God bless us and keep us, each one according to our burdens.

## *B'ha'alotecha* (Numbers 8:1-12:16)

### Like Manna from Heaven

Most if not all of us have heard of the expression, "like manna from heaven." When we feel something is an unexpected or undeserved gift that has fallen into our laps, we use this biblical reference. A wonderful thing has fallen out of the sky.

And yet, when we look back at the sacred story in the Torah, we see that the ancient Israelites did not greet the substance they called manna with such enthusiasm. The Torah reads:

> The riffraff in their midst felt a gluttonous craving; and then the Israelites wept and said, "If only we had meat to eat! We remember the fish that we used to eat free in Egypt, the cucumbers, the melons, the leeks, the onions, and the garlic. Now our gullets are shriveled. There is nothing at all! Nothing but this manna to look to!" (Numbers 11:4-6)

But what exactly was this stuff called manna? The Torah continues:

> Now the manna was like coriander seed, and in color it was like sap. The people would go about and gather it, grind it between millstones or pound it in a mortar, boil it in a pot, and make it into cakes. It tasted like rich cream. When the dew fell on the camp at night, the manna would fall upon it. (Numbers 11:7-9)

Apparently, this stuff called manna descended with the dew, enough to feed the Israelites throughout the next day. Tradition has it that none fell on Shabbat, but a double portion fell on Friday so that the people would not have to work on Shabbat but could gather two days' worth. (This is, incidentally, the source of why there are traditionally two loaves of *challah* on Shabbat.) Faithfully, the manna would appear, and no one went hungry.

Now, I can understand that too much of anything will not taste good. Economists call this the law of diminishing returns. The first piece of cake tastes great. The next one is okay, but the fifth makes you sick. Perhaps the people just couldn't stand the taste of this creamy stuff anymore.

A close reading of the Torah, however, reveals a more subtle and profound lesson. When the people complain, they do not actually cite the taste of the manna as the source of their disgust. Instead, the people complain that they had it better in Egypt, where there was fish, cucumbers, melons, leeks, onions, and garlic. The fact that there was also slavery, persecution, degradation, and the murder seems to have been forgotten. It is a trick of human nature that sometimes we remember only what we want to remember, and we hear only what we want to hear. Dissatisfied with the manna, the Israelites only recall perhaps the one pleasant thing about being in Egypt.

Of special note was the claim that they got the fish "for free," as if there was anything that was really free in Egypt. Back in Egypt, when the Nile overflowed, it is easy to catch fish. Never mind that these were the same waters in which the Egyptians drowned the Hebrew baby boys. At that moment, in the hot sun of the wilderness, standing in the waters of the Nile grabbing fish was a pleasant mirage. The fact that this is what the Israelites choose to remember shows just how skewed their memories were.

A rabbinic teaching tells us that manna tasted like anything people imagined it to be. The Talmud teaches, "Whenever Israel ate it, they found many flavors in it" (*Yoma* 75a). If it tasted bad, it was because of their own inner discontent, not because of the flavor of the food in their mouths. The manna tasted bitter because the people were longing for an imaginary past when they were able to grab free food. The sages continue that what the people really meant by "free" was that, back in Egypt, the food was free from *mitzvot*. Back when they were slaves, they didn't have to fulfill any of God's commandments.

The idea that they longed for food that wasn't free of charge but free of the obligations of *mitzvot* reveals a natural part of the human character. As a slave or as a child, when we are only allowed to do as we are told, we do not have the responsibility to control our impulses or necessarily think of other people. We can indulge our appetites. Civilization, however, as symbolized by God's commandments, demands a certain amount of self-discipline. It was easier to grab the nearest food doled out by the taskmasters, suffer, and complain then to hear God's call, obey God's commandments, and have a certain amount of self-respect. Back then, we ate fish for free, free from the burdens of civilization and thinking of others. Now God asks us to be responsible for ourselves and our families. With real freedom comes real responsibility, or what the rabbis called the "yoke of the *mitzvot*."[59]

But perhaps what troubled the Israelites most was not eating the same thing every day or that it was free from the constraints of God's commandments but that they had to depend upon the manna to appear each morning. Vegetables or some other foods could be kept for several days. It gave them a feeling of security that they could touch, smell, and taste. The manna, however, appeared overnight and disappeared every day. Relying upon it for survival required that hardest task of all, the task of faith.

What would happen if God did not supply the manna each day? The people would go hungry. How would they feed their children? Such questions must have caused them tremendous anxiety. We can imagine that they were constantly waiting for the other shoe to drop.

We live with this kind of anxiety as well. "What if?" is a question that haunts us, if we let it. This, however, is no way to really live. We need to go forward with a certain amount of trust that we will greet each day with whatever it will bring, or, as the sages say in tractate *Berachot* 60a, you should say a blessing on that which is in front of you. If a good thing turns bad or a bad thing turns good, that can be dealt with in its time. For now, we can thankfully greet each day and deal with what life deals us, step by step.

My prayer for all of us is that when we eat the manna of our days, it tastes pleasant to us. Let us not engage in nostalgia for the taste of something that never really existed. And let us not constantly wonder "what if" to the detriment of enjoying the passing of time. Instead, let the flavor of each day be sweet because it reflects back the sweetness within our own souls. Let each day taste good because we have faith in the goodness around us. If this is true, then we will certainly enjoy a double portion.

[59] Rabbi Nosson Scherman, *The Complete Artscroll Siddur* (Brooklyn: Mesorah Publications, Ltd., 1984), 90.

## *Shelach Lecha* (Numbers 13:1-15:41)

### A Different Spirit

As we read the Torah this week, we reach perhaps the most disastrous story of the Jewish people in the Five Books of Moses, and it can be understood as a problem that confronts us still today.

This week we read the story of the *m'raglim* – the twelve spies who were sent into the Land of Israel to check it out before the Israelites entered as a whole. The spies go into the land for forty days, and they return with a report that the land does indeed flow with milk and honey, but it is also a harsh land that devours its inhabitants. The people there, the spies claim, are giants, and the spies felt like insects in comparison. Mass hysteria spreads, and the people then lack the courage to enter the Land. In response, God does not force them into the Land but instead tells them they will live the rest of their lives in the wilderness outside its borders for 40 years, one year for every day the spies scouted.

From where did this failure of confidence and courage and this break-out of mass hysteria come?

Perhaps we get a clue from the opening line of the portion. The title of the portion is *Shelach Lecha*, which means, "Send for yourselves" (Numbers 13:1). God tells Moses he may send the spies into the Land, but God makes it clear that they are sending these spies "for themselves," not for God's sake. God already knows the Land is a good land. They need to see and check it for themselves in advance. While there is nothing wrong with being cautious, we can already see evidence that the people lacked faith and were fearful. If someone tells you something is already taken care of but you have to check it out anyway for yourself, it shows a lack of trust and a fear within.

But there was not unanimity among the spies. Only ten of twelve spies brought back a discouraging report about the Land. Two of the spies, Joshua and Caleb, brought back a positive report. Upon returning, they said to the people, "Let us by all means make *aliyah*! We can do it!" But the people did not listen to this minority report.

Why were Joshua and Caleb so confident while their companions were so fearful?

With regards to Joshua, the Torah says his name was Hoshea, but Moses called him Yehoshua, adding the *yod* in front, so that the letters of God's own name would be a part of his. Moses was saying that Joshua was a more Godly man than the others. Joshua had a certain kind of faith. Later in the Torah, Joshua is described as a man *asher ruach bo*, "who has spirit in him" (Numbers 27:18).

And as for Caleb, the Torah says that he distinguished himself. The narrative goes that when the spies went into the land, "they went up the south side, and he arrived at Hebron" (Numbers 13:22). The rabbis noticed the change in the sentence, "they" went up, but only "he" went to Hebron. Who was "he"? The Sages say this was Caleb, who separated himself from the others in order to go to Hebron, for Hebron is the place where the ancestors were buried. Caleb went on a separate side trip by himself to see the graves of Abraham & Sarah, Isaac & Rebecca, and Jacob & Leah. The Talmud elaborates that whereas the other spies were there to evaluate the land for conquest, Caleb was motivated by a *ruach acheret*, "a different spirit" (*Sotah* 34b).

What was this "different spirit" that was "in" both Joshua and Caleb? What was it that gave them faith while the others panicked?

There is a big difference between going into a Land in order to pay respect to your ancestors versus going into a place to evaluate it for conquest. The first is an act of love; the second is an act of aggression and competition. How much would the history of the Land of Israel be different if all the peoples of the world approached it out of love instead of out of fear?

Consider the long history of Jerusalem. Over several thousand years, Jerusalem has been destroyed twice, besieged 23 times, attacked 52 times, and captured and recaptured 44 times.[60] At the crossroads between Asia and Africa, this tiny stretch of land seems destined for conflict.

We can all approach our lives either through love or fear. The Hasidic masters call the approach of fear *mochin d'katnut* – a small mind. It is a mind of competition, that what is your gain must be my loss, a mind of limited and diminishing resources, a zero sum game. The approach of love, however, is called *mochin d'gadlut* – an expansive mind. It comes with the perspective of cooperation and sharing what little there is. And the reason I called this story the most disastrous one in the Torah is because when it comes to the Land of Israel, the approach of love is still the minority report.

---

60 Archeological Institute of America: archaeological.org/lectures/abstracts/9873

Logic says that if you both have equal claim to something you either split it or share it. If not, you are stuck in a small, constricted mind-set. And the tragedy is that people of an expansive mind keep reaching out and getting burned. The Land of Israel is the rightful Jewish homeland. Its only future is eventually to become two states for two peoples. But there are many who are still stuck in 1947 if not in thousands of years before.

Rather than give up, however, the seekers of peace must keep reaching out. There is always an opportunity to make things better, to insist on approaching a challenge from the perspective of love and not fear because we insist on being loving people. We need to have tireless and infinite faith that one day it will pay off. We love our land. So do others. Let us meet in that different spirit.

I offer this prayer for the Land of Israel, translation of word from the well-known Hebrew song, *BaShanah HaBa'ah*:

> Next year we will sit on the porch and count the migrating birds. Children on vacation will play catch between the house and the fields. You will yet see how good it will be next year. Red grapes will ripen till the evening and will be served chilled on the table. And lazy winds will carry to the crossroads old newspapers like a cloud. Next year we will spread our own hands in the radiant light. A white heron will spread her wings in the light as the sun shines through them.[61]

## Fringes and Reminders

Just recently, we moved my grandfather from his home in Florida to live with my aunt in New York. As all of you know, many from first-hand experience, such a move is very difficult. Change is hard. But one of the tasks that all of us face when we move is the choice about the collection of things. Inevitably, the occasion of moving becomes a time to sort through and throw away certain items. Others, however, we choose to keep, often for purely sentimental reasons. Everything from toothbrush holders to *Kiddush* cups may serve as reminders of something, and without their physical presence, an intangible memory might get lost.

---

[61] *Mishkan T'filah*, 349.

This, incidentally, is the wisdom behind the concluding paragraph of this week's Torah portion. In this last section we read about the tradition of *tzitzit*, that is, the fringes that we find located on the corners of our prayer shawl, the *tallit*. Some of you might be more familiar with the Ashkenazic pronunciation of these terms, *tzitzis* and *tallis*. In any case, these fringes on the corners and hanging from the sides of this garment are supposed to serve as reminders, physical symbols of intangible ideas that might otherwise get lost. Like a memento from a by-gone era, we are supposed to be able to look at the fringes of our garment and recall a custom from our ancient past. The *tzitzit* are symbols from long ago. There is one crucial difference, however: the *tzitzit* are supposed to be part of a garment that isn't kept in a drawer but is worn in living, breathing, everyday life. The *tzitzit* aren't just supposed to literally tie us to our past. They are supposed to make us look to our everyday actions in the present.

There are three meanings to what the *tzitzit* are supposed to symbolize. The first one is the commandments. The Hebrew numerical equivalent of the word *tzitzit* is 600, plus the eight fringes and five knots on a corner equal 613, the number of commandments there are supposed to be in the Torah. The second paragraph of the *V'ahavta* prayer, which we recited earlier this evening, actually refers in its context to the *tzitzit*, to these ritual fringes. "Therefore remember and fulfill all of My commandments and be holy to your God" (Numbers 15:40). The *tzitzit* are reminders to fulfill the commandments. Each one hangs and says: Honor your father and mother. Do not murder. Do not commit adultery. And on and on.

Often we need to be reminded of the commandments, of our duties and obligations. There is a wonderful story about the character of Joseph in the Bible when he was tempted by Potiphar's wife who wanted to seduce him. The biblical story says that she was literally tearing at his clothes when he had a vision in the window of his father's face. Perhaps it was his own reflection, but at that moment he saw his father's visage in his own. It was then that he remembered himself and ran from the room, so as not to disappoint his father or his tradition.

The *tzitzit*, then, serve as a reminder of our ancestors and their values. Just the way a person might tie a knot around one's finger so as not to forget something, the knots of the *tzitzit* remind us of the *mitzvot.* Wearing them can be a visual prompt to behave well. If we get carried away doing something in the back of our minds we know we shouldn't, catching a glimpse of our *tzitzit* can pull us up short.

The second meaning of the *tzitzit* comes from passages in the prayer book where it says that God will one day gather all of the exiles from the four corners of the earth. In Judaism, there is the promise that one day, all those people in exile, no matter how far flung, are going to be brought home again. For the Jewish people, many believe this means returning to the Land of Israel. In many traditional synagogues, before chanting the *Shema*, you may see people gather the four corners of their *tallit* in their right hand before singing of the oneness of God, linking a belief in God with the promise of the ingathering of exiles.

The act of homecoming is physically attached to us by hanging *tzitzit* from the four corners. This was of vital importance to fortify our people's faith when we felt alienated and lost. While we know people can be refugees and physically in exile, we also know people can feel forsaken or abandoned, even at home. People who are lost are literally on the fringe, the marginal members of society, who we pray will one day be brought home again, will find a place of safety and promise. Wearing the *tzitzit* is an act of aligning ourselves with the promise of a future redemption. It is a declaration of hope.

Finally, the third meaning of these fringes requires us to look back at how they were once worn even though we do not wear them in this fashion today. Once, long ago, there was a thread of blue that was woven among the fringes at the corner of the garment, made from a special dye so that it would be a specific shade and color. This blue thread, interwoven with the white, was part of the ancient symbolism of the *tzitzit.* We have, however, lost the formula to make this special blue dye, and so rabbinic sages long ago said that we shouldn't have a blue thread in our *tzitzit* until we discover this secret once again. In the Ethiopian community, however, they still have a thread of blue in the corner of their prayer shawls.

The meaning of this blue thread is described in the Talmud (*Menachot* 43b, *Sotah* 17a). There we read: "What distinguishes blue from all other colors? Blue is like the sea, the sea is like the sky …and the sky is like [God's] Throne of Glory." The blue thread ties us from earth to heaven, one kind of blue reminding us of another. Through this chain of association, we connect to God's glory. Personally, I understand this passage in the Talmud to also carry us from the physical to the abstract. We establish a link between the solid woolen thread of the *tzitzit*, through to the liquid form of the sea, to gusts of air of the sky, to the most intangible and abstract of feelings, the feeling of God's presence. The *tzitzit* are to remind us that, through many dimensions, reflections, and ways unseen, God is continually with us, just beyond our comprehension.

The *tzitzit*, then, are powerful symbols, once we understand them. They are reminders of the commandments recalling our duties as Jews. They are symbolic of people who are marginalized or on the fringe in exile in some way, to whom it is our obligation to help bring them back to home and safety. And the *tzitzit* are the tail ends of a feeling of our consciousness just beyond our reach, a glimmer of a feeling that the God of all the universe is with us, close by, at the edge of our understanding.

Wearing a *tallit* in the morning or on the *bimah* is a beautiful and meaningful way to actively engage in worship and embrace these values. The *tallit* that I am privileged to wear was woven for me by a wonderful woman, Terry Tarnow, from Traverse City, Michigan where I served as a student rabbi. She is a weaver and weaves a *tallit* for every *Bar* and *Bat Mitzvah* student, as well as every student rabbis, who comes through her doors.

There is a story that even God wears a *tallit*. Before putting on a *tallit* in the morning, some recite the verses from Psalm 104:1-2, "Eternal One, my God, You are very great. You have put on majesty and splendor, cloaked in light as with a garment, stretching out the heavens like a curtain." The heavens themselves are God's *tallit*.

The rabbis of antiquity expound upon this idea that the heavens are God's *tallit* with a story (based on *Sifrei* Deuteronomy 307). God once said to Moses, "Take heed of the heavens." Look at them and see them as God's creation. Just as the sun came up in the east today and will set in the west, so has God not abandoned you or forgotten you. In other words, know that the heavens are God's garment, the cloth from which God made the universe. The sun rejoices in its place in God's *tallit*, and we are part of that fabric. Just as the body has a soul, so is God the soul of the universe, wearing the universe like a cloak of light. The heavens are a mere covering for a greater splendor, a brighter light, beyond them. We are threads woven into God's world, a stitch of light in the *tallit* of the universe.

However, we need not limit the power of reminders of what is most meaningful in life strictly to these threads that hang from the prayer shawl. Reform Jews may or may not choose to wear a *tallit*, depending upon their own artistic expression when they pray. We must not, however, lose the value of what a *tallit*, with the *tzitzit* hanging from it, represents and does for us. We have to ask ourselves what it is in our homes or on our persons that go beyond just sentimental value, that actually point to something meaningful in our lives. What are the everyday reminders in our lives that lead us and link us to God and the Jewish people? What do our symbols mean, and do they lead us and renew in us faith and hope?

Consider how David Wolfson, a Zionist who attended the First Zionist Congress in Basle, Switzerland, answered this last question, not just for himself but for the whole Jewish people. Theodor Herzl, in preparation for the Congress, asked him to propose a flag for a Jewish State. Wolfson thought and thought, wondering what would unite Jews from all over the globe. He records his answer in these words: "Then it flashed upon my mind; but we have a flag indeed! It's white and blue: the *tallit* in which we wrap ourselves during prayer. This *tallit*, with its *tzitzit*, is our coat of arms, our emblem. Let us take the *tallit* and unfurl it before the eyes of Israel, before the eyes of all nations."[62] And so the Israeli flag is a *tallit* with threads of blue running through it.

And so we pray to God: When in doubt, let us remember the *tzitzit* of Your universe, the commandments. When feeling lost, help us know that You, God, will gather in all exiles by taking in the four corners of the world. And when feeling alone, may we have the strength and gentleness to know that God's threads reach everywhere, knotting and tying us to the divine presence both as a nation and as individuals. "Adonai, my God, You are very great. You have put on majesty and splendor, cloaked in light as with a garment, stretching out the heavens like a curtain." May we always see our world as such a beautiful vision as this.

---

[62] knowledgedb.org/?pageid=23568

## *Korach* (Numbers 16:1-18:32)

### Real Freedom

We of American society are predisposed to favor revolutionaries. Rebellions against authority in the name of the equality of all people have direct ties to the mythology of the United States. It is easy for us to identify with those who claim that all are equally holy under God, and that no one should raise him or herself above the people in the fashion of royalty.

The Torah portion entitled *Korah*, however, teaches that not all revolutions are good, nor are all revolutionaries honest. Numbers 16-18 gets its title from its chief villain, Korah. Korah and his followers, Dathan, Abiram, and On, as well as two hundred and fifty chieftains, lead a rebellion against Moses and Aaron. Korah, the great grandson of Levi, and Dathan, Abiram, and On, of the tribe of Reuben, challenge Moses in the wilderness. They say to Moses, "You have gone too far! For all of the community are holy, all of them, and God is in their midst. Why do you exalt yourselves over the community of God?' Moses falls on his face in a strong show of emotion. He then retorts to the rebels that they should bring a sacrifice in fire pans come the next morning, and God will make known who is God's chosen. Moses then uses the rebels' words in kind: "You have gone too far!"

Korah essentially accuses Moses of being undemocratic. "All the people are holy," he says. His accusation, however, is disingenuous, and he does not appear to be looking out for the people so much as simply wanting power for himself. But even if we accept him at his word, that he really was interested in the equality of all, the problem is that we may all be equal before God, but that does not mean that we all have the same abilities and qualifications. Whether he likes it or not, Moses' is God's chosen.

Because of our love of equality and fairness, Moses' words may not sit well with us. Aren't we all made in God's image? Aren't we all equal before God? They answer of course is yes. But being equal before God does not mean being equally qualified for all things. I may like to sing, but that does not mean that I should be a cantor.

So we ought to ask, what is it that distinguished Moses that made him more qualified for leadership than all the other people? At one point, Moses wistfully wonders aloud, "Would that all of God's people were prophets!" What made Moses different that made him a prophet among prophets?

I believe the qualification and lesson for us this week is this: Moses was willing to take responsibility for the people. Time and again he mediated between the people Israel and the Almighty. He was truly their servant. What made him God's chosen and made him stand out above the majority was that he humbly felt himself a servant of the people. He put the people first. The Torah describes him as the humblest man on earth. It is precisely his humility as seeing himself as the lowest of the low that actually made him the highest of the high.

It is natural for all of us that we are willing to enjoy the beauties of freedom. We understand this as our right and our due. But with freedom comes responsibility. It does not come without sacrifice. Korah may have spoken eloquently about freedom and equality, but when it came to presenting his sacrifice, it was not acceptable. We too as an American society love to talk about our rights, but when it comes to sacrifice, we sometimes forget the meaning of the word.

Occasionally I have the privilege of talking to World War II veterans. They often have mixed feelings when they look at our society today. On the one hand, they want their grandchildren to grow up in a world of prosperity, where they do not have to serve and fight in a tragic war. On the other, they cannot help but notice that many of us do not know what it really means to serve and to sacrifice. The two things our country asks of us is to pay our taxes and serve on a jury when called. We often do our best to get out of both as much as possible. We may love to quote Kennedy, "Ask not what your country can do for you but what you can do for your country," but what do we really do for our country?

In the coming years, I predict that we are going to be asked to sacrifice more for our society than we have in the past. We are going to have to sacrifice because we don't have much choice. Our economy is going to dictate that we make do with less. Deficits on all levels must be confronted. The destruction of the environment and our habitat is going to inconvenience us and affect how we use our resources and our love affair with our cars. More inclusive health care may mean all of us spending more money so that we have a healthier society. If we go into these challenges with high sounding words but not much sacrifice, as Korah did, we are not going to make it. But if we are willing to take responsibility for each other in the way that Moses took responsibility for the people, then we are all going to get through this together.

Let us pray to back up our ideals with actions. Let us know that real freedom and community means real service and sacrifice. And let us remember the notion that the Jewish philosopher Viktor Frankl: On one coast, he said, we have the Statue of Liberty. On the other coast we should erect a statue of equal importance, a Statue of Responsibility.[63] Freedom and responsibility need to go hand in hand, much the way our American Bill of Rights ought to be counterbalanced with our Jewish understanding of commandments. What sacrifices must we all make that will be pleasing in God's sight?

## Flowers and Almonds

As I sat to write this short sermon, I was cognizant of the fact that tonight would be a Shabbat with an *aufruf* or wedding blessing. When I looked to the week's Torah portion, I discovered that it was Korah. Korah is a character who leads a rebellion against Moses. He is punished by being swallowed by the earth. The parallels between the sensation of having the earth open up beneath your feet and being sucked into oblivion and marriage are so obvious that I need not go into them. Instead, let us look to another part of our Torah portion:

> Moses spoke to the Israelites. Their chieftains gave him a staff for each chieftain of an ancestral house, twelve staffs in all; among these staffs was that of Aaron. Moses deposited the staffs before the ETERNAL, in the Tent of the Pact. The next day Moses entered the Tent of the Pact, and there the staff of Aaron of the house of Levi had sprouted: it had brought forth sprouts, produced blossoms, and borne almonds. (Numbers 17:21-23)

After the rebellion against Moses and his brother Aaron, God affirms Aaron's role with a miracle. Aaron and his family served as priests for the Tabernacle, or portable sanctuary in the wilderness. His descendants would minister in the Holy Temple in Jerusalem. But after challenges to Aaron's authority, God asks a representative

---

[63] Frankl, 156.

of each tribe to put their tribal staff in the Tabernacle, and behold: all the staffs remain unchanged except for Aaron's, which brings forth not only blossoms but also fruit. Specifically, it sprouts almonds.

Why did God choose to affirm Aaron in this way with this miracle? A staff was used as a tribal banner. It was also used for walking, for steadying one's feet and finding one's way. It is a tool of leadership, to help tap out a path when we are blind. And the idea of a dead piece of wood growing again reminds us of many theological themes: rebirth, renewal, and even resurrection. It also tells us of vitality, that under Aaron's leadership, no matter how cut off or dismal things may seems, the Jewish people will always come back to life, that we will continue to grow and thrive in keeping with God's commandments.

But it is the added detail of the almond that is most instructive. The almond tree is the first to blossom in the Land of Israel. Around Tu B'Shvat, or the beginning of spring, the almond tree begins to flower. It is for this reason that the almond has become a symbol in Israel for wakefulness and industriousness. While all the other trees are still sleeping, the almond tree is working hard. It wakes up early and gives its fruit.

At Kibbutz Beit Alpha in the Galilee is a mosaic floor approximately 1500 years old. Among the symbols of the Ark, the menorah and the lion of Judah is a depiction of Aaron's staff. On the left there is a plain plant, and on the right the plant has flowered with a little bird on top of it. We might imagine that, to those who built this floor, the staff meant the sovereignty of the Jewish people in Israel would one day return. In my mind, the bird might be a dove, a symbol of peace. We have witnessed the miracle of the rebirth of the State of Israel, but we have not yet experienced peace which was the artisans' hope. Still, it is comforting to know that the wood of Aaron's staff is still alive, that the miracle of renewal endures.

The question remains, however, of what this blossoming staff might mean personally to each of us. There are times in our lives when we feel like the wood, cut down, when we are lost and we do not know what the future will bring. It takes an act of will to grab hold of this staff with both hands and to go forward. Our vision gets blurry as we are flailing about with our staff in hand. There are people we need to lean on to help show us the way. But our staff also blossoms. We count our blessings, counting each blossom and eating each fruit with gratitude and appreciation. We take little for granted and pray more fervently.

But perhaps we can also strive for the attribute of wakefulness that the almond represents. Perhaps we can rush to be the first ones to bring blessings to others. Perhaps we can pursue diligence in our relationship to God. And perhaps we can strive to be ever more giving in our relationships with others, to listen with more empathy and to reach out with more kindness.

Let us endeavor to feel the vitality that was contained in Aaron's staff. Let us pray for renewal and rebirth in our bodies and souls. And let us also pray for each other in our Temple family, that we can stand together under the God's banner of love, tradition, and loyalty.

## *Chukat* (Numbers 19:1-22:1)

### The Rock that Turned into Water

Did you ever do something that you regretted? Did you replay the memory of that scene in your mind over and over, wishing you could undo it or somehow take it back? It is probable that Moses felt that way about an incident in this week's Torah portion.

Moses's sister Miriam has died. Moses, undoubtedly grieving, tries to go "back to work" dealing with other people's problems. Their first complaint is that there isn't enough water. Moses consults God who tells him to speak to a rock and it will produce water for the people. Moses goes before the people, and he apparently completely loses it:

> Moses and Aaron assembled the congregation in front of the rock; and he said to them, "Listen, you rebels, shall we get water for you out of this rock?" And Moses raised his hand and struck the rock twice with his rod. Out came copious water, and the community and their beasts drank. But the ETERNAL said to Moses and Aaron, "Because you did not trust Me enough to affirm My sanctity in the sight of the Israelite people, therefore you shall not lead this congregation into the land that I have given them." (Numbers 19:10-12)

The punishment is harsh and absolute: Moses, full of understandable grief and anger, loses his temper, and he is told that he may not enter the Promised Land.

Doesn't God's punishment of Moses seem a bit unfair? Aren't we allowed to lose our temper once in a while? Is Moses really not allowed into the Promised Land because of this one transgression?

Rashi understands Moses' sin to be that he hit the rock, not once but twice, when God actually told him to speak to it. In addition to deviating from the commandment, symbolically this means that Moses relied upon force rather than dialogue to solve a problem. Nachmanides, on the other hand, says that Moses' sin was that he took credit for the miracle, saying, "Listen you rebels, shall **we** get water for you from this rock?" By saying "we," Moses is implying the miracle is coming from him and Aaron and not God. Still another explanation comes from Maimonides who believed that the real sin was Moses' anger itself; rather than hit the rock, what he really wanted to do was hit the people. And Isaac Abravranel comes up with no less than ten different explanations, which usually means that none of them are quite satisfying on their own.

But if we look back to the story of the Torah itself, we find that God gives an explanation for the punishment. God says, "Because you did not trust Me enough to affirm My sanctity in the sight of the Israelite people…" Aviva Zornberg notices that the verb "to trust" is actually in the causative in Hebrew. It is not so much that Moses did not trust God, but rather should be translated, "because you did not cause them to trust Me, to believe in Me, to have faith in Me."[64] Moses led them to water but not to God.

One might read the entire book of Deuteronomy as a response to this one event. Let us imagine that Moses was allowed into the Promised Land. Perhaps the people would have started to worship Moses instead of God. The liberation from physical slavery would have been meaningless if the people still remained trapped in idolatry. They would have been led to a land flowing with milk and honey but not to God. And so Moses, realizing that he by necessity is a limited human being, that he will die and there are boundaries and borders that he cannot cross, learns from this experience and tells the people at the edge of Canaan: "Choose life – that you and your offspring will live – by loving the Eternal your God, heeding God's commandments, and holding fast to God." (Deuteronomy 30:19-20) I am not certain that the book of Deuteronomy would ever have been written if Moses had been able to enter the Promised Land.

The scene is a painful one to watch, much like taking the car keys away from an elderly person who no longer should be driving but insists that they can. And yes, one dramatic act of sin can undo years of goodness and giving. Yet all of us at all ages experience disappointments and regrets, things we wish we could take back or that worked out differently. Occasionally we all stub our toes on a rock or we hit a stone wall that will not let us pass. We desperately want something, as desperate as Moses was to enter the Promised

---

[64] Avivah Gottlieb Zornberg, *Particulars of Rapture: Reflections on Exodus* (New York: Doubleday, 2001), 242.

Land, and the world says "no." How we live with disappointment is a test of our character.

Yet that same rock appears elsewhere in Jewish writings, and sometimes we can learn a valuable lesson from the very obstacle we are facing. can turn into a lesson to be learned. In Psalm 114 in the Hallel Psalms we praise God who "turned the rock into a pool of water, the flinty stone into a fountain." (Psalm 114:7-8) The rock keeps us from our desires, but water flows from it, if we have the courage to drink it. Not getting the job or the career we hoped for can teach us about what we really need to survive. Illness and physical limitation can tell us to slow down and appreciate the miracle and gift that is each day. Loss can move us to renew relationships and ask for and offer forgiveness. It is at the graveside that we call God *hatzur tamim poalo* – the Rock whose works are pure, and each Shabbat we pray to God as *tzuri v'goali* – our Rock and our Redeemer. The same rock, looked at differently, can be a lesson in how to live better.

After all, aren't our regrets and our mistakes our greatest teachers? Don't we learn the most from the places where the universe didn't conform to our wishes? Aren't we ultimately thirsty not for water easily found but for meaning, for a firm foundation, the bedrock of God's purpose in our lives?

The greatest lessons in life are earned, often through sacrifice. Let us pray that we have the strength to drink Moses' water, to learn from our mistakes and disappointments. In doing so, maybe we can each pass on our own personal book of Deuteronomy of what we have learned from experience. We can teach our own affirmation of faith, goodness, and wisdom from all the lessons we have learned within the confines of our limitations. To do so requires faith that God has made us in such a way that we can grow into better people.

**Confronting Our Fears**

"Snakes. Why'd it have to be snakes?" So says Indiana Jones, played by Harrison Ford in *Raiders of the Lost Ark*. The brave hero of the movie has a phobia of snakes. And so have many people for thousands of years.

This week's Torah portion contains a story that involves snakes. In Numbers 21, the Israelites are complaining as they are traveling through the desert, and God sends snakes to attack them. The Torah says that many people died of snakebites. God, however, tells Moses to create a staff with a serpent on it, and anyone who looks up at the snake will be healed. Moses creates a copper snake on a staff, and the people who look at it are cured.

This story is clearly rooted in ancient mythology. Today, we can see the symbol of a snake coiled around a staff as a symbol of healing at many medical establishments. It is the Rod of Asclepius, belonging to the Greek god in charge of medicine. The snake was seen as a symbol of healing because a snake sheds and rejuvenates its skin, and yet it was also a symbol of medicine because medicine taken improperly could be poisonous. This symbol was also found in Egypt, and a copper idol of a snake was even found in Israel near the copper mines of Timna, dating back to about 1000 BCE.

The snake is also prominent in the Torah. We can remember the snake of the Garden of Eden as well as the staffs that turned into snakes when confronting Pharaoh. And here we have the snakes of the wilderness and the copper snake that heals them. The English words "copper snake," however, miss the alliteration of the original Hebrew. The Hebrew word for snake is *nachash*, the Hebrew word for bite is *nashchu*, and the Hebrew word for copper is *nechoshet.* In other words, *nachashim nashchu*, and the *nachash nechoshet* cures them.

But even with all of this background, this is a very puzzling passage to be included in our Torah for many reasons. Let's name just some questions:

- Isn't the punishment of killing the people with snakes over-the-top with cruelty? What kind of God is this?
- We know we are forbidden to make idols or graven images, but isn't a copper snake an idol?
- And doesn't this seem like some kind of magic? What could this possibly be here in the Torah to teach us?

The punishment does seem to be especially harsh, but we have to remember that our Torah is filled with stories of plagues and miracles. And we are left to wrestle with the idea that the God who sends the snakes is also the one who sends the cure. God creates life which has both which has both snakes and staffs. "I create light and darkness," says God (Isaiah 45:7). For Jews, the Source and Soul of the Universe is all One. Life, it seems, is a package deal, and like the dual nature of the snake, it both hurts and heals. Over and over, God says to us that we must confront life as both a blessing and as a curse, and we must be strong enough to "choose life."

The rabbis, however, had a much harder time with the idea that Moses made an apparent idol to cure the people. Unable to accept the story in its plain sense, they ultimately resorted to a psychological interpretation, explaining the story not literally but metaphorically. Read symbolically, the snakes attack the people when the Israelites are complaining. These are the snakes of their toxic, negative minds. The snakes represent the evil inclination, going all the way back to the Garden of Eden. Some scientists refer to the oldest parts of our brains as our "reptilian brain" because of its development in evolution. It is where some of our most primitive fears and instincts come from.

But the cure is to not give in to this spiritual venom, to stare the snake down, represented by the elevated staff with the shining, copper serpent. Moses tries to lift up our affliction, face the hardship, and hopefully be healed. You must confront that which frightens you and rise above it.

Understood this way, this Torah story represents something that happens inside each one of us. When we are behaving at our worst, our evil inclination or primitive fears come back to bite us. But we must be willing to look at our fears straight on, confront them, and elevate these impulses to a higher plane. We must raise them up on Moses' staff. The drama of this story, therefore - according to the rabbis, is an everyday struggle inside of ourselves.

Today, there are many medicines people take that have horrible side effects. A universal side effect of illness is anxiety. It is hard to live with fear every day. Healing comes from each other, from someone who can be a Moses for us, help us face what we need to, and lift our spirits.

Our task is to confront our fears and do our best to change the *nachash* into *nechoshet* that which bites into that which heals. It is not magic; it's hard work. And the Torah gives us a symbolic story that is a prescription for inner strength and living courageously.

## *Balak* (Numbers 22:2-25:9)

### Seeing the Blessing

One characteristic of the Torah is that it teaches through pairing opposites. Right from the start in the story of creation, we see that the world is made of opposites: light and dark, sea and sky, dry land and ocean. Adam and Eve are split one from the other, and so forth.

This idea of pairs continues in a moral dimension. Moses is paired opposite Pharaoh. Whereas Pharaoh thinks he is a god, Moses is described as the humblest man on earth. When Pharaohs are buried, they get a pyramid, but Deuteronomy tells us no one knows where Moses is buried.

The rabbis looked at this week's Torah portion similarly. The Torah takes an unusual turn by focusing the movie camera, so to speak, not on the Israelites but on another scene altogether in the land of Moav. The king of Moav, Balak, is afraid of the Israelites passing by his land, so he hires a sorcerer, Balaam, to cast a curse on them. It is the one story in the Torah whose main character is not a patriarch or an Israelite but actually an enemy of Israel.

Balaam the sorcerer tries to do what the king says. He tries several times to stand on different hilltops and cast curses on the Israelites, seeing their tents from far away. However, before he tries he warns the king that though he may attempt to call down God's wrath, God is the one who decides what words will come out of his mouth as the spell is cast. Sure enough, words of blessing come out of his mouth, not words of curse. One of those curses turned into blessings is part of our morning prayer service: *mah tovu ohalecha ya'akov mishkenotecha Yisrael.* "How good are your tents, O Jacob, your dwellings O Israel!" (Numbers 24:5) Despite Balaam's best efforts to cast a curse, his spell was turned into its opposite.

Knowing that the Torah often teaches through pairs and opposites, the rabbis went looking for Balaam's opposite. Who stands at the other end of the spectrum? They insightfully came up with none other than Abraham. Abraham is told that he is supposed to be a blessing. In God's opening words to Abraham, the Torah says:

> I will make of you a great nation,
> And I will bless you;

I will make your name great,
And you shall be a blessing.
I will bless those who bless you
And curse him that curses you;
And all the families of the earth
Shall bless themselves by you. (Genesis 12:2-3)

Whereas Balaam is a caster of curses – effective or not – Abraham and his descendants are impervious to such spells because they are commanded to be a blessing. Blessing and curse, these are the opposites that the rabbis notice.

The rabbis expand upon the moral dimension of this comparison in Pirkei Avot 5:19, "One who has a good eye, a lowly spirit, and a humble soul is a disciple of Abraham, while one who has the opposite characteristics is a disciple of the wicked Balaam." Rashi explains that a "good eye" is someone who lives without jealousy and that a "lowly spirit" is someone who exhibits self-control over his or her desires. Again, we see that for the rabbis, blessing and humility win out over cursing and arrogance.

But it is Rabbi Yehudah Leib Alter of Ger who brings perhaps the most relevant message for us today.[65] Commenting on the pairing of Abraham and Balaam, he says that every day is always a mixture of blessings and curses. There is no time and there is no soul that does not have a blend of both good and bad. The difference between the righteous and the wicked, therefore, is that "the righteous seek to find that point of grace or time of good will," whereas "the entire goal of the wicked is to find that [moment of] wrath" and exploit or capitalize on it.

The Gerer Rebbe continues, each day is usually filled with far more blessings than curses. He says that despite the wicked impulse, "we still find that goodness is more plentiful." How we choose to see things is up to us.

I think we can all remember conversations we have had when we were discussing an occasion, and despite the ninety-nine things out of a hundred that were good we chose to focus and discuss the one

[65] Arthur Green, *The Language of Truth: The Torah Commentary of the Sefat Emet, Rabbi Yehudah Leib Alter of Ger* (Philadelphia: The Jewish Publication Society, 1998), 257-258.

thing that did not go well or was bad. Such a negative view offers a skewed version of reality. This is all the more troubling when we inevitably talk about other people. A wicked or jealous impulse in us seeks to meditate on another's flaws instead of seeing their obvious strengths or virtues. This Torah portion reminds us that we are to never stop seeing the blessings in each day and in each person and to keep the bad in perspective.

We are supposed to let the blessings overwhelm us and let go of the bad. This is, in fact, what Balaam eventually does after having his curses turned into blessings three times. He surrenders and lets himself sing out God's blessings a fourth time, not instigated by the king.

> Word of Balaam son of Beor,
> Word of the man whose eye is true,
> Word of him who hears God's speech,
> Who beholds visions from the Almighty. (Numbers 24:3-4)

Might we all merit the ability to see the world as a place of blessings, who have eyes that are true, who can see and hear God's speech in everything, and have the vision to focus on goodness out of a deep sense of humility.

## When Praising Can Be a Curse

*Mah tovu ohalecha Yaakov! Mishkenotecha Yisrael!*

How good are your tents, O Jacob! Your dwellings, O Israel! (Numbers 24:5)

Our Shabbat morning services begin with these words, words of praise for the houses of the people Israel. They are put at the beginning of the service so that people can acknowledge the synagogue, the ultimate House of Israel, as they enter. They come from this week's Torah portion, but their source is unusual.

In this week's Torah portion, a sorcerer named Balaam is hired by the king of Midian to curse is Israel. Apparently, he is very talented at pronouncing curses. However, he tells the king that there is a catch; he can try to curse, but he still must say words of truth that God approves. He is not in complete control over what comes out of his mouth.

Balaam stands on a mountaintop and attempts to curse Israel, which would somehow weaken their spiritual power. The reverse happens, however, and out of his mouth comes words of blessing. Time and again, from different vantage points on different mountains, Balaam tries to curse them, but instead only blessings come out. These include the words of *Mah Tovu*, the Shabbat morning opening song.

How are we to understand Balaam today? Sorcerers and cursing seem foreign to us. Few of us believe in magic and spells.

Actually, we have an all-too-familiar correlation in today's world to Balaam and his profession. People, politicians especially, regularly hire people to curse their enemies. They hire media experts and image consultants to give our words the right spin. Candidates are regularly torn down by negative campaigning, and people are tried in the press before they get to sit in front of a judge or jury. Balaam is with us on an everyday basis, each time we watch television, read a newspaper, or look to the Internet. The only real difference is that God is not editing the messages that are coming out, holding us accountable to the truth.

But we don't have to look to the media or our political process to see how relevant this story is today. We just have to look honestly at ourselves, each one of us into our hearts.

Today, people have access to social media. They can bring people together, such as for the funerals of the teens slain in Israel, from all around the globe. They can also start riots. Is Balaam, the power share words of curse or blessing, to be found in our Internet as well? What of the knee-jerk reaction, the story without the facts, the slander and the hatred that have permeated the airwaves this week?

In the Talmud, the rabbis say that Moses wrote this story in particular, the Book of Balaam, which we know as Numbers 23 and 24 (*Bava Batra* 14b). Aviva Gottlieb Zornberg says that in writing this story about Balaam, the prophet who likes to curse, Moses was actually acknowledging his down dark side, his wicked impulses and secret desires.[66] Moses, in leading the people, always had to be polite and say the right thing. But underneath it all sometimes he really wanted to let people have it, to let himself lose his patience and vent

66 Heard at a lecture by Dr. Zornberg at Temple Sinai, May 28, 2014.

his frustration and anger. Nevertheless, he had to make sure that he uttered blessings and found the good in others, even if sometimes he didn't genuinely feel it. In this reading, Balaam is a character representing Moses' shadow that he attempted to exorcise through the writing of the Torah.

And so it is, teaches Zornberg, with all of us. Each of us have tremendous power, and the "Balaams" we repress can come out in the worst ways. But words can also heal. The words we speak matter.

## *Pinchas* (Numbers 25:10-30:1)

### Zealotry Today

Judaism is not what the Torah says. Judaism is what the rabbis of antiquity say what the Torah says and also what we have inherited and interpreted from them. Not everything that the Torah says is holy.

Sound like blasphemy? Actually, all forms of Judaism, including Orthodox, Conservative, Reconstructionist, or Reform, follow the principle that Judaism is not what the Torah literally says but the traditions that we take based upon the Torah. Judaism is not a fundamentalist religion but a religion with a long history of metaphor and interpretation.

Consider the following statements, all found in the Torah:

"Love your neighbor as yourself." (Leviticus 19:18)

"You shall not suffer a witch to live." (Exodus 22:18)

"God made male and female in the divine image." (Genesis 1:27)

"You shall take out a rebellious son and stone him to death." (Deuteronomy 21: 18-21)

"You shall be holy, for I, the Eternal One, am holy." (Leviticus 19:2)

"The Eternal One is a man of war." (Exodus 15:3)

Now, the Torah says all of these things, but not all of these things are Jewish. Beware of someone who says that we should believe something just because it is in the Torah. The Torah says a lot of things, and it was written by a lot of people. Some of them said things that have stood the test of time and feel like eternal truths to us; other statements seem like a throwback to primitive human behavior.

Jewish tradition, like it or not, has chosen to embrace some of the passages in the Torah and to leave others behind. Some verses we choose to understand in their plain sense, and others we either ignore or interpret out of existence. Thus we understand the commandment to "choose life" quite literally, but the phrase "eye for an eye" has always meant monetary compensation in Jewish tradition, far from its literal meaning. We Jews choose to embrace the principle of loving our neighbor as ourselves, the idea that all are made in the image of God, and striving for holiness, and you will never hear in Hebrew School that we should stone witches and loud mouth sons and that

God is a man of war.

This is especially true for this week's Torah portion. In this week's portion, a gentleman named Phinehas catches an Israelite engaged in a forbidden fertility rite with a Midianite idolatress. In his zeal and fury, he spears them both through like a shish-kabob. In response to this act of capital punishment without a trial, which the rabbis of antiquity found very problematic as do we, the Torah says that God rewards Phinehas with an everlasting covenant of peace. Now that is a story you will not hear in Hebrew School!

What shall we do with such a difficult story today? We cannot ignore it, for it reveals to us a side of human nature from which we cannot turn away. We have all imagined vengeance at one time or another. We cannot teach it to our children, for the values of revenge and hasty execution are not ones we want to instill in the next generation. And we cannot take up the Torah and throw the whole thing away, which would uproot our civilization and dismiss the very document in which our most precious values can be found.

So what to do? What we can do with this week's Torah portion is that we can understand that Phinehas and his actions are part of the human condition, but they are not Jewish. We all feel righteous anger at times, and we also long for vengeance. But how can we, in the 21st century, read a passage about religious zealotry and violence, we who encounter terrorists in the daily news, and think of it as what God wants and commands of us? The mind rebels against the thought.

Instead, we can oppose this part of the Torah with another part of the Torah, and we do not have to go far to find a passage that contradicts the zeal of Phinehas and gives us footing to stand on. Later in this same portion, it says that Moses should pick Joshua, a man who has the spirit of God in him, to lead the Israelites after he is gone, that Joshua should go out and come in before the people. Joshua is described as a man of courage who cares about the people and will lead them into the future, like a shepherd. It is striking that God does not instruct Moses to select Phinehas to be the next leader of the Jewish people, but rather Joshua, a man of spirit. We can reject Phinehas not because we reject the Torah but because the Torah gives us another voice and perspective on the issue of leadership and self-control. We can reject Phinehas in favor of Joshua.

This idea of selective reading and interpretation, which everyone does, might, however, make some of us feel uncomfortable. Who are we to decide which passages of the Torah should be our guide and which should not? How are we to know what God is commanding and what is a throwback to another, harsher time?

The only thing we have is that other gift that God gave us in addition to the Torah, which is our conscience. If we as a community read the Torah with our divinely-given conscience, if we read prayerfully for guidance, including all of the wonderful commentaries and interpretations that have been handed down to us through the generations, then we will find the way through the Torah to the way that God wants us to go. Judaism has always encouraged us to challenge and to question, and we must continue to do so, especially with our most sacred books. With our hearts and minds wide open and well educated, we can hear God's voice through the Torah, if only we trust our conscience as a community.

Perhaps we might understand the Torah better through another metaphor. Imagine that the Torah is like a mirror, the kind that a person can hold by a handle in one hand. Imagine that, looking into the mirror, we see all that humanity has to offer, the good and the bad. We see the holiest heights of universal responsibility, one for the other, in the name of God, and we see the darkest lows of genocide and idolatry. God is holding this mirror up to us and asking us to take a good, long look. What shall we see, and what shall we do about it?

Let us pray to be able to read our Torah, in the way of fundamentalists and zealots who cause so much harm in our world, but as caring people searching for God. Let us not just look into the depths of our Scriptures but also into the eyes of another and see God in both places. Let us pray to never forget the face within the pages of our religion, and the religion in the face of another person.

## *Matot-Masei* (Numbers 30:2-36:13)

### The Most Troubling Passage in the Torah

To me, there are many troubling passages in the Torah. There are stories of God sending plagues and fire. There is the command to Abraham to sacrifice his son. But this week's Torah portion contains the most troubling passage.

In this week's portion, in the opening verses of Numbers 31, the Israelites go to war against the Midianites. The Israelites are victorious and wipe out the Midianites, sacrificing them to God. Phinehas, the zealous priest, leads the charge. And when Moses finds out that the Israelites spared some of the Midianite boys, Moses sends them back to kill them all.

Our Torah, which tells us to love our neighbor and ourselves, that all people are made in God's image, and that we shall not murder, records a genocide carried out by Moses and the Israelites with God's apparent approval.

The rabbis were very disturbed – as you must be – by this passage. It is for this reason that they modified the passage, reading into it that Moses made provisions for those among the Midianites who wanted to flee to have a way to do so. Rabbi Natan in *Midrash Sifrei* says that they conducted the war "as Adonai commanded Moses," and the only way God commands a war is to attack from three sides, not four. In other words, according to the rabbis' radical rereading of the text, "God arranged for anyone who wanted to flee to have peace." Later, this approach to war was codified by Maimonides in the *Mishneh Torah* (*Hilchot Melechim U'milcheihem* 6:7), who said Jewish law rules that when you attack a city, you may only attack it from three sides, not four, so that anyone who wants to escape can get away with his or her life. Hasidic teaching in Torah Temimah reinforces this interpretation, saying that this was an oral tradition from Moses to Joshua, for later we find before Joshua entered the land of Israel, he "sent three announcements, and one was for anyone who wanted to flee to safety." With this mode of interpretation, we find again the general rule that Judaism is not what the Torah says; Judaism is what the rabbis say the Torah says (even if we might consider it a very forced interpretation).

Modern scholars have also been disturbed by this story of genocide in the Torah. They point out that this story, along with other stories where the Israelites wipe out the Canaanite nations, most likely never happened. There is no archeological evidence of the burned destruction of these cities. Furthermore, if you look at the events recorded in the book of Judges, you find these people who were supposedly wiped out are alive and well and living next to the Israelites. This intermingling causes all sorts of conflicts and tensions, but the fact of the slaughter of these peoples is cast in doubt.

While I think the rereading of the rabbis was ethically necessary, teaching us that God always has mercy and so should we, and the findings of modern scholars is reassuring, letting us know that this probably never happened, there is a deeper point to this disturbing story. It goes to the essence of Torah. Torah is neither a God-given ethical rule book nor is it a flawed account of history. Torah at its essence is the recorded dreams of our ancient ancestors. It reveals fragments of their collective unconscious, including their darkest desires. They may have never murdered every man, woman, and child of the Midianite people, but some of them probably wanted to, dreamed of doing just that, and wrote it down.

And what does the fact that we piously read this story year after year say about us? We read this passage as part of the Torah reading cycle because we, too, have dark fantasies of wiping out other people, people we wish would just go away and leave us alone. In our polite conversation we say it is horrible, but our darkest dreams are uncensored.

People who do not own their own darkness cause the most damage. The writer Parker Palmer in his essay, "Leading from Within," teaches, "By failing to look at our shadows, we feed a dangerous delusion…: that our efforts are always well-intended, our power always benign, and the problem is always in those difficult people…. [There is] darkness that we carry within ourselves—the ultimate source of the shadows that we project onto other people…."[67]

The Torah is sacred because it holds up a mirror to the human condition. It tells us the truth about ourselves, including our most murderous urges that we thankfully subdue, and asks us to own them

---

[67] Parker J. Palmer, "Leading from Within," *Let Your Life Speak: Listening for the Voice of Vocation* (San Francisco: John Wiley & Sons, Inc., 2000), 79-80.

and take responsibility for them. "Do not forget for a moment that you are really a predatory animal," the Torah reminds each one of us. "It is only law and conscience that keeps you in the image of God."

Once we acknowledge that we have fears and fantasies inside of us, we can then choose not to act on them. We can project not our darkness but our light, not act out of anxiety but out of trust, and not to react from our fantasies but from our faith.

God, teach us the truth about ourselves, so we can grow into better people.

## Journeys

In this week's Torah portion, we read the last chapters of the book of Numbers. The Torah portion is called *Masei*, meaning "journeys," and it is taken from the first sentence of the portion, "These are the journeys of the people of Israel." Indeed, the idea of journeying or traveling seems to be the theme of the whole portion. All of the journeys of Israel over the past forty years are recounted, naming them after their starting points. Our Torah portion thus lists all of the places that the people Israel have left behind.

But then the Torah takes up another theme, apparently unrelated. The narrative goes on to explain that the people of Israel are finally about to enter the Promised Land, but when they do they must set up cities of refuge. These cities are sanctuaries to which those convicted of capital crimes may flee. That is, the first concern of the Torah before the Israelites enter the land of Canaan is that they must set up safe-houses for people on the run. Moreover, these cities are to be outside of the Promised Land. They may be cities of refuge, yet they are also places of exile.

So the Torah begs the question, what is the relationship between these topics? On the one hand, we have a list of all the places that Israel has left. Israel first left Egypt. From there they left Sukkot, then Etam, then Pi-hahirot, and so on for fifty verses, reviewing all of their wanderings for forty years. It is an extremely lengthy passage which concludes with a description of the land they are finally going to enter, a place they can call home, a place that they will not leave behind.

And then in a disjointed fashion there is a piece of legislation demanding that the Israelites set up these cities of refuge, these sanctuaries for exiles. These refugees are people who have unintentionally committed murder. The next of kin of the victim, translated by some as "the blood-avenger," has the right to execute them. The condemned thus have to flee from the blood-avenger of the bereaved family, but where to? Thus the cities of refuge must be established, places where the redeeming kinsman cannot legally enter, city-sized prisons where the condemned may live out their lives safe from the revenge of capital punishment. It is, at first look, an odd transition.

A connection between these two topics is offered by the rabbis: When the Israelites were journeying from place to place, they were really fleeing from place to place. They were people on the run, much like the condemned fleeing from the blood-avenger. The *midrash* says that when one is pursued, one may do nearly anything to save one's life. The interpretation then continues:

> The Holy One said to Israel, My children, Be cautious concerning my *mitzvot* and protect the Torah, and see how many miracles and wonders I did for you from the moment you left Egypt. I brought down those who hate you and brought you through the sea...I destroyed the Emorites. And all these forty years in the wilderness, I did not leave you for a single moment. How many enemies...And how many snakes and scorpions I killed from before you...Therefore, God said to Moses, write down all of the journeys that Israel has traveled in the wilderness so that they will know the miracles that I performed on their behalf. (Numbers Rabbah 23:1)

In this way, the fleeing of the people Israel and the fleeing of the condemned are melded into one. Just as the condemned may flee for his life, so has Israel been fleeing from place to place, from danger to danger. Israel has fled from the slavery of Egypt, hostile kings, and even the natural dangers of wild animals. The list of portion *Masei* thus isn't so much a list of journeys but of narrow escapes, a list of dodges and flights. The Torah calls these places "*motzeihem*," the places they have left, never the places that they journeyed toward. It is not a list of destinations; it is a list of places better left behind.

And yet, there's a problem. So long as the Israelites are fleeing, they are stuck wandering in the wilderness. Their orientation is always backward, toward the place they just left. They are never concerned about where they are going. They have fled from, not journeyed toward, and they haven't made it to the Promised Land in forty years. They have no destination. They can only run away from what is behind them, from their past.

And it is the same with the condemned running away from the blood-avenger. The cities of refuge are outside of the Promised Land. They are places of exile. They may feel safe, but they are not the kind of security that one calls home. They have the safety of a prison.

It is as if the Torah is trying to say that so long as someone is running away, that person will never reach his or her destination. So long as one's orientation is backward, to what one is leaving behind, one will never make it to what is ahead. Someone who is always running away is like someone condemned to exile. All of the miraculous escapes and excuses in the world are no replacement for a promised land, a home which involves commitment and an unflinching look ahead.

As the Torah continually demonstrates, very little has changed in the nature of humanity between the time of its narratives and our modern era. The Torah is a book which illustrates the essence of the human condition, in all its glory and ugliness, its good and evil, and we, too, suffer from the same faults from which the Israelites suffered. Often, we spend a great deal of our lives running away and never getting anywhere.

Sometimes, we are running away from our careers. We stubbornly cling to the way we want things to be and do not deal with the realities of the way things are. It is difficult to face the fact that one may be unhappy in one's job, or in one's workplace, or in a certain field. It seems safer to pretend that everything is okay and spend forty years wandering in a wilderness.

Or sometimes we flee from the education we wish we had gotten, whether it be secular or Jewish. I have often heard of how hard it is to go back to school after years of working or to go back and finish a degree left uncompleted. In regard to Jewish learning, it is especially daunting to be an educated professional in the outside world and in the synagogue classroom be painfully ignorant. But often we would rather flee from facing a fear rather than take the worthwhile risk.

And of course, it is often easier to run away from the commitment that a loving relationship demands rather than be willing to fight for it. Such commitment by its very nature demands that we let down our defenses, make ourselves vulnerable, and face the future. One must eventually stop running away and be willing to make a promised land, a secure home with one's partner.

Whether we have fled from the commitments of a career, an education, or a relationship, to run away, the Torah teaches, is a kind of exile. We must eventually stop listing the places we've left behind and start making the place we would like to journey toward. The Israelites, at the end of the book of Numbers, are finished running away. They have had enough of fleeing. They are ready to enter the Promised Land, and they are ready to fight for it. And that is where the next book, the book of Deuteronomy, picks up, with Moses's final address as the Israelites prepare to conquer the land of Canaan. As they were ready to face the future and travel head to a difficult destination, so should we in our journeys.

May God guard your journeys, your going out and your coming in now and always.

# *DEVARIM* - DEUTERONOMY

## *Devarim* (Deuteronomy 1:1-3:22)

### Moses' *Devarim*

The book of Deuteronomy consists of Moses' last words before he dies. It is a kind of ethical will which he is leaving to the Israelites. In the words of Rabbi W. Gunther Plaut, "the speaker pleads and urges, threatens and comforts, exhorts and – at last – invokes the very heavens to be witnesses."[68]

The end of the book tells us that Moses was buried in a humble place, and no one knows his grave site. It leaves unsaid what material wealth he passed on to his children. We are to guess that it probably wasn't much. After all, Moses lived most of his life as a desert nomad, and you only owned what you could carry with you. Instead, Moses' legacy is his words. The book of Deuteronomy in Hebrew is *Devarim*. *Devarim* doesn't just mean "words" but also "things." Moses' words are the things he has left behind. And we are all the inheritors.

In giving this last series of speeches, we might well hear the later words of Ecclesiastes that would fit neatly into Moses' mouth: "As you emerged naked from your mother's womb, so will you return." Moses' basket as a child, the riches of Egypt, his staff with which confronted Pharaoh and split the sea, the tablets of the Ten Commandments – all eventually are gone. All he has left are his words.

Summertime is a time to be outdoors, to walk around the lake, and to inevitably witness nature's growth and decay. My children have pondered the new flowers, the growth of raspberries, and the death of a snake on the road. We cannot help but see that life is a process of becoming. God, the Source and Soul of the universe, takes new shapes and forms and then dissolves, coming together briefly and then falling apart, only to come together again for new shapes and games. Occasionally, a piece of God manifests itself as a human being. We are fortunate to exist for a while, to be conscious and even self-conscious and hopefully conscientious, and to notice the glory of

---

[68] Dudley Weinberg and W. Gunther Plaut, "Introducing Deuteronomy" in *The Torah: A Modern Commentary*, Revised Edition (New York: Union for Reform Judaism), 1146.

everything around us. Hopefully also we are moved to protect the uniqueness of each manifestation of the divine, and to not only notice it but to hold it in loving kindness.

But, like Moses, we cannot take anything with us. All that we leave behind are our *devarim*, our things that are as intangible as words. On the verse from Ecclesiastes I just quoted, that "naked you came into the world and naked you shall leave it," the *Midrash* tells the following parable:

> There was once a fox who found a vineyard that was fenced in on all sides. The fox could see the delicious grapes high above, but needed to pass through the fence to get them. Finally, the fox found a small hole in the fence, but he could not fit through. What did he do? He fasted for three days until he was skinny enough to fit through the hole. Frail and weak, he crawled through. And what a reward on the other side! He ate the grapes to his heart's content, filling his belly. Never before did he have such a feast. Finally it was time to go home, but the fox discovered that he had grown so fat, he could not fit through the hole in the fence. He fasted again for three days, and lean and frail, he crawled back. The fox exclaimed, "Vineyard! O vineyard! You are so lovely and so beautiful! But in the end, just as I came to you, so do I leave you…" (Ecclesiastes Rabbah 5:20)

What are we to make of the message of Moses and Ecclesiastes, of the fox and the vineyard? Perhaps it is only this: that we should wake up each morning and thank God for a new day, that we should make the most of it and decide to be happy, that we should enjoy what we can when we can because we can't take it with us and we only go around once, that we should love powerfully and forgive easily, and we should remember that the only thing we really leave behind are our *devarim*, our words. And who knows? Those words might just make a difference in someone else's life. As Rabbi Rami Shapiro says in summing up Ecclesiastes: "Eat well, drink smart, do what you love, and love who you can."[69]

**Forty-two Journeys**

When Douglas Adams wrote in his famous novel, *The Hitchhiker's Guide to the Galaxy*, that the secret of life, the universe, and everything was the number forty-two, he meant it as a joke.[70] He said he just wanted to show how absurd it was to pick out meaning in random numbers, and so forty-two popped into his head. Since then, geeks have been trying to find great significance in the number forty-two, from the page on which Harry Potter discovers he is a wizard to the percentage of the daily allowance of salt found in an average fast food hamburger.

All joking aside, Judaism has chosen to use some numbers as symbols of significance. Seven for Shabbat is a number of perfection and completion – possibly taken from the number of planets visible by the naked eye. Sets of ten, taken from the fingers, were a good way to remember commandments and plagues. And forty meant a generally long time, possibly symbolizing the average life-span in the ancient world, as well as days and nights on the ark, years in the wilderness, and days spent by Moses on top of Mount Sinai.

While we may smile at the arbitrariness of finding meaning in certain numbers, numbers were serious business to the ancients, especially the Israelites. In Hebrew, the same symbols are used for numbers and letters, with aleph indicating 1, bet indicating 2, and so on. Therefore, when God speaks the world into being, God is making the universe out of letters and numbers, not unlike the numbers scientists assigned to elements. And when the Torah became written down, great care was given to the letters and numbers used.

For instance, we read this week about the journeys of the Israelites. Moses recounts them to the second generation of the Children of Israel who are about to enter the Promised Land. He reviews these travels one-by-one as they traveled from Egypt to Israel

---

[69] Rabbi Rami Shapiro, *Ecclesiastes: Annotated & Explained* (Woodstock: Skylight Publications, 2010), xvi.

[70] "Why 42 ? – alt.fan.douglas-adams – Google Groups". Retrieved 1 September 2007.

through the Sinai wilderness. Rashi points out that forty-two journeys are listed in all at the end of the book of Numbers. (Maybe Douglas Adams was on to something after all, and he didn't know it!) For this reason, to mirror the forty-two segments of the journey of the Israelites, tradition has it that there are forty-two lines of Torah in each column in a Torah scroll. I personally checked our Torah scrolls, and it is correct. (By the way, the first book printed with movable type, the Gutenberg Bible, also has forty-two lines per page. In further uses of this numerology, there are also forty-two additional cities of refuge the Israelites are to set up when they settle in the Land of Israel, and forty-two words in the *V'ahavta* prayer. Many of these uses of symbolic numbers were deliberate.)

The Baal Shem Tov taught that it is not only the journey of the Israelites from Egypt to Israel that had forty-two stages. Each life has forty-two journeys, the first being birth and the last being death. Birth corresponds with the Exodus, and the World-To-Come corresponds with reaching the Land of Israel. That leaves the forty journeys of a life-span in between that each of us must go through.[71]

The Baal Shem Tov's great-grandson, Rabbi Nachman of Breslov, took this idea one step further. The Torah says, "These are the journeys of the Children of Israel." Rabbi Nachman teaches that the use of the word "these" is supposed to remind us of the earlier use of the word these, when they made the Golden Calf and said, "These are your gods, O Israel!" (Exodus 32:8). This use of the word "these" must atone for that use of the word "these," he teaches (*Likkutei Moharan* I:40). To mitigate the idolatry and the anger that is in the world, we must now go on journeys of compassion and repentance at each stage of our life. To be a Jew is to bring compassion to ourselves and others wherever we may go or be.

While these uses of symbolic numbers may be interesting or fun, it is helpful to think of our lives as journeys that are being written on a scroll or book. After all, as we are approaching Rosh Hashanah and Yom Kippur at the end of the summer, we imagine that each of our lives is a Book of Life, and we review that book and judge what we see.

So imagine your journeys with me. What were your starts and

---

[71] Yitzhak Buxbaum, *The Light and Fire of the Baal Shem Tov* (New York: The Continuum International Publishing Group, Inc.), 131.

stops so far? Where did you rest, and where did you keep going? What are some of the stages that were hard, and what are some of the ones that you wish you could relive for a while?

After all, this week's portion is called *Devarim*, after the words or things that Moses said as he recounted their journeys. But the Haftarah by Isaiah is *Hazon* (Isaiah 1:1-27), meaning a vision of the future. It is by reviewing the *devarim* of the past that we are able to have a *hazon* of the future, to think about where we want to journey next, or perhaps where we want to make our camp and stay a while. How many of us are happy to be right here, ready to plant our staff and stand with our tribe in this place? How many want to pick up and go, to change, and are eager to move on? And how many of us are a combination of the two, feeling the push and pull of life?

Shabbat is a pause in the forty-two journeys. It is time to breathe in and take stock. And as we read down the lines of text of not only this past week but this past year and anticipate the next page in the Book of Life, let us learn from our tradition and pray that we read with compassion and bring compassion to others.

## *Va'etchanan* (Deuteronomy 3:23-7:11)

### The *Shema* as a Spiritual Journey

We have reached the climactic moment in the Torah when Moses addresses the people before they reach their destination of the Land of Israel. He declares the *Shema*, the statement that the Eternal is our God, the Eternal is one. It is a statement that we continue to echo on our journeys, whether it is while we close our eyes in prayer, when we take out the Torah, when we put a child to sleep, or when we are at the final moment of someone's life at a bedside. These are some of the first Hebrew words our children learn, and converts memorize them in their studies. If the Jewish people's journey has a repeating theme, it is the *Shema*, words we have uttered in every time and place and under all circumstances.

Yet too often I fear we recite these words by rote without thinking about what they mean and what they have meant to others in our history. They are words that we all know, but it is hard to be thoughtful in today's world while speeding by in our SUV at 80 miles an hour with our headset connected to our cell phone. We are so busy that the things that are most sacred to us are too often taken for granted. How ironic that the first word of the *Shema* is to "hear," to listen. It doesn't just mean to listen in the way that we listen for a number from Information or wait for our name to be called. It means to pay attention, to listen deeply, to hear the forces of history and faith that reverberate through these Hebrew words.

I believe that we Jews ought to talk more about our history and faith. Many liberal Jews have a hard time talking about God. If you don't believe me, have a brief conversation with an evangelical Christian and compare for whom God is more of a reality in their daily life. For Jews, the simple six words of the *Shema* can be the start of a conversation, perhaps the launching point for a personal journey that echoes the journeys of the Israelites that we read about today from long ago.

Consider, for instance, that there is a strong possibility that what Moses meant when he said the *Shema* was not so much that God is one, but that we should worship God alone. Moses was addressing the Israelites before they entered the Promised Land, and he was very fearful that they would be lured into the idolatry that surrounded them. In a time when polytheism was the norm, the idea of compromising and making treaties with other gods was natural. Instead, Moses cautions them to listen, that the Eternal is our God, the Eternal alone. It is to this God, the Eternal One, that we are to worship singularly and exclusively. The force of *echad* is not so much a metaphysical statement of theology but rather a political demand that the Israelites stay loyal to the covenant.

We can feel a spiritual connection to that time and place when we realize that idolatry is still with us. Whenever we are tempted to put an excessive premium on fame and fortune, whenever we idolize hotel heiresses who get out of jail early or sports figures who may or may not be on drugs, Moses' words might come to us saying that we have crossed the line. The things that bring us wealth and power are profoundly different than the ones that bring us contentment, peace and meaning, and the *Shema* can remind us of that.

There is a *midrash* that essentially tells us that Moses could not have predicted all of the meaning his words would have for future generations. In this story, God enables Moses to see into the future, and he sees the classroom of Rabbi Akiba, the famous sage who we invoke each year in our Passover Haggadah. Moses is magically transported there, and Akiba is lecturing about the *eiruv* and milk and meat dishes, and Moses confesses to God that he doesn't understand a word. Nevertheless, when Moses hears Rabbi Akiba tell his students that this is the Torah that God gave Moses on Mount Sinai, and Moses feels some comfort in that he got some credit. But then Moses sees Akiba become martyred by the Romans. Akiba is tortured to death, and with his last breath he is able to say the *Shema*. Moses is stunned by Akiba's faith (*Menachot* 29b).

Moses could have never predicted what the *Shema* would mean to Akiba, yet we can also identify with Akiba's understanding of the *Shema*. When it is time for us to meet our Maker, many of us strive to have the kind of faith that Akiba did. It is not commonly known that there is a form of "last rites" in Judaism, a miniature Yom Kippur, a *vidui* that includes the *Shema*. Sometimes we can say it on behalf of another as a way of saying goodbye. I will never forget those moments in my rabbinate when I have had the privilege of holding the hand of another, when I have rubbed my thumb across their knuckles and said someone's last *Shema* either for them or with them.

Can you imagine what Moses would have said if he could have seen even further into the future, if he saw Maimonides proving that

God is one in a dialogue with Aristotelian philosophy? Or perhaps if he saw the mystics of Tzfat immerse themselves in meditation through the *Shema*'s words, trying to establish oneness with God and with creation, to lose themselves in infinity? Or how about when Abraham Joshua Heschel marched for Civil Rights, claiming that we need to listen to the fact that humanity is one, black and white together, just as God is one, and that there will be either "one world or no world"?[72]

The *Shema* has meant different things to different people in different times and places. It reverberates with the pushes and pulls of each era. It makes demands on us and asks us what we ultimately believe. It is both timely and timeless. And there is room for each person to choose what they believe. Some figures may appeal more to one person than another. Judaism has always been flexible, including a variety of avenues for struggle, doubt, and faith.

One last story: another journey and take on the *Shema.* The story comes from Victor Frankl, a Jewish psychologist and survivor of Auschwitz.

In his memoir, *Man's Search for Meaning*, Frankl recalls when he arrived at the concentration camp. Having neither wife nor children, all that he had that he felt gave his life meaning was the manuscript of his first book tucked into his coat. The first thing that they did when people arrived in Auschwitz was that they took people's clothes. Frankl felt despair as he saw his coat with the manuscript taken from him, that nothing of him would now survive, neither a physical nor a mental child. In return he received the ragged uniform of a prisoner who had just been gassed. He reached into the pocket, and there he found a page torn out of the prayer book, a page that had on it the *Shema.* He felt that his was not a coincidence but instead a call to life, to live his ideals rather than simply put them on paper. In that moment, he felt God commanding him.[73]

We are the blessed inheritors of all of this history. We are all on spiritual journeys, whether we realize it or not. Let us think about the words we pray and to use this as an opportunity for learning.

---

[72] Abraham Joshua Heschel, *Man Is Not Alone: A Philosophy of Religion* (New York: Noonday Press, 1951), 112.

[73] Frankl, 137-138.

## The *Shema* Ethic

"Once a photograph of the Earth, taken from outside, is available … a new idea as powerful as any in history will be let loose."[74] Thus said astronomer Fred Hoyle in 1948. Perhaps it turned out to be not so much an idea as a feeling, one that shuttle astronaut Nicole Stot described as true awe. And while the feeling of awe is ancient, we have gained a critical new perspective and hopefully urgency.

Or maybe not. I grew up with a photograph of the Earth on my wall. Most days as a kid I didn't even think about the meaning behind it. Perhaps even this amazing vision can be taken for granted.

A new documentary has come out, a portion of which is available for free on the Internet. The video is called "Overview," and it interviews astronauts who have had the rare experience of seeing the Earth from outer space. In 1968, when the Apollo mission circled the moon, the astronauts were very focused on going to the moon and seeing the stars. Unexpectedly, the most profound experience was when they turned around and looked behind them and saw the Earth, which for the first time looked like a small ball floating in a huge vastness of black space. All the astronauts interviewed tried to describe the feeling of awe that an actual overview of the planet brought out in them. Philosopher David Loy explains it in these words:

"To have that experience of awe is to at least for the moment to let go of yourself, to transcend the sense of separation, so it is not just that they were experiencing something other than them but that they were at some very deep level integrating, realizing their interconnectedness with that beautiful, blue-green ball."[75]

Astronauts come back profoundly changed. They have less patience with political boundaries. From outer space those lines don't exist. The space explorers want to tell us that if we could see what they have seen, we would cooperate a lot more and work much harder to preserve our shared home. We would understand that we are all in this together. We would appreciate our planet more. What is

---

[74] Fred Hoyle, 1948. Quoted in independent.co.uk/arts-entertainment/science-a-new-view-of-home-1306095.html.

[75] overviewinstitute.org

in the everyday mundane and seemingly forever is from outer space fragile, small, and precious. The experience has even given birth to The Overview Institute, which wants us to hear the message that, "From space, the astronauts tell us, national boundaries vanish, the conflicts that divide us become less important and the need to create a planetary society with the united will to protect this 'pale blue dot' becomes obvious and imperative."

This realization gives new meaning to the slogan, "Think globally. Act locally." Seeing as how most of us are not going into outer space, how do we live with this knowledge locally without having had such an "Aha!" experience? It is one thing to know something, it is a deeper level to feel something, but the deepest impact is if we internalize a truth and actually live it.

Jewish wisdom says that we are of two-minds when it comes to our lives. Most of the time, we worry about finishing a project at work, getting along with the boss, bringing home the groceries, and whether we have gas in the car. We also worry about our children, our marriages, our parents, and what people think of us. We think of the bills we have to pay or the things we want to buy. We try to get through the to-do list. These things are, of course, important.

But various Jewish thinkers call such a mind-set *mochin d'katnut*, or a constricted mind. This is a mentality of getting-by, buying and selling, consumerism, manipulating, conquering, fixing, solving, and getting through. It is necessary for survival, but if this is the totality of life, it feels empty.

On the other hand, there is also a Jewish religious mentality of living with a sense of transcendence, what is called *mochin d'gadlut* or an expanded mind. We relate to the world and to each other, open and vulnerable. These are made of fleeting moments of relationship, of noticing, being amazed, and wondering. We live in relationship with and feel addressed or called to something higher or deeper. And this feeling, what the astronauts call the Overview Effect, makes us realize we are all interconnected.

Rabbi Levi Yitzhak of Berdichev says that this is the true meaning of the *Shema*. He points to the order of the Hebrew words: *Shema Yisrael: Adonai Eloheinu Adonai Echad*. The words mean: *Shema Yisrael* - Listen, you Israelite: *Adonai* - which means, "the Infinite," is *Eloheinu*, our God who we relate to personally, but is still *Adonai*, the

Infinite, and everything is all *Echad*, One (*Kedushat Levi Vaetchanan* Deuteronomy 6:4). Rabbi Arthur Green explains:

> "[The *Shema*] means that endless Being was there before each and all of us came into existence. It is *our* God for the brief instant we flash across life's screen. But then we let go, and it is...endless Being once again.[76]

Think of the *Shema*'s Hebrew words as a number line. There is an arrow pointing in one direction, a dot indicating a point, and then another arrow pointing the opposite direction. The first *Adonai* of the *Shema* points to infinity going one way, the dot is where we happen to be which is *Eloheinu*, our personal, rather small and limited definition of God, and then the next *Adonai* is the arrow pointing to infinity in the other direction. We are one small dot in between in space. We are a part of the world, the world is part of the universe, and the universe is a part of an Infinity we call *Echad*, Infinite Oneness, or God. *M'olam ad olam, atah El* - From eternity to eternity, You are God. (Psalm 90)

And because we are all One, we become responsible for one another. Each of us is unique: a fragile, precious manifestation of the universe seeing itself, never having been here before and never being replicated again. We must protect each other and the home we live in. We might call this the *Shema* Ethic, which is the Jewish version of the Overview Effect.

But just to bring this back down to reality, to our constricted life of turmoil, wars, and limited options, let me put our interconnectedness in the everyday terms of the Rev. Martin Luther King, Jr.: "It really boils down to this: that all life is interrelated. We are all caught in an inescapable network of mutuality, tied into a single garment of destiny. Whatever affects one directly, affects all indirectly. We are made to live together because of the interrelated structure of reality. Did you ever stop to think that you can't leave for your job in the morning without being dependent on most of the world? You get up in the morning and go to the bathroom and reach

---

[76] Arthur Green, *Radical Judaism: Rethinking God and Tradition* (New Haven: Yale University Press, 2010), 130-131.

over for the sponge, and that's handed to you by a Pacific islander. You reach for a bar of soap, and that's given to you at the hands of a Frenchman. And then you go into the kitchen to drink your coffee for the morning, and that's poured into your cup by a South American. And maybe you want tea: that's poured into your cup by a Chinese. Or maybe you're desirous of having cocoa for breakfast, and that's poured into your cup by a West African. And then you reach over for your toast, and that's given to you at the hands of an English-speaking farmer, not to mention the baker. And before you finish eating breakfast in the morning, you've depended on more than half the world. This is the way our universe is structured, this is its interrelated quality. We aren't going to have peace on Earth until we recognize this basic fact of the interrelated structure of all reality."[77]

The *Shema* Ethic can thus be summarized as follows: Just as God is One and Infinite, we must strive to be one in a way that recognizes our interconnectedness and respects the uniqueness of each individual.

So, my-fellow-unique-manifestations-of-the-Infinite-God, our challenge is this: we can either live our lives entirely as ego-centric consumers, in the mentality of constricted *mochin d'katnut*, thinking our personal dot is the center of the universe, or we can live a life informed by the fleeting glimpses of unity and interrelatedness, of the *Shema*, of expansive *mochin d'gadlut.* We try to move, however so slightly, from narrowness to openness.

This is what the Hasidic text *Torey Zahav* teaches is the true meaning of the shofar. The breath moves from the narrow end of the shofar to the broader, more open end where the sound comes out. We, too, as Rabbi Arthur Green puts it have to be like the shofar and "have to move from our narrow, constricted places into a realm of greater breadth and open-heartedness."[78]

We have precious few moments of transcendence that help open us up; we have to recognize them and let them teach us and live out their wisdom in our everyday lives. And we as a global society badly

---

[77] Martin Luther King, "A Christmas Sermon on Peace" (ecoflourish.com/Primers/education/Christmas_Sermon.html)

[78] As taught in a lecture and heard by the author.

need an ethic of interconnectedness, what from a Jewish point of view is the *Shema* Ethic, because we are all in this together.

How are we going to think of our world, ourselves and each other? Perhaps we should start by looking back at ourselves and seeing how beautiful, fragile, and amazing we really are. If we do, we might be a little more appreciative, a little less destructive, and a bit more open-minded. We might be kinder, more compassionate, and more patient. We might want to take care of the big picture and worry less about the petty.

If only we would learn how to look and listen. It would change everything.

## *Eikev* (Deuteronomy 7:12-11:25)

### The Alphabet of Your Being

A hundred years ago in Jewish time is a very short time indeed. The Jewish people have a history that goes back some 3,500 years, and compared to that a century seems like a drop in the well. But also from a Jewish point of view, a hundred years ago is a tremendous amount of time because of this past century's events. Before the Holocaust and before the State of Israel, in a land now largely empty of Jews called Poland, there was a different world of Jewish life called Polish Hasidism. What we sometimes see imitated today in the black hat and black coat outfits of the Lubavitch are mimics of the outfits of Polish aristocracy of the seventeenth to early twentieth centuries. The Hasids, once upon a time, were people who demanded a revolutionary breakthrough against the establishment of institutionalized Judaism. In a Jewish world that prized scholarship and legal debate over all else, the Hasids declared that, in addition to study, one could also find God by praying outside in the woods and by singing ecstatically while dancing. Eventually, the Hasidic world itself became institutionalized and lost its revolutionary nature, and this is what we see today in Brooklyn and in the settlers on the West Bank. If you want to read about what happened when Hasidism met the modern world, read a novel by Chaim Potok, of blessed memory, who died earlier this week.

The last great teacher of Polish Hasidism was a man named Rabbi Yehudah Leib Alter of Ger, who was so wise and whose writings were so profound that they called him the "*Sefat Emet*," that is, he was the "Words of Truth," as if he were the living embodiment of Torah itself. The *Sefat Emet*, this speaker of truth, or, as Rabbi Arthur Green might have it translated, this "honest talker," served as the Gerer Rebbe, that is, the leader of his community, from 1871 to 1905. And when he looked at this week's Torah portion, here is what the *Sefat Emet* saw a hundred years ago.

"If you surely listen to My commandments that I command you…" (Deuteronomy 11:13). The Torah portion tells us that there are consequences for our behavior that we must listen to the voice of God and keep God's commandments because blessings or curses will surely follow. If we devastate the land, the land will pay us back in kind. If we empty ourselves of God, we will be left without much meaning. But if we protect the land and seek out God in every branch, river, and field and in every face, then we will enjoy endless blessing.

The Lesson of the Text: The Alphabet of Your Being

However, in accordance with the mystical traditions of Hasidic Judaism, the *Sefat Emet* read this phrase in a radically different way.[79] Unfortunately, in order to understand the *Sefat Emet*'s insight we have to take a brief detour into grammar, but I promise it will be brief.

"If you surely listen to My commandments that I command you (*etchem*)…" The Hebrew word for "you" is *etchem*. It has two syllables, *et* and *chem*. The second syllable, *chem*, is easier so we will look at that first. *Chem* refers to the audience in the second person plural. In simpler language, a more literal translation of "*chem*" would be "y'all." If you surely listen to My commandments that I command y'all (*etchem*)…

The first part, the *et* part, has no equivalent translation in English and usually simply indicates a direct object. But not for the *Sefat Emet*. In Hebrew *et* is spelled *aleph-tav*, that is, with the first and the final letters of the Hebrew alphabet. Which means that, according to the *Sefat Emet*, God is commanding y'all with your whole being, from *aleph* to *tav*, the whole alphabet of your soul, every single line, curve, dash, and point. If you surely listen to My commandments that I command y'all with the entire alphabet of your being…

Holy Potential Within Us

Now, we have to ask ourselves, when was the last time that we ever did something with the "entire alphabet of our being"? Did we even know that we had an alphabet inside of us? One might picture a bunch of Hebrew letters, swimming around inside our heads and limbs. What is the Hebrew alphabet doing there inside of us in the first place?

The *Sefat Emet* must have been trying to say that we have the potential to listen and to act with every fiber of our being, with the very DNA of which we are made. We have, each of us, within us, a series of letters deep in our souls that can make endless numbers of combinations and gives us unlimited potential, both for good and for

[79] Green, *Language of Truth*, 295-296.

evil. In the alphabet of our being, we decide which combinations of letters will come out, which words will be formed by our mouths, and these words will determine our path and the consequences that we face. If you surely listen to My commandments that I command y'all with the entire alphabet of your being… Each one of us is but a bunch of letters thrown together, and it is up to us what words and actions they will produce. Our soul is an alphabet, and what people will remember of us are the words we leave behind.

Holy Potential Within Others

This freedom that we enjoy, freedom in the choices we make, who we are, and who we are going to become, also must make us cautious and respectful of each other. Our individual freedom might seem unlimited, but alongside us are others with equal power and equal possibility. We must treat each other with respect, for the person alongside of us is also brimming with holy potential.

Consider the rabbinic proverb, "Despise no one and dismiss nothing, for there is no one who does not have his or her moment and nothing that does not have its place" (*Pirkei Avot* 4:3). I personally believe that this is the most important teaching of the Talmud. I will repeat it: "Despise no one and dismiss nothing, for there is no one who does not have his or her moment and nothing that does not have its place."

This sentence says far more than "every dog has his day." It means that we must be careful and respectful of others because each person and each thing has a role in God's universe. Holy potential resides in all things and in everyone. A cup of wine on Tuesday can become *kiddush* on Friday night. A candle during a thunderstorm can provide light during a power outage, but after the death of a loved one it can provide a different kind of light and warmth. And each person who we might otherwise take for granted, whom we might step over on the sidewalk on our way to the metro, is actually a creature of God, is someone made in the divine image and deserves respect. That person, given a different place and time, given a chance at a different future, might be able to fulfill a holy possibility, might find a meaningful reason for existence. Who knows? A Polish Hasid would teach that that person might even be the Messiah.

According to this understanding, the world does not need anything added to it or taken out of it. The world is what we make of it. Good and evil, the holy and the profane, the blessing and the curse exist potentially in all things and in everyone, and given the right place and the right time, miracles can happen. The alphabet of our being can be rearranged, and we can start again, creating new words and different paths to travel.

## The Holy Potential of our Freedom, Even in Death

I would like to read a poem to you. It is a poem written by the great Israeli poet Yehuda Amichai, and he wrote it in memory of his mother. It was read by my rabbi, Rabbi Gustav Buchdahl, at the funeral of my grandmother. It is an original translation by Rabbi Steven Sager. I invite you to think about your loved ones who have passed away and the alphabets that made up their lives. One might want to understand this poem as a kind of prayer, a prayer invoking the holy potential of our freedom, even in death.

> She is free, free. Free from the body
> and free from life and from the blood which is life,
> free from desires, free from sudden fears and from fear for me,
> free from honor and free from shame
> free from hope and from despair, from fire and water,
> free from her eye color and free from her hair color
> free from furniture and free from cups knives and forks,
> free from Jerusalem above and from Jerusalem below
> free from identity and from identity papers,
> free from round stamps
> and from square stamps
> free from photographs and free of clips
> She is free, free.
>
> And all of the numbers and all of the letters
> that ordered her life are also free
> for new combinations, new destinies, and for new games
> of all the generations that would come after her.[80]

---

[80] Translated by Rabbi Steven Sager, sichaconversation.files.wordpress.com/2010/08/she-is-free-holding-loss.pdf.

## *Re'eh* (Deuteronomy 11:26-16:17)

### Giving *Tzedakah*: A Sacred Act

I slow down as I approach the intersection. It is a busy intersection, and I am the fourth or fifth car in my lane back from the red light. There are rows of traffic on either side of me. And that's when I spot him.

There he is, the man in the torn camouflage jacket, holding the cardboard sign. On the sign, written in black magic marker, is scrawled the following words: "Homeless Veteran. Please help. God bless you."

The man is disheveled with a straggly beard and deeply tanned skin from sitting in the sun. He makes his way dangerously from the concrete median strip in between two lines of cars and begins limping his way up the row, holding his cardboard sign in one hand and a Styrofoam cup in the other.

What do I do? A sudden sense of discomfort grabs me, and my mind fills with questions. Should I give him something? Do I put the car in park and roll down the window? What if the light turns green? Is he dangerous? Is he going to get hit by a car? Is he really a military veteran? Maybe if I don't look at him, he will just walk by me and go away. I'll just look terribly interested at the odometer. If I give him something, is he just going to use it for booze? Or maybe he genuinely needs my help and needs food to eat? Aren't I supposed to give to the poor? Isn't that what Judaism says? Am I neglecting my duty as a Jew? How do I know the money is going to go for something good? I'm sure there are other beggars to give to, just at the next intersection. I can't give to everybody. What do I do?

If you are like me and have inevitably passed by a beggar on the street or at an intersection looking for a hand-out, you probably have asked yourself some of these same questions. It is easy for good people to feel conflicted about this situation. We all want to do the right thing, but what is the right thing to do? How can we guard against our own selfishness and laziness by making the effort to give to the less fortunate while at the same time not be taken advantage of and really do something constructive in this world?

In this week's Torah portion, taken from the Book of Deuteronomy, the fifth and final book of the Torah, we read the following passage:

> If, however, there is a needy person among you, one of your kinsmen in any of your settlements in the land that the Eternal your God is giving you, do not harden your heart against your needy kinsman. Rather, you must open your hand and lend him sufficient for whatever he needs… give to him readily and have no regrets when you do so, for in return the Eternal your God will bless you in all your efforts and all your undertakings. (Deuteronomy 15:7-8, 10)

Based upon this passage, Judaism has a long tradition of giving to the poor. The Hebrew word for this kind of giving, *tzedakah*, does not actually mean "charity." Its roots are in the concept of "righteousness" or "justice." Giving to the poor, therefore, is the right thing to do in God's eyes.

From biblical times, people left portions of their harvest for the poor. The individual Israelite farmer was commanded to leave the edge of the field standing for the poor to come and harvest themselves. Similarly, the individual Israelite was obligated to leave the forgotten sheaves, the overlooked gleanings, and the misshapen and separated produce for the poor to pick up. These categories of food to the poor, the edge of the field, the forgotten, the overlooked, the separated or misshapen, do not just tell us about kinds of produce. They also remind us of the kinds of people who tend to be poor: those who we want to forget or ignore, those separated from their families or suffering from some kind of mental or physical disability, and all of those who society pushes to the margins and the edges of our consciousness.

As time passed, Jewish giving became even more sophisticated. From the individual Israelite farmer, Jewish giving to the poor became a corporate responsibility. The community as a whole felt an obligation to take care of those who are poor and less fortunate than others. Compassion became institutionalized. Daily and weekly distributions to the poor became commonplace, so common that one Jewish authority once wrote that he didn't know of a Jewish community that didn't have at least one soup kitchen and a weekly collection for the poor.

To this day, institutions like Jewish Federation, the Jewish

Foundation for Group Homes, the Hebrew Home for the Aged, Magen David Adom, Hadassah, Mazon, and so many others exist so that we can continue to fulfill our obligations as Jews in giving *tzedakah*. We not only do the right thing in God's eyes by giving, we also uphold an ancient Jewish tradition.

The status of giving today, however, is not like it was just a generation or two ago in America. Jews who came to America and found a new life here felt genuinely grateful to this country for taking them in and also a sense of solidarity with the larger Jewish community that made giving *tzedakah* an assumption of Jewish life. The American Jewish community built hospitals and founded charities to help both the larger world and specifically other Jews as a sign of their Jewishness, as a characteristic of their identity as a Jewish American. Our present generation does not have the same kind of ethnic tie that their grandparents did, in the crush of taxes, health insurance, and saving for college educations and retirement, give proportionally less than previous generations. Ironically, the present generation is financially much better off than those Jewish immigrants who first came to America, but they feel pressure to succeed and achieve as never before. In the words of one graduate student, "Everything has been handed to me. If I fail, I will have no one to blame but myself. I must succeed, but to surpass the achievements and status of my parents is simply impossible."

By chasing a certain image of success and social standing, we have become less giving. So what happens to our beggar on the street corner of questionable background who is asking for our money?

I cannot tell you a perfect solution to the awkwardness of facing a beggar. I can only tell you what I do. I personally do not feel confident about giving handouts to strangers, for I do not know if I am helping someone or contributing to a problem. Sometimes I am prepared enough to have a gift certificate to McDonald's or something else in my wallet precisely so I can hand it out when asked and in that way I know that I am giving food to the hungry. But often I am not prepared that way. Perhaps I am not selfless enough, and I hope that I am not guilty of hardening my heart or averting my eyes.

But I do know that we would all feel a great deal better about not giving to the beggar on the street if we knew that we had done our part in giving *tzedakah* institutionally. If we give *tzedakah* in a substantial way to the plethora of charities that beg for our attention, if we make giving a part of our identity and a regular part of our annual budgets, then we can face the beggar and say, "I may not be giving now, but I do give in a way that I feel does some good in the world and makes a difference in other people's lives." If we give as a member of the Jewish community, then we can feel we have done our part as we walk down the street and can look our fellow human beings in the eye.

It was the thinker Moses Maimonides who described the giving of *tzedakah* as a Jewish virtue, something to be done not because of getting a heavenly reward but because it is simply the decent thing to do.[81] Before we cease to give because we feel the recipients are undeserving, we can listen to Maimonides' words. He compared giving *tzedakah* to the way that God gives to the world. God gives to us despite what we deserve. God unconditionally sustains this beautiful world that can supply all of our needs, if only we would use our resources wisely. In the same way, perhaps we can give to others, despite what we presume they deserve. Perhaps we can open our minds as well as our hearts in realizing that success is not measured in how much we accumulate and if we have become wealthier than our parents. True success is measured in what we give and the difference we make in others' lives.

On Shabbat, especially, we might want to remember the words of this week's Torah portion about giving. On Shabbat, we light two candles. We share a cup of wine from a silver *Kiddush* cup. We say a blessing over bread and eat a big and beautiful meal. But before all that, there was a sacred object that once stood alongside the candlesticks, the *Kiddush* cup, and the cutting board that seems to have disappeared. It has diminished in popularity. On Shabbat, before any blessings were said, people used to pass around the *pushka*, a can for *tzedakah*. Giving *tzedakah* was a ritual act, just as holy as the rest. The coins that were collected did not add up to much. But the value of giving was sanctified, and those around the table were reminded that it was a religious duty to give what we can. Giving tzedakah was seen as a sacred act.

---

[81] See my introduction in my translation of Maimonides laws on giving, *Gifts for the Poor: Moses Maimonides' Treatise on Tzedakah* (Williamsburg: The College of William and Mary, 2003), xxx-xxxi.

It is time for the return of the *pushka*. Before we enjoy our Shabbat meal, let us remind ourselves to give *tzedakah*. Let us emulate previous generations not in how much wealth they accumulated but in how money they gave. If we do our part, especially as the New Year approaches, than our minds will be settled and our souls will be content when we are faced with that beggar on the street. Then we will know that we have done our part in working for a day when no one is marginalized or forgotten, and everyone is provided for in the way that God intended.

**From Curse to Consequence**

The opening words of this week's Torah portion reads, "See, this day I set before you blessing – *bracha* – and curse – *klalah*: blessing if you hearken to the commandments of the Eternal your God that I command you this day, and curse if you do not hearken the commandments of the Eternal your God, but turn away from the path that I command you this day and follow other gods who you do not know" (Deuteronomy 11:26-28).

This statement has been used in the past as a classic example of the theology of reward and punishment. This reading says that if we do the commandments, we are rewarded, and if we do not, we are punished. The rabbis of antiquity believed this is how God operated in the world, handing down verdicts from a throne on high.

There are merits to such a way of thinking. It makes us feel humble, and it indulges our need to surrender to a Higher Power. Many of us today, however, have a great deal of trouble believing in such a theology. The reasons are straightforward. First, it does not represent our experience. Any child soon figures out that the world is often unfair. Those who follow the commandments do not necessarily get rewarded, and those who disobey do not necessarily get punished. The world simply does not work that way. Second, whereas all suffering brings such a way of thinking into question, the Holocaust especially makes it repugnant. Simply put, the murder of millions and the evil of others cannot be rationalized as an instrument of God's wrath. To put it in the terms of the *Midrash*, we do not justify the people at the expense of God, and we do not justify God that the expense of the people. Lastly, a punishing God is not any kind of God I would like to pray to. On a basic emotional level, it feels false.

Our experience, with the Holocaust in the center of our memories, cannot permit us to believe the way that many of the rabbis did two thousand years ago. But I do have faith that we can constantly find new meaning in our Torah, as Jews have done for centuries, from the earliest rabbis to the philosophers to the Kabbalists to the Hasidim to the scholars of the Enlightenment. Let's reread our text and see, if we read closely, if the rabbis' theology is the only acceptable interpretation.

The first line says, "See, this day I set before you blessing and curse." The words "this day" do not just refer to the time the speech was delivered. It refers to right now. Moses' speech was recorded in a scroll so it would not be lost, so listeners in the future would also feel addressed. "This day" means today, right now, in this very room.

What is also interesting is that the words that follow are *bracha* and *klalah*: blessing and curse. Notice that they do not say reward and punishment. There are blessings if you *tishm'u* – listen or hearken, as in *Shema* – and there are curses if you do not. The translation in your *chumashim* says "obey," but that is not entirely accurate. It literally means to hear and do. Think about a time when you had an argument and you felt that the other person wasn't listening to you. "You're not listening!" you may have shouted in frustration. Most like they were listening, but they were ignoring you. As a father trying to raise children, I can feel Moses' pain here. They hear everything; whether or not they do what they are supposed to is another matter.

Blessing if you hear and do and curse if you don't does not necessarily have to mean reward and punishment. It could also mean good consequences and bad consequences. If you hear and do what I am telling you, there will be good consequences. If you refuse, there will be bad. Other things may also happen to you, but we are not talking about that. We are talking about the consequences of your own actions and your responsibility for them. Some of those consequences may be materially evident such as the loss of a job or a wrecked car; others may be only felt in the world of emotions, such as lingering anger or a ruined relationship.

It is appropriate that we meditate on this passage at this time of year because we are approaching the Days of Awe. During these holidays especially, the image of the rewarding and punishing God on a throne appears most prominently. The central prayer is *Unetaneh Tokef*, which states that our deeds are measured, and we are either inscribed for blessing in the book of life or left out, and you know what that means. All sorts of imaginative deaths were recorded in order to scare people straight: strangling, stoning, drowning, etc.

As much as scaring someone straight might capture the imagination, there are unintended results. We might dream that God will personally reward us if we do well and hurt us if we do badly. We might think of God as a kind of sadistic Santa Claus, checking if we were naughty or nice. Worse, if our loved ones pass away, we might wonder why God took them from us unfairly.

But if we think of the drama differently, we can understand it to mean not whether we physically live or die or about all suffering in the world but only if we are truly living the life we should for the things we can control. Are we living lives of vibrancy, filled with spirit and goodness, or have we deteriorated to a spiritless existence of appetite and callousness?

There are more ways to live and die then physical existence, and there are more ways to believe in God than reward and punishment. We can believe in a Soul of the Universe that wants us to live fully, taking into account the rabbis' words: "one *mitzvah* leads to another, and one transgression leads to another" (*Avot* 4:2).

Let us take responsibility for the consequences of our actions. Let us not exist with unnecessary fear or the death of the spirit in our hearts. Let us be truly alive while we are here.

## *Shoftim* (Deuteronomy 16:18-21:9)

### Judging with *Tzedakah*

The time of returning is upon us. The Hebrew month of *Elul*, which leads up to Rosh Hashanah and Yom Kippur, is our communal time of personal reflection. It is individual and personal as each of us looks inward at ourselves, but it is communal in that we draw support in doing this together. What is one thing you can do to prepare for Rosh Hashanah, besides cooking or setting up extra chairs? Can you talk about it and share it with a friend at the *oneg* or some other time? Don't be afraid to ask each other how your personal preparation for the High Holy Days is going.

Rabbi Levi Yitzhak of Berdichev understands the opening verses of this week's Torah portion in light of getting ready for Rosh Hashanah (*Kedushat Levi Shoftim*). For him, Rosh Hashanah was Yom Din, a day of personal judgment. We judge how we are supposed to be in the world, we spend the next ten days apologizing, forgiving, and changing, and then we come before God with a clean heart on Yom Kippur.

But it takes preparation to make the most out of Rosh Hashanah. You get out of it what you put into it. And so we are all invited to start thinking about how we want to change or goals we want to set now.

The opening words of the portion are *shophtim veshotrim titein lekha bekhol she-arekha... veshaphtu et ha-am mishpat tzedek* - "You shall appoint judges and officials for you in all of your gates [that *the Eternal* your God is giving you,] and they shall judge the people with due justice" (Deuteronomy 16:18). While this verse in its plain sense is about setting up courts to judge the people fairly, Rabbi Levi Yitzhak asks us to take the verse personally. How do you judge others? How do you judge yourself?

In his commentary, he rereads the verse with a series of wordplays and puns. Instead of *she-arekha*, your gates, add different vowels into this word in the Torah and you get *shiureka* - your assessments. Be just when you find yourself being judgmental in your assessments and "sizing up" of others. We tend to think that "they" are so much more or less at something, but is this an illusion?

Rabbi Levi Yitzhak teaches further: judge the people with *tzedek*, with due justice. Instead, he asks us to read, judge the people with *tzedakah*, with just giving. When judging someone else, judge charitably. Think generously. Rabbi Levi Yitzhak concludes with a warning from the Talmud: "The way a person measures (others) so is he measured" (*Megillah* 12b).

According to this teaching, how we think about and treat others comes back to us. If we are strict or envious of others, then we will find we are treated with that same harshness. But if we just, generous, and compassionate with others, we create space for that instead.

Modern psychology would reverse this teaching to show another side of this truth: How you judge and treat yourself often comes out in what you project onto others. Rewriting Rabbi Levi Yitzhak's teaching this way, we might read: But just when you are assessing and "sizing up" yourself. Be charitable and generous with yourself the same way you might be with a friend. When you treat yourself this way, you will then treat others similarly. If you can think of yourself with compassion, you will be able to find compassion for others.

I believe that we who are hard on others are usually just as hard if not more so on ourselves. If we can find a way to ease up on ourselves, we will naturally start treating other people in our lives more gently.

Our teaching on the Torah portion suggests these Elul questions:

How harshly do you judge yourself? Can you laugh at yourself? Has there been a time when you have gotten angry when instead you could have laughed at yourself? Are you easily embarrassed? Why?

The Torah insists that compassion and loving kindness are a part of justice. Justice, *tzedek*, is just one letter away from *tzedakah*, giving. What small step can you take to be more giving? Can you be content that being generous is the just thing to do?

And finally, how can you get ready for Rosh Hashanah and Yom Kippur emotionally? On these holidays, we ask God to judge us with generosity and kindness. When thinking of others and ourselves, shouldn't we do the same?

## *Ki Tetzei* (Deuteronomy 21:10-25:19)

### The Respect for Life

The number one selling musical compilation in this country right now is a collection of music remembering September 11. The album is by Bruce Springsteen, an American icon of the 1980s and now, it seems, of the turn of the century. Regardless of one's opinion of Bruce Springsteen's music, the lyrics to the songs have struck a deep chord in how we are going to remember 9-11, and they are words of faith, love, and duty. Springsteen has long been respected as a spokesperson of the working class and often as a representative of the forgotten poor and the marginalized in society. In this musical collection he turns to the lives of everyday people on September 11, and in one song, called "The Rising," he imagines all of the souls of the departed, firefighters and all, rising to heaven through the smoke and flames. Many of the songs qualify as prayers.

There is an irony that is raised by this CD and by all of the memorial services in which we will participate in a little less than a month. The irony is that those who perpetrated the crimes of 9-11 considered themselves martyrs and prayed to God continuously even as they carried out their suicide missions. Now, we are memorializing our martyrs from that day and offer up all of our prayers. Indeed, we need to pray, or else Springsteen's CD would not have provoked such an emotional reaction. Both terrorist and victim have their martyrs and pray to God. I cannot even imagine what it must be like for the Almighty to have to sort these prayers out.

Jewish tradition can provide a guide to help us sort out the ethics of martyrdom. We can begin by looking at this week's Torah portion, which tells us a great deal about a Jewish respect for life. Of course, we have to be sure to not only read what the Torah portion says but also how subsequent Jewish tradition transformed these words into values that we would recognize.

In this week's Torah portion, we read laws about an astonishing variety of topics from marriage to capital crimes. Moses Maimonides counted 72 commandments read this week.[82] Among these are what to do with the body of a criminal who has been executed. It seems that many in ancient times would display the executed criminal as a

[82] Plaut, 1320.

grisly reminder to the people not to break the law and perhaps give some the satisfaction of revenge. The law in the Torah, however, says that this is forbidden. "An impaled body is an abhorrence to God" (Deuteronomy 21:23). Even the worst of human beings must be buried on the same day as the execution because even the lowliest criminal bears the divine image.

Another law from this week's portion speaks of preventing cruelty in any shape or form, even to animals. It says that, when collecting eggs for food, one must send away the mother bird so she will not see you actually take the eggs from her nest. To take away a living creature's young, even an animal's, must be done with sensitivity, so we do not cause any unnecessary distress in the creature, and we are careful to learn compassion in all things ourselves. The famous commentator, Rashi, wrote that if this is what we should do for animals, all the more so should be we sensitive not to cause grief in our fellow human beings.[83]

Finally, there are laws in this week's portion that tell us to take care of the poor by leaving them produce that otherwise would be forgotten, left over grapes or olives, which were staple products at that time. The Torah names the vulnerable members of society: the stranger, the orphan, and the widow. These people, despite their powerless status, have to be given their due as human beings. Their rights to life and well-being as children of God must be acted upon.

What ties all of these laws together, in my opinion, is a great sensitivity for the sanctity of life. Even at the extremes of society, from the criminal to the poor person to the everyday action of gathering food, we are supposed to remember the great value that all life has. It is telling that, earlier this year, a member of Hamas was quoted as saying that they will win this conflict because the Jews love life too much.

Despite the sanctity of life, however, Jews also have their martyrs. There are people in Jewish history who are remembered just as much for their deaths as for their lives. We read about many of these people on Yom Kippur during the Yizkor service. Among these were rabbis who chose to teach Torah even though the Roman authorities had forbidden it. Jewish sources describe their torture and their deaths in horrific detail. Most famous of these martyrs is Rabbi

---

[83] Rashi on Deuteronomy 22:6-7.

Akiba, who was asked why he continued to teach Torah even when he knew that if he got caught he would be executed. He answered in a parable. He said that there were once fish living in a lake, and a fox came up and told them that they were no longer safe in the water. He told them that they needed to jump out onto dry land to be saved. Akiba then explained that to stop living a life of Torah was to be a fish on dry land. He would take his chances in the water for a life of meaning, but to abandon Judaism was certain death (*Berachot* 61b).

Akiba was caught, however, and tortured and executed. The Roman commander, a man named Rufus, ordered all kinds of horrible things to be done to Akiba's body in front of a large audience. Akiba was so dignified, however, that legend has it that the crowd was silent. Before he died, he is supposed to have said that all his life he wanted to be able to fulfill the words, "You shall love the Eternal your God with all your heart, with all your soul, and with all your being," and now he is able to do just that. He then recited the *Shema* and died.

We can still learn from this story a great deal about how Jewish tradition views martyrdom. There are times in Jewish history when people have chosen to die rather than give up certain principles. There are times when we have chosen to go to war. Sometimes, our only choice is not if we are going to die, but how we die. This is the choice of the martyr.

However, there is a crucial difference between this kind of martyrdom and the suicide attacks that we see today. Judaism does not encourage us to seek out martyrdom. It is not something glorious to reach for. Martyrdom, instead, is a final option when no other choices are left. The real goal is to seek out a meaningful life, a life of sanctity with respect for the lives of all others.

This, most of all, separates the terrorist and the victim. The terrorist sought out martyrdom. The victim did not. As we memorialize our martyrs on September 11, whether it be through music or ceremony, it is important that we emphasize this difference, for as we will read on Yom Kippur morning, God commands us:

"I call heaven and earth to witness against you this day that I have set before you life or death, blessing or curse; choose life, therefore, that you and your descendants may live" (Deuteronomy 30:19).

## Concerning Birds, Rooftops, and Enemies

The question is: what kind of person do you want to be?

That is what seems to be at the heart of this week's Torah portion, *Ki Tetzei*. This portion contains a list of mitzvot commanded upon the Israelites. The topics range widely. Just consider a few of them:

First, there is a commandment that when you want to take eggs from a nest, presumably for your breakfast, you should send away the mother bird first. You shouldn't take the eggs while the mother bird is watching. Rabbi Moshe ben Nachman says the reason is the Jewish value of *tzar ba'alei chayim* - not causing needless pain to any creature.[84] If there is a way to limit suffering, even towards animals, we should do it. Cruelty to animals is against Jewish law.

But Maimonides says the question goes deeper. If we can learn to be kind to a bird, then hopefully we can learn to be kind to another human being. But he puts it in an "all the more so" fashion: If God wants us to show compassion for a simple bird, then all the more so should we show compassion for other people.

A second commandment is that when we build a new house, we should make sure to build a fence around the roof. Now this only makes sense if you know something about the Ancient Middle East. Not worried about too much about rain, ancient people had flat roofs. People lived in their homes of a few rooms, but then a ladder led up through a hole in the roof, and the roof served as a balcony. In the summer, people would sleep up there to cool off. And there were also other things on the roof, such as tubs for laundry. The *Mishnah* - the earliest compilation of Jewish Law - has prohibitions about dumping water off the roof into an alley and creating a hazard.

So as a precaution, Jews invented the first building code. The Torah insists that everyone needs to have a fence around their roof to keep people from accidentally falling off, whether they were rolling over in their sleep or doing their laundry.

Finally, there is a commandment that happens when you are on the road. If you pass by and see that a person whom you consider to be your enemy has had an accident, you are obliged to help him or her. If their donkey has fallen and cannot get up under its load, even if its owner is your enemy, you must stop and help them lift it.

---

84 Ramban on Deuteronomy 22:6-7.

Another similar commandment says that if you see your enemy's animal has gone astray, you must fetch it and bring it back. "Do not turn aside and pretend you don't see," says the Torah. The Torah clearly had great insight into human nature. How convenient it would be to claim later, "I'm sorry. I didn't notice."

One of the things all of these commandments have in common is that they guarantee nothing. So you send the mother bird away. Are you really limiting the bird's distress? Can you read the mind of a bird? So you build a fence around the roof. Does that really mean that accidents won't happen? So you help your enemy on the side of the road or return their lost property, despite the hard feelings. Does that really mean that you are guaranteed to get a thank you, or even to bury the hatchet and no longer be enemies? The answer to all of these questions is no.

But the heart of the lesson is: what kind of person do you want to be? Do you want to be the kind of person who is cruel to animals or to others? Do you want to be the kind of person who didn't at least try to do everything possible to make your home safe? Do you want to be the kind of person who is incapable of virtuous behavior, who cannot rise above a quarrel to be helpful or make a gesture of peace? The answer to these questions is no as well.

As we approach Rosh Hashanah and Yom Kippur, we are asked to sit in judgment on ourselves and see ourselves as God sees us. If we start measuring our worth against other people or things beyond our control, then we are locked in an ill-fated game. But if we measure ourselves against the mitzvot, then they provide a standard against which we can see how much we have grown or need to grow. God's standards are rooted in compassion. With that in mind, each of us should ask ourselves, 'Can I look at myself in the mirror with a clear conscience?' Of course, remember that God's compassion extends to you as well.

At the end of the day, it is just you as an individual in the sanctuary facing God, *HaRachaman* - the One who Commands and Gives Compassion. That is the only real standard, and it is the only one that can provide peace.

## *Ki Tavo* (Deuteronomy 26:1-29:8)

### Saying "Amen"

There are times in our lives, perhaps in the morning as we sit with a cup of coffee and watch the day begin, that we feel truly blessed. We are grateful for what we have, and we reflect on the goodness we have known. And then there are other times in our lives where it seems that we are working under a dark cloud. Anything that can go wrong does go wrong, and it is hard to feel the joy of life. Our Torah portion this week brings up these feelings, feelings of either being blessed or cursed.

The drama that our Torah portion describes is as follows: there are two mountains. On one side is Mount Gerizim, and on the other is Mount Eival. Mount Gerizim is lush and fertile with vineyards and streams. Mount Eival is desolate, a wasteland. In between the mountains stand the people Israel as they prepare to enter the Promised Land. On Mount Gerizim, the fertile mountain, representatives of the tribes of Shimon, Levi, Yehudah, Issachar, Joseph, and Benjamin stand. On the desert mountain are positioned representatives of Reuven, Gad, Asher, Zevulun, Dan, and Naphtali. The people of Israel stand at attention in between.

Moses begins the drama by telling the people that they must obey God's will. If they obey, they will be blessed. If they do not, they will be cursed. With that, the representatives on each of the mountains begin chanting. The ones on the fertile mountain sing out all of the blessings that will come upon the people if they obey God's will, and the ones on the desert mountain chant the curses that will come as a consequence of their disobedience. In between, the people hear both at the same time, in stereo, so to speak. What at first seems very clear, blessing and fertility on one side, curse and waste on the other, suddenly becomes difficult. The words get entangled with each other. One has to strain to make out the blessing from the curse, and one hopes that the people who are singing the blessings would sing a little louder. That cacophony of sound is the drama that the Torah depicts.

Today, however, we read through these lists one after the other as we read from the Torah scroll. The lists of curses are long and gruesome, while the lists of blessings are powerful and inspiring. In many traditional synagogues today, it is a custom to read the lists of curses as quickly as possible and in a low voice. The reading of the blessings, however, is supposed in a manner that is long and thoughtful. In a sense, we reenact the drama of Mount Gerizim and Mount Eival in the synagogue, but we skew it towards the blessings. The problem of reading these lists one after the other, however, is that one misses the point of the drama. They are supposed to be heard simultaneously. The point is to feel the confusion, the blessing and the curse at the same time, for life is made of both.

We may, in life, be tempted to hear only the curses. Perhaps we even listen for them and do not even realize that we are doing it. The glass is always half empty. When we meet people, it is easy to show mistrust. We may have been hurt in some way, are depressed about something, and we have learned to survive through cynicism.

On the other hand, others may want to hear only the blessings. Our idealism is necessary and inspiring, and we must always cling to hope. But if we are naïve, we can get beat up pretty quickly. We can become vulnerable to any obstacle that comes along. Living in a fantasy world, we rarely get things done.

And so, like our ancestors, we must try to stand in between the mountains. It's awfully confusing in between there. We often do not know what to do. The right path is not so clear cut. Inside our heads are these mountains of blessings and curses. Our experience heaps them up, builds them, and makes them towering. As children, we often have very simplistic notions of right and wrong. Mount Gerizim is green and fertile, while Mount Eival is desolate and wasted. As we grow, however, what at first appears easy to distinguish eventually becomes more difficult. Things become more ambiguous as we grow older. Nothing seems to be either a complete blessing or a complete curse. To use a secular example, we can see this mixture of good and bad in all aspects of entertainment. Moving from the drama of the Torah to the dramas of Shakespeare, there is not a single play that Shakespeare wrote that is entirely tragedy or entirely comedy. He always included elements of both in every play. The reason? Life is never so simple as to be entirely one or the other.

Moreover, the Torah adds another element that may be very surprising to some. As the Torah lists the curses, there is an instruction to all of the people to say, "Amen," after each and every curse. It is the only place where the word, "Amen," which means, "I believe," appears in the Torah. As the blessings are listed, however, there is no such requirement. No one is required to say, "Amen." Why would that be? Why are we required to say "Amen," to the curses and not to the blessings?

The reason is that the Torah only requires something if there is a need. Our rabbis teach that we will naturally say "Amen," to the blessings. No one has to require us to do so. It's the acknowledging of the curses that's the difficult part. When we say the Motzi at the oneg, it is easy to say, "Amen," thanking God for food and community. But when someone dies, and we say, "*Baruch Dayan Haemet*," Blessed is the only true Judge, then it is more difficult for the "Amen," to come out of our mouths.

Nevertheless, we must acknowledge the reality of the curses, but we also must listen and hope for the blessings. We can't let those blessings go by. More importantly, along with the rest of the people Israel standing in between the mountains, we hope that the blessings get louder and louder.

We cannot make the world more clean cut. We have very little control over what each day may bring, whether it be blessing or curse. Our world is a mixture of the two. What we do have control over, however, is what we listen for. Shall we listen for only the curses, or shall we seek out the blessings? The Torah seems to be teaching us that what we should do is say "Amen," to the curses, and then sing out those blessing with all our might. There is nothing that is forcing us to be passive listeners. We, too, can sing.

As we approach the Days of Awe, the days where we take stock of our lives and renew our relationships, let's listen to what this Torah portion has to teach us. Life gives us both good and bad, often in the same day. It would be foolhardy to ignore one and only focus on the other. With a firm grounding in reality, however, we can still sing out the blessings of our lives so that they fill our world from one mountaintop to the other.

## Lost and Found

Recently I lost my glasses. I had to put on another pair, and they never felt quite right. Not like my favorite pair. And the prescription must be slightly different. I didn't see the world the same way. Then I found the old pair which had fallen out of a suitcase in the bottom of a closet. Putting them on, I felt the familiar fit. There is something magical about finding something that was once lost.

This idea of lost and found is found in this week's Torah portion. Instead of losing an object, even if it is the kind of thing that helps you see the world, the Torah is about how we see ourselves and each other. The words are familiar, for we recite at the Passover *seder*:

> My father was a fugitive Aramean. He went down to Egypt with meager numbers and sojourned there; but there he became a great and populous nation. The Egyptians dealt harshly with us and oppressed us; they imposed heavy labor upon us. We cried to the Eternal, the God of our ancestors, and the Eternal heard our plea and saw our plight, our misery, and our oppression. The Eternal freed us from Egypt by a mighty hand, by an outstretched arm and awesome power, and by signs and portents, bringing us to this place and giving us this land, a land flowing with milk and honey. Wherefore I now bring the first fruits of the soil with You, Eternal One, have given me. (Deuteronomy 26:5-10)

The opening phrase, "my father was a fugitive Aramean," could be translated any number of ways. *Arami oveid avi. Arami* – an Aramean, that is, one who spoke the main language of the land, Aramaic, which shares the same alphabet as Hebrew. *Oveid* – fugitive, wandering, lost. For some, "perished." *Avi* – my father. In other words, "My ancestors, even my parents, were lost." But the rest of the passages summarizes the story of the Torah, and it reveals that now we are found. "Bringing us to this place and giving us this land, a land flowing with milk and honey." In gratitude, we bring our first fruits. We say thanks before we enjoy.

To this day, when one visits the land of Israel, many people when they find out you are Jewish will say, "Welcome home." It is an amazing thing to think that one is a tourist and to find out that you have a place where you belong. To be found when you didn't know you were lost. And I hope as many return to the synagogue for the Days of Awe, often for the first time in a long while, that they have the same feeling of being at home.

But the fact is, home is a feeling, and exile is a state of mind. One can be in downtown Jerusalem and be in exile. One can be in one's own kitchen and feel like a fugitive. One can be surrounded by people and feel utterly alone.

Starting on Saturday night, we start the journey home again. With *Selichot*, we ask how far we have wandered and what it might take to return. These are open-ended questions of a lifetime, but each year we try to come closer, to end our exile, to make *teshuvah* and return in repentance. We imagine God to be a shepherd who seeks out lost sheep and makes them pass under the divine staff, as it says in Gates of Repentance: "As the shepherd seeks out his flock, and makes the sheep pass under his staff, so do You muster and number and consider over soul…"[85]

How do we "get found"? If we are feeling alienated, how do we find our way home? That answer is a mystery, as individual as each person who asks it.

But I would like to share at least one possible direction one can go in order to find a sense of connection or belonging. If exile is truly a state of being and not a matter of geographic location, then the answer is within each of us no matter where we are. We cannot move to another coast to escape our problems, nor can we sit still and hope to be saved. Instead, we need to open up our lives to others and share what is within. We pray together, for this is a shared experience.

Locked in the prison of the self, we can impose our own sense of exile. Too often, when we feel lost, we stare into ourselves, looking for insight, trying to find a way out. Instead, perhaps we need to look outward. We cannot necessarily free ourselves but must reach out to another, for it is love and connection and trust that are liberating. In reaching out our hand toward another, we may find that help coming back in return.

So it is taught in a parable from the Talmud:

Rabbi Yochanan was a healer. By reaching out his hands, he could touch others and raise them up. People were in awe of this holy man.

Once day, however, Rabbi Yochanan fell ill. His disciples gathered around him. Why couldn't he heal himself the way that he had healed others? Why couldn't those magic hands lift up his own soul?

Then, Rabbi Yochanan's friend, Rabbi Chanina, pushed through

[85] *Gates of Repentance*, 108.

the crowd and came to his bedside. He reached out and took Rabbi Yochanan's hand, and, the Talmud says, he raised him up. As the disciples looked on in wonder, the men explained, "A prisoner cannot free himself from prison." (*Berachot* 5a-b)

Even healers need to be healed by others. Even people accustomed to giving all the time need to receive. Even the greatest and most talented among us can get lost and occasionally need to be found.

We were not meant to live life in isolation. It is only in community that we make connections and find a sense of belonging. Then we can fulfill the words of Ezekiel 34:11-12: "I will search my sheep, and seek them out… I will seek the one which was lost, and bring back the one which was driven away."

## *Nitzavim-Vayelech* (Deuteronomy 29:9-31:30)

### All of us Standing Together in the Dark

We gather in the night, and we pray together. There is a hidden irony in this. The irony is this: historically, the evening prayer service has always been an optional prayer service with no fixed time for the community. The morning and afternoon prayer services were best said with a *minyan* in synagogue, but it says in the *Midrash*: "*Ma'ariv hi reishit*" – the evening service is not mandatory (*Mishnah Berachot* 4:1). It has no fixed time. The reason was simple; it was not safe in ancient times and in the Middle Ages to go out at night. God knows what criminals, or, in the imagination, what demons and ghosts, lurked outside in the nighttime black. The darkness was dangerous, and so one was allowed to say the evening prayers at home. When weighing the endangerment to life against the commandment to pray with a *minyan*, the sanctity of life, of course, won out. Nevertheless, communities still strove to have evening services together as a community. It was not because they dismissed the risk; it was simply better to be in the dark together. Reform Judaism has even made the Friday night service the main service of prayer.

But perhaps there was another reason for making nighttime community prayers optional in Jewish law. Perhaps it is because it is simply difficult to pray in the dark. By "dark" I do not mean physical darkness but spiritual. We might remember that the ninth plague of Passover was one of darkness, where each person was trapped in the fears of their imagination, a plague tailor-made for each soul.

Rabbi Yehudah Leib Alter of Ger, who lived about 100 years ago in Poland, looked at this week's Torah portion, *Nitzavim*, and he read the opening words: "You stand this day, all of you, before the Eternal your God, your tribal heads, your elders, and your officials, all the men of Israel, your children, your women, even the stranger that is within your camp from woodchopper to water drawer… (Deuteronomy 29:9-10).

This first thing to notice about this opening passage is that the entirety of the Jewish people is described as *nitzavim*, standing before God. *Nitzavim* is a special kind of standing, for it means "standing at attention." They are standing rigidly before God. Are they standing that way out of respect? Out of fear? We don't know. But everyone is included, from the richest and most powerful – the officials and tribal heads – to the laborers and the poor – the woodchoppers and water drawers. Men, women, and children, are all equal standing before God.

But what interests Rabbi Yehudah in his commentary is not just the equality of the people before God or their posture but that the text says "this day." "You stand this day, all of you, before the Eternal your God." Read radically, "this day" means today, right now, at this very moment. The Torah speaks to us in the present, for all of us stand before God at every moment, wherever we are. And it is for this reason that ultimately we can say there is no fixed time and place for our prayers, for God hears us and watches us everywhere. Moreover, it is the spontaneous prayer, the prayer that often comes out of spiritual darkness at no fixed time, which is most piercing to God. Rabbi Yehudah writes:

"The darkness in the human heart causes us to call to God…This outcry opens the gates of prayer more than any fixed time, since [the people] Israel ever stand before the Eternal, in a way that is beyond time."[86]

We stand always beyond time before God, and it is the spiritual reaching out to God in our darkest moments when we speak the truth. Perhaps there is something mysterious about the nighttime that simply makes us more prayerful, for it brings out the shadow in each of us that longs to be redeemed by God.

It is for this reason that not only our Shabbat evening prayers are opportunities for reflection and worship but also our special *Selichot* service that will take place at the conclusion of Shabbat tomorrow night. The word "*selichot*" means "prayers for forgiveness," and it comes before Rosh Hashanah to ease us in to the heavy work of self-examination. The Sephardim recite *selichot* from the first of the month of Elul, but the Ashkenazim, whose customs we follow, say these prayers the week before. We do so late at night, when our minds are more susceptible to influence. It is held during the midnight hour, deliberately placed to help cast out our demons and face the challenges of repentance and reconciliation. *Selichot* are prayers that we say in the dark – highlights of High Holy Day liturgy that ask us to look at our misdeeds and return to the path God has chosen for us. We chant *Avinu Malkeinu* and, at midnight, sound the

---

[86] Arthur Green, *Language of Truth*, 329.

shofar for the first time of the season.

Let us embrace this and every opportunity to reach out in the darkness for each other and draw closer in prayer. We stand, all of us, before God, wherever we are, but it is always better if we can stand before God together. It is better to be together, especially in spiritual darkness. We share each other's joys and sorrows and lighten each other's burdens.

As we start on the hard work of repentance, as we think of the people to whom we should apologize and the people to whom we ought to finally grant forgiveness, as we think of the grudges in our heart that weigh us down and the darkness that blinds us, let us join together before the High Holy Days to try to purify ourselves. Repentance takes more than a day; it is a process that takes time. Apologies and words of forgiveness are things that must be thought through. But we can do so more easily if we realize that we are not alone, that we all face such challenges and such darkness together, year after year, and standing before God, we are only human.

## *Ha'azinu-V'zot HaBerachah* (Deuteronomy 32:1-34:12)

### I Believe

An Orthodox Jewish friend asked me, with some real perplexity in her voice, why I wasn't Orthodox. "You love Torah study. You *davven* [pray] regularly. What keeps you from being Orthodox? I don't understand it."

This is my stuttering, inadequate response. I will try to answer as best I can.

I am a religious Jew, but I am not Orthodox. For some that is an impossible contradiction in terms. It is not for me. For me, it is a matter of belief and integrity.

I am a religious Jew because I believe in God as the One, *HaBorei Chei Haolamim* – the Source and Soul of the universe. I love Torah study and try to find a way to learn something sacred every day. I believe in prayer. I take the *mitzvot* – the commandments – very seriously as an everyday part of my life. I am a passionate supporter of the State of Israel as both the Jewish homeland and a democracy open to all. I also have an instinctive love of Jewish people as members of my family.

But I do not believe the Torah was written by God and literally dictated. I believe it was told and retold by the ancient Israelites about their experiences and then eventually written down over time. After centuries the Torah was edited together, most likely in the time of Ezra. The Torah isn't fiction, and it isn't nonfiction; it is in the in-between place called autobiography of real memories passed down through the generations. It is sacred to us because it is the vocabulary that Jews have used for centuries to talk about God, and it mirrors the human condition. We learn Torah to understand what our ancestors believed, to learn what the Rabbis taught, and to know ourselves.

I do not believe that Jews are *am segulah*, God's treasured, chosen people. I believe that we are people, with an identity that is unique and remarkable, but I don't believe our souls are different from others. I believe that all people are made in God's image.

I also do not believe in the literal resurrection of the dead, or that a *moshiach* [messiah] will appear on the top of the Mount of Olives to save us. I do not pray for the rebuilding of a Third Temple and the reinstitution of animal sacrifice. I believe that *Olam Haba* is not the World to Come but is the World that is Potentially Already Here, not in heaven but on earth. I believe our job is to make our world into that world by relieving suffering.

I believe in a Zionism committed to Israel's security and eventual coexistence.

I believe in free will and consequences. I believe that there is no conflict between religion and science. I do not believe God rewards and punishes, either on a macro or personal level. I believe that often you reap what you sow, but also that the world is imperfect. Sometimes the most important *beracha* [prayer/blessing] we can say is: *Baruch Atah Adonai Eloheinu Melech Haolam Borei* [Blessed are You the Eternal our God Ruler of the universe who creates] Good Enough. Sometimes it just has to be good enough.

I believe in inclusion. I do not believe that gays and lesbians are sinners, as some ignorant people still claim, or that women are "so holy" that they have to be kept away from certain public aspects of Judaism. I believe that God made every soul unique and precious, and I am responsible to whoever is before me. I believe that ethics comes first.

I love the rituals of Judaism, but I believe that some rituals, namely keeping kosher, keeping Shabbat strictly, and following the order of the entire traditional *siddur* [prayer book], have become so overly complicated that they alienate rather than bring together, which is contrary to what they were intended to do in the first place. The letter of the law has often become divorced from the spirit of the law. I believe that sometimes simpler is better.

I believe in the beauty of Judaism. I love the sound of the *shofar* [ram's horn] on Rosh Hashanah, the challenge of fasting and the melodies on Yom Kippur, building a *sukkah* [hut/tabernacle], and sleeping outside on Sukkot. I get an electric charge from reading the end of the Torah and immediately starting it again on Simchat Torah. I love staring at Hanukkah candles. I love eating dates – the Biblical honey of the land flowing with milk and honey – at a Tu B'Shvat seder. I love being ridiculous on Purim. I love hearing children sing the four questions on Passover. (I do not love gefilte fish, but I tolerate it with horseradish.) I love seeing our youth chant the Ten Commandments on Shavuot for Confirmation.

Most importantly, Shabbat – with family meals, study, and prayer is – my most sacred time. The most important moment is when my wife and I bless our children.

I believe in speaking in the name of the prophets at Capitol Hill in Washington, DC. I believe that Judaism is more than just going to services and lighting candles of various kinds; it is about social justice and actually doing something to make the world a better place. I believe not only in a Promised Land but a Promised World. I believe in *tikkun olam* -- the obligation and the dream of fixing the world. I feel much better about myself after I have brought food to our local food pantry or having delivered free groceries to someone in need.

And I believe in praying and studying every day. Every single day without exception. For me, prayer is also *tikkun olam* – fixing the world – but on the inside. My inner world needs fixing too. I believe in loving and serving God and loving your neighbor as yourself.

So you see, I am a deeply religious Jew, but belief separates me from the Judaism of previous centuries and the Judaism of some of my present-day family members.

God gave each one of us two amazing gifts: a religious tradition to guide us, and a conscience with which to make decisions. I thank God for both, and I will abdicate neither.

What do you believe?

# ABOUT THE AUTHOR

Rabbi Joseph Meszler is the spiritual leader of Temple Sinai in Sharon, MA. He is active in interfaith and social justice work. He is also a noted Jewish educator to both youth and adults.

Rabbi Meszler is the author of several books, including: *Facing Illness, Finding God: How Judaism Can Help You and Caregivers Cope When Body or Spirit Fails* (Jewish Lights Publishing 2010), *A Man's Responsibility: A Jewish Guide to Being a Son, a Partner in Marriage, a Father and Community Leader* (Jewish Lights Publishing, 2008), and *Witnesses to the One: the Spiritual History of the* Sh'ma (Jewish Lights Publishing, 2006).

Learn about Rabbi Meszler at www.rabbimeszler.com.

Made in the USA
Middletown, DE
15 November 2015